M000209342

UNDERSTANDING CASE STUDY RESEARCH

SAGE was founded in 1965 by Sara Miller McCune to support the dissemination of usable knowledge by publishing innovative and high-quality research and teaching content. Today, we publish over 900 journals, including those of more than 400 learned societies, more than 800 new books per year, and a growing range of library products including archives, data, case studies, reports, and video. SAGE remains majority-owned by our founder, and after Sara's lifetime will become owned by a charitable trust that secures our continued independence.

Los Angeles | London | New Delhi | Singapore | Washington DC | Melbourne

UNDERSTANDING CASE STUDY RESEARCH

Small-scale Research with Meaning

MALCOLM
TIGHT

Los Angeles | London | New Delhi
Singapore | Washington DC | Melbourne

Los Angeles | London | New Delhi
Singapore | Washington DC | Melbourne

SAGE Publications Ltd
1 Oliver's Yard
55 City Road
London EC1Y 1SP

SAGE Publications Inc.
2455 Teller Road
Thousand Oaks, California 91320

SAGE Publications India Pvt Ltd
B 1/I 1 Mohan Cooperative Industrial Area
Mathura Road
New Delhi 110 044

SAGE Publications Asia-Pacific Pte Ltd
3 Church Street
#10-04 Samsung Hub
Singapore 049483

Editor: Jai Seaman
Assistant editor: Alysha Owen
Production editor: Katie Forsythe
Copyeditor: Sarah Bury
Proofreader: Victoria Nicholas
Marketing manager: Sally Ransom
Cover design: Shaun Mercier
Typeset by: C&M Digitals (P) Ltd, Chennai, India
Printed and bound by CPI Group (UK) Ltd,
Croydon, CR0 4YY

© Malcolm Tight 2017

First published 2017

Apart from any fair dealing for the purposes of research or
private study, or criticism or review, as permitted under the
Copyright, Designs and Patents Act, 1988, this publication
may be reproduced, stored or transmitted in any form, or
by any means, only with the prior permission in writing of
the publishers, or in the case of reprographic reproduction,
in accordance with the terms of licences issued by
the Copyright Licensing Agency. Enquiries concerning
reproduction outside those terms should be sent to the
publishers.

Library of Congress Control Number: 2016945296

British Library Cataloguing in Publication data

A catalogue record for this book is available from
the British Library

ISBN 978-1-4462-7391-3
ISBN 978-1-4462-7392-0 (pbk)

At SAGE we take sustainability seriously. Most of our products are printed in the UK using FSC papers and boards.
When we print overseas we ensure sustainable papers are used as measured by the PREPS grading system.
We undertake an annual audit to monitor our sustainability.

Contents

List of Boxes and Table

BOXES

TABLE

About the Author

Malcolm Tight is Professor of Higher Education at Lancaster University in the UK, where he has worked since 2004. He was previously Professor of Higher Education at the University of Warwick, and has also worked at Birkbeck College and the Open University. His research interests include social research designs and theories, the history of higher education and the developing state of higher education research.

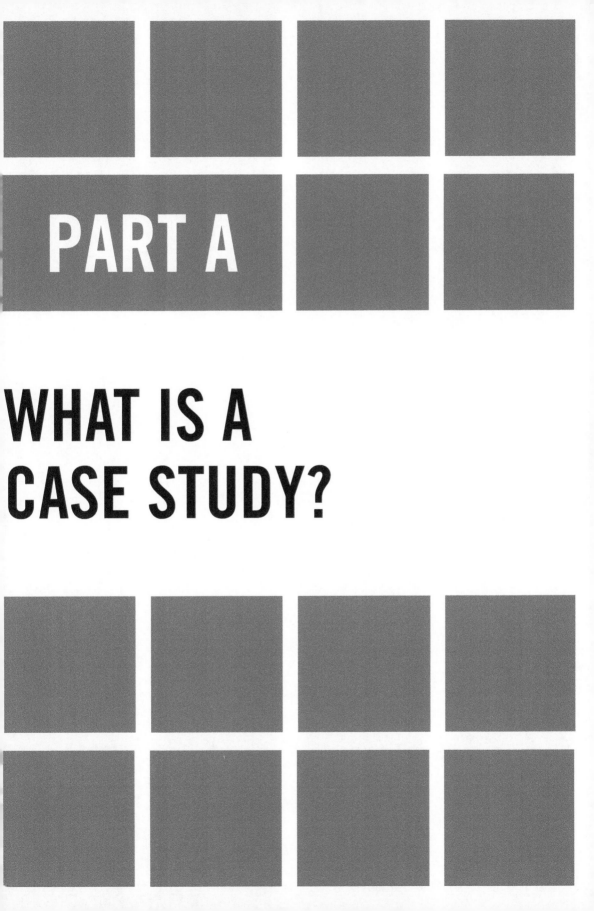

PART A

WHAT IS A
CASE STUDY?

Introduction

AIMS AND AUDIENCE

This book provides a comprehensive guide to the nature and use of case study research. It is designed primarily for students – final-year undergraduate students, master's students and beginning doctoral students – who are learning about research methods and/or undertaking small-scale research projects of their own, and who might be interested in undertaking case study research. It will also be useful, therefore, to academics involved in instructing and/or supervising such students, who may not all be as familiar with case study research as they might like to be.

The focus of the book is primarily on the social sciences, as this is both the subject area with which I am most familiar, and also the area in which case study is most commonly employed as a research design. However, as case study is widely used in many disciplines, the book also explores that varied usage, so it should be useful beyond the social sciences as well.

The book has been written in what you will hopefully find to be an accessible and relatively jargon-free style. In part this has been a deliberate strategy, as most things can be explained fairly simply and there is generally no need to use obscure language. In part it is also because this is the only way I know how to write. There is, though, some specialist language involved in case study and related research, so this has been used and explained as necessary.

The book takes as its central position that *case studies are small-scale research with meaning*. In other words, while it is clear that case studies are, by definition, limited or bounded in their scope, they nevertheless aim to produce valuable data and analyses which are of broader interest and usefulness. It is in this way that they have the potential to make significant contributions to our understanding.

We don't, of course, all have the time, funding and access to undertake larger-scale research. However, much can be achieved through smaller-scale research projects such as case studies. The trick, then, is to make the small-scale research that we undertake both useful and meaningful. This book aims to assist you in doing that.

THE CONTENTS OF THE BOOK

In the succeeding chapters, you will find discussion of, and answers to, the following questions:

- What are case studies (see Chapter 2)?
- What kinds of case study are there (see Chapter 2)?
- How does case study compare to other research designs (see Chapters 3 and 6)?
- What are the advantages and disadvantages of case study (see Chapter 3)?
- How can case study research be meaningful and valuable (see Chapter 4)?
- How are case studies used in different disciplines (see Chapter 5)?
- How are case studies used in combination with other research designs (see Chapter 6)?
- How can I access and use published case study research (see Chapter 7)?
- How do I carry out a case study (see Chapters 8 and 9)?
- What is the future for case study research (see Chapter 10)?

Each chapter begins with an outline of its contents, and ends with a summary of the main points made and a list of key readings. Boxes are used in some chapters to present examples or summarise material, and plentiful quotations from the extensive literature on case study research are provided.

One key feature of the book is its extensive discussion of selective case study publications: this is a particular feature of Chapters 4, 5, 6 and 7. This has been done to better exemplify the kinds of research that case study designs have been used for, to show their potential, and to illustrate the kinds of conclusions that such research can come up with.

I hope you find the book both enjoyable and useful.

2

Origins and Applications of Case Study

INTRODUCTION

This chapter seeks to provide an overview of case study as a research design (i.e. a way of pursuing a particular research project; the status of case study is considered in more detail in Chapter 3). Its five main sections consider:

- what we mean by 'case study'
- how case study has developed over time
- how it is interpreted and applied in different disciplines
- the different types of case study
- the relations between research case studies (the main focus of this book) and teaching case studies.

All of these issues are discussed further, and illustrated by the use of example case studies from a range of disciplines, in the remainder of the book.

WHAT IS A CASE STUDY?

All research studies cases: instances or examples of particular things (e.g. people, animals, planets, companies, schools, works of art, elements, policies, ideas). This does not mean, however, that all research projects are case studies.

Much research takes an alternative approach, and focuses on specific and limited aspects of cases (commonly referred to as variables: e.g. people's opinions, animals' habits, planets' orbits, companies' balance sheets), measuring and exploring their variation, and relationships with other variables, for a given sample of cases. This is the more typical approach taken in scientific and/or quantitative research.

The term 'case study' is, or should be, reserved for a particular design of research, where the focus is on an in-depth study of one or a limited number of cases. In practice, however, its use is rather messier and more complex:

> To refer to a work as a 'case study' might mean: (a) that its method is qualitative, small-N, (b) that the research is holistic, thick (a more or less comprehensive examination of a phenomenon), (c) that it utilizes a particular type of evidence (e.g. ethnographic, clinical, nonexperimental, non-survey-based, participant-observation, process-tracing, historical, textual or field research), (d) that its method of evidence gathering is naturalistic (a 'real-life context'), (e) that the topic is diffuse (case and context are difficult to distinguish), (f) that it employs triangulation ('multiple sources of evidence'), (g) that the research investigates the properties of a single observation, or (h) that the research investigates the properties of a single phenomenon, instance or example. (Gerring 2007, p. 17)

To compound matters further, Gerring (2007, p. 18) goes on to note that case study has a large number of variants or synonyms: 'single unit, single subject, single case, N=1, case-based, case-control, case history, case method, case record, case work, within-case, clinical research'.

So what is a case study? Box 2.1 contains eleven definitions of case study, selected from among the many available in the literature, and organised by date. It illustrates both the development of our understanding of case study over time (the subject of the next section), and the similarities and differences in these understandings at any one time.

■ ■ ■ Box 2.1   Definitions of Case Study ■ ■ ■

A case study, basically, is a depiction either of a phase or the totality of relevant experience of some selected datum. (Foreman 1948, p. 408)

A case study is expected to catch the complexity of a single case... Case study is the study of the particularity and complexity of a single case, coming to understand its activity within important circumstances. (Stake 1995, p. xi)

[T]he single most defining characteristic of case study research lies in delimiting the object of study, the case... If the phenomenon you are interested in studying is not intrinsically bounded, it is not a case. (Merriam 1998, p. 27)

An educational case study is an empirical enquiry which is: conducted within a localized boundary of space and time... into *interesting* aspects of an educational activity, or programme, or institution, or system; mainly in its natural context and within an ethic of respect for persons; in order to inform the judgements and decisions of practitioners or policy-makers; or of theoreticians who are working to these ends; in such a way that sufficient data are collected for the researcher to be able... to explore *significant* features of the case... create *plausible* interpretations... test for the[ir] trustworthiness... construct a *worthwhile* argument... [and] convey *convincingly* to an audience this argument. (Bassey 1999, p. 58, emphasis in original)

A case can be an *individual*; it can be a *group* – such as a family, or a class, or an office, or a hospital ward; it can be an *institution* – such as a school or a children's home, or a factory; it can be a large-scale *community* – a town, an industry, a profession. All of these are single cases; but you can also study *multiple* cases: a number of single parents; several schools; two different professions. (Gillham 2000, p. 1, emphasis in original)

A case study is a research strategy that can be qualified as holistic in nature, following an iterative-parallel way of proceeding, looking at only a few strategically selected cases, observed in their natural context in an open-ended way, explicitly avoiding (all variants of) tunnel vision, making use of analytical comparison of cases or sub-cases, and aimed at description and explanation of complex and entangled group attributes, patterns, structures or processes. (Verschuren 2003, p. 137)

A 'case study'... is best defined as an intensive study of a single unit with an aim to generalize across a larger set of units. (Gerring 2004, p. 341)

[C]ase study is a transparadigmatic and transdisciplinary heuristic that involves the careful delineation of the phenomena for which evidence is being collected. (VanWynsberghe and Khan 2007, p. 80)

A case study is a study in which (a) one case (single case study) or a small number of cases (comparative case study) in their real life context are selected, and (b) scores obtained from these cases are analysed in a qualitative manner. (Dul and Hak 2008, p. 4)

A case study refers to the study of a *social phenomenon*: carried out within the boundaries of one social system (the case), or within the boundaries of a few social systems (the cases)... in the case's natural context... by monitoring the phenomenon during a certain period or, alternatively, by collecting information afterwards with respect to the development of the phenomenon during a certain period... in which the researcher focuses on process-tracing... where the researcher, guided by an initially broad research question, explores the data and only after some time formulates more precise research questions, keeping an open eye to unexpected aspects... using several data sources, the main ones being (in this order) available documents, interviews with informants and (participatory) observation. (Swanborn 2010, p. 13, emphasis in original)

Case studies are analyses of persons, events, decisions, periods, projects, policies, institutions or other systems which are studied holistically by one or more methods. The case that is the subject of the inquiry will be an instance of a class of phenomena that provides an analytical frame – an object – within which the study is conducted and which the case illuminates and explicates. (Thomas 2011a, p. 23)

The first three definitions usefully focus on key elements of our common understanding of case study. Thus, Foreman, in the earliest of the definitions given, stresses that case study is about a particular item, thing or case; or, in his words, 'some selected datum'. Stake points out that the case being studied is both particular and complex; after all, if it were not the former, it would not be a case, and, if it were not the latter, it would scarcely be worth studying. And Merriam notes that the case needs to be bounded or delimited; as she says, if it isn't, it isn't a case, and you are not then engaged in case study but in some other kind of research.

Seven of the other eight definitions stress other aspects of case study which most of its proponents would agree with. Thus, Bassey, Verschuren, Dul and Hak and Swanborn all emphasise that the case is to be studied in its 'natural' or 'real life' context. Cases are not artificial entities, they are not experiments, but are part of our reality, from which – even though, as cases, they are bounded – they cannot be separated.

Both Verschuren and Thomas point out that case study is a holistic research strategy. We study (or, at least, attempt to study) the entirety of the case, not selected aspects of it. In practice, this may mean that we study as much of the case as we can in a given period of time. Gillham, Dul and Hak and Swanborn stress that case study need not be confined to single cases, but might involve the comparative study of two or more cases.

Some of the elements of the different definitions could, however, be said to fall into the categories of desirable or idealistic. Bassey writes of case studies focusing on 'interesting aspects' and 'significant features', leading to the construction of a 'worthwhile argument', all of which is definitely a desirable quality, and most probably sought for at the outset of the case study, but not necessarily guaranteed. What is interesting or significant for one researcher may not be so for another, though all would hope and aim for their arguments to be worthwhile.

Gerring states that the aim of case study is 'to generalize', which might not always be feasible, and indeed would be rejected as an aim by some case study researchers. The case might be of interest for its own sake, or might be too particular, or the researcher might be unsure about whether their findings were generalisable. The issue of generalisability is a key one in discussions of case study, and we will return to it in more detail in Chapter 3.

Verschuren's argument that case studies should be observed in 'an open-ended way' might also be questioned in terms of its practicality. Most researchers do not have indefinite time to devote to a piece of research, and, after all, one of the main attractions of case study research is that it is small-scale and focused. In Verschuren's definition, it is also by no means clear what is signified by 'an iterative-parallel way of proceeding', which seems to introduce unnecessarily complicated jargon to what is meant to be a straightforward definition.

Other elements of some of the definitions are more particular, and might be debated or disagreed with. Thus, when Dul and Hak specify that case studies are to be analysed 'in a qualitative manner', they are revealing both their own preference and the most common strategy (although their preference seems to be immediately compromised by their reference to 'scores'). It is also possible to analyse case studies, either wholly or partly, in a quantitative manner; though, as we shall see, Dul and Hak are not alone in their view.

Something similar is going on when Swanborn unnecessarily restricts case study to the study of 'social phenomenon' which is presumably his focus and interest. Other kinds of natural phenomena (e.g. the dissemination of diseases, weather patterns, the hunting strategies of particular animals) might also lend themselves to a case study approach.

Perhaps the most unusual of the eleven definitions offered is that of VanWynsberghe and Khan, who describe case study as a 'transparadigmatic and transdisciplinary heuristic', or, in other words, a way of researching that can be applied in almost any circumstance. That seems rather an obscure way of setting out a definition. While the second part, 'the careful delineation of the phenomena for which evidence is being collected', seems more straightforward, it could be applied equally well to many research designs.

Of course, when we are discussing anything of significance, which case study certainly is, there are bound to be differences of opinion and variations in understanding. This is how academics and researchers work to advance and develop our thinking. So it is not surprising that we can readily identify differences and disagreements between these definitions (and there are many others that could have been used). But the commonalities between them are stronger, and, as well as clarifying what case study is, they also help to make it clear what case study is not.

We can be reasonably confident, then, in stating that case study involves the following:

- The study of a particular case, or a number of cases.
- That the case will be complex and bounded.
- That it will be studied in its context.
- That the analysis undertaken will seek to be holistic.

Case study is not, as we have already noted, an experiment (though it might be combined with an experimental research design: see Chapter 6). Nor is it a survey or a large-scale analysis. Case study is *small-scale research with meaning* (this interpretation is discussed in more detail in Chapter 4).

THE ORIGINS AND HISTORY OF CASE STUDY

The history of case study is a long and complicated matter: only a brief overview will be given here.

The development of case study as a research design both encompasses and illustrates the issues and critiques (these are discussed at greater length in Chapter 3) which it has had to deal with throughout its history. It also further demonstrates the diversity of usage to which the term case study (and analogous terms) has been put, and its application in a wide variety of disciplines (the subject of the next section and of Chapter 5).

Burgess (1927) offers an account of the early application of case study in American sociology. He notes that 'The case-study method was first introduced into social science as a handmaiden to statistics' (p. 114), with the latter long regarded – as it still is in many quarters today – as the most desirable way of undertaking research. In other words, case study was seen largely as a means for fleshing out and providing detailed illustration or exemplification to complement quantitative analyses, rather than as an alternative to them.

Burgess considered that 'the actual introduction of the case-study as a method of sociological field research was made by Thomas and Znaniecki in *The Polish Peasant in Europe and America*' (p. 116), which was first published in 1918 (see also Adelman 2015). This places case study (at least in its sociological context) as being about a century old. Unsurprisingly, then, Burgess, writing when case study was less than a decade old, concludes that 'it is apparent that case-study as a method in sociology is still in its infancy' (p. 117). Others, however, date the origin of case study research as rather earlier, with Scholz and Tietje (2002, p. 4) referencing the work of the French sociologist Le Play in 1855, adding more than half a century to Burgess's reckoning.

Writing nearly 20 years after Burgess, Symonds (1945) reports on what was then recent work on the use of case study, in particular with respect to personality research. It is apparent from his argument and conclusion how important, despite the greater development and acceptance of the method, statistics and 'objectivity' remained:

> [M]uch remains to be done to improve its methodology so that case materials may be amassed and treated in a manner that includes, on the one hand, objective appraisal and statistical integrity and that, on the other hand, never loses sight of the integrated, dynamic, holistic picture of human personality which the case study approach to research uniquely may give. (p. 357)

To survive alongside more 'scientific' methods, particularly statistics – with which it was constantly compared – case study had to be carried out in a suitably rigorous fashion (Burgess 1941; Cottrell 1941; Maxfield 1930; Stouffer 1941). From its beginnings, therefore, a great deal of attention has always been given to trying to devise common standards or approaches to case study.

Thus, Foreman (1948) sought to develop a theory of case studies. He argued that case studies use three sorts of data – personal documents, participant observation and third-person reports (a rather partial listing to the modern eye) – and that they may be used in five ways in sociological research: 'They may serve purposes of: (1) illustration; (2) concept and hypothesis development; (3) hypothesis testing; (4) prediction or postdiction; (5) methodological testing or refinement' (p. 410). He goes on to consider the adequacy of case records and their interpretation, how this may be judged, and the thorny issue of generalisation.

In the 1950s, however, case study became less popular for a period in the social sciences. As Platt (1992) notes, in her analysis of the history of case study in American methodological thought:

> The term 'case study' has played a variety of roles, changing over time, in American methodological discussion... Its use has often been imprecise, carrying ideological connotations rather than analytical denonation. (p. 17)

She associates the post-war decline in the popularity of case study with a variety of other factors as well, including continuing concern with the issues of generalisation and prediction, problems with the articulation of case study analysis, and increased competition from the development of more sophisticated quantitative techniques and associated databases (an area in which American social science led the world).

Case study research began to make a comeback in the late 1960s and 1970s (Simons 1980, 2009), as qualitative techniques assumed a greater importance and popularity, particularly outside North America:

> In the last 25 years the shift away from quantification and large scale survey methods in the social sciences, alongside the increasing attention being given to language and meaning in constructing identity and social relations, has seen a significant revival in case study methods. This has led to a range of reappraisals of the method, and an increased emphasis upon lived experience, the life-story and the biographical/autobiographical in social research. (David 2006, p. xxxix)

The increased development and diversification of qualitative methods (e.g. Denzin and Lincoln 2005a) both helped to build up the contemporary popularity of case study as a research design and led to its mistaken identification in some quarters as solely a qualitative approach. Its scale and accessibility as a research design resulted in its increasing usage by the growing numbers of final-year undergraduates, postgraduates and small-scale researchers in the social sciences and beyond.

CASE STUDY IN DIFFERENT DISCIPLINES

Swanborn (2010) identifies several disciplinary sources of importance in the development of case study:

- The growth and development of many sciences, such as the health sciences, clinical psychotherapy and law [not usually considered a science], went hand in hand with the study of cases...
- A specific source of inspiration in social science is constituted by the traditional study of a village or local setting in cultural anthropology...
- A third source is the sociological Chicago School...

- In political science, historical roots include a strong tradition building on case studies…
- Well-known from the field of psychology are the studies of Sigmund Freud and other psychoanalysts. Later on, the study of individual persons (cases) on other domains, such as personality psychology and clinical psychology, developed.
- More recently, the study of cases in many policy fields (e.g. social work, youth support, labour market intermediary, the integration of ethnic minorities) presents new impulses. (p. 11)

In other words, there are many diverse 'traditions' of case study research, which have been developed and pursued often with little reference to, or even knowledge of, each other. This is, however, by no means unusual in academic research. What case study means, therefore, in political science will be at least subtly different from what it means in sociology (as will the sources referred to), and significantly different from its practice in disciplines which are further removed, such as psychotherapy or health care.

The importance of case study to a range of disciplines has been maintained up until the present day. It is particularly evident (and prevalent) now in the business/management area; for example, in accounting (Cooper and Morgan 2008), industrial marketing management (Beverland and Lindgren 2010), international business (Piekkari, Welch and Paavilainen 2009), operations management (Voss, Tsikriktsis and Frohlich 2002), public administration (Barzelay 1993) and small business studies (Chetty 1996).

Outside the business/management field, case study is most closely associated with other professional disciplines, which have come to dominate provision in most universities and colleges. The most prominent, after business/management, are health/medicine (Jones and Windholz 1990; Lukoff, Edwards and Miller 1998; Yin 1999) and education (Snyder 2012; Stenhouse 1979). Other professional disciplines with strong traditions and current usages of case study include development (Vellema, Ton, de Roo and van Wijk 2013), information systems (Cavaye 1996; Dube and Pare 2003), law (Caulley and Dowdy 1987) and social work (Lee, Mishna and Brennenstuhl 2010).

Case study research is not, however, as already indicated, solely the preserve of professional disciplines, but is also widely practised in what might be termed the 'pure' (as opposed to applied) disciplines. These include geography (Curtis et al 2000), philosophy (Ruzzene 2012), political science (Gerring 2006), psychology (Stewart and Chambless 2010) and sociology (Burrawoy 1998).

Some of the studies referenced offer practical guidance on how to apply case study in the discipline in question, while others offer surveys of the ways in which case study has been applied. Examples of case study analyses from different disciplines, and from around the world, including those referred to here, will be presented and discussed in more detail in Chapter 5.

TYPES OF CASE STUDY

Proponents of case study have long recognised that there are different sorts of, or approaches to, case study. Box 2.2 sets out nine alternative typologies of case study: eight of them were suggested during the last two decades, along with an earlier categorisation. These are by no means the only typologies that have been suggested, although they include some of the most influential and most widely cited. It is clear that the more recent examples draw on the earlier examples (compare, for example, Eckstein and Levy). The nine examples given do, however, usefully illustrate the variety of considerations that different authors bring to bear, and the different terminologies used, as well as their common concerns.

■ ■ ■ Box 2.2 Types of Case Study ■ ■ ■

1 Configurative-idiographic study – dealing 'with complex collective individuals'
2 Disciplined-configurative study – 'application to cases of frameworks of inquiry'
3 Heuristic case studies – 'serving to find out'
4 Plausibility probes – to establish whether broader, more painstaking studies might be valuable
5 Crucial case studies – tests of theory. (Eckstein 1975, pp. 97–113)

1 The intensive case study (including interpretative and explanatory)

'The goal is to provide a history, description or interpretation of unique and typical experiences or events. These events become the basis for developing theory from an understanding of the context in which certain events occurred.'

2 Comparative case studies (case surveys, case comparisons, creative interpretations)

'…emphasize the use of contrasting observations from varied settings and highlight the development of clear concepts.'

3 Action research

'[A] term for describing a spectrum of cases that focus on research and learning through intervening and observing the process of change.' (Cunningham 1997, pp. 402, 405)

1 Descriptive (exploratory-descriptive, focused-descriptive)
2 Theoretical-heuristic (grounded theory building, hermeneutic work)
3 Theory-testing (testing propositions within grounded theory, metatheoretical construction). (Edwards 1998)

(Continued)

(Continued)

1   Holistic

'A holistic case study is shaped by a thoroughly qualitative approach that relies on narrative, phenomenological descriptions. Themes and hypotheses may be important but should remain subordinate to the understanding of the case.'

2   Embedded

'Embedded case studies involve more than one unit, or object, of analysis and usually are not limited to qualitative analysis alone.' (Scholz and Tietje 2002, p. 9)

1   Intrinsic, 'if the study is undertaken because, first and last, one wants better understanding of this particular case';
2   Instrumental, 'if a particular case is examined mainly to provide insight into an issue or to redraw a generalization';
3   Multiple or collective, when 'a number of cases may be studied jointly in order to investigate a phenomenon, population or general condition'. (Stake 2005, p. 445)

1   Typical
2   Diverse
3   Extreme
4   Deviant
5   Influential
6   Crucial
7   Pathway (i.e. chosen to elucidate causal mechanisms)
8   Most-similar
9   Most-different. (Gerring 2007, pp. 89–90)

1   Idiographic (inductive or theory-guided) –

'which aim to describe, explain or interpret a particular "case" and which can be either inductive or theory-guided'.

2   Hypothesis-generating
3   Hypothesis-testing
4   Plausibility probes (pilot or illustrative studies) –

'an intermediary step between hypothesis generation and hypothesis testing and which include "illustrative" case studies'. (Levy 2008, p. 3)

1   Explanatory or causal
2   Descriptive
3   Exploratory

All of which may be single or multiple. (Yin 2009, pp. 19–21)

1   Subject 'the case itself' and object 'the analytical frame or theory through which the subject is viewed and which the subject explicates'
2   Purposes and approach – theory-centred or illustrative
3   Comparative/non-comparative – employment of time. (Thomas 2011c, p. 511)

The classifications are all fairly simple, most involving no more than two, three, four or five categories, though Gerring's includes nine. Some, however, then break the categories down further in another hierarchical level, or identify a series of dimensions or spectra along which the characteristics of case studies vary.

Thomas's classification is probably the most complex, as it involves at least three distinctions: whether the focus is on the subject (the case itself) or the object (the theoretical framework adopted), whether the case study is theory-centred or illustrative, and whether a comparative or non-comparative approach is adopted. The last two of these distinctions are common to, though differently expressed in, many of the typologies.

The comparative/non-comparative distinction concerns whether the focus of the study is on a single case or more than one case (a point highlighted in their definitions of case study by Gillham and Swanborn: see Box 2.1). Cunningham also refers to this distinction as comparative, while both Stake and Yin use the alternative terms 'multiple' or 'collective', while for Scholz and Tietje this element is wrapped up in their 'embedded' category.

Levy, following Eckstein, offers 'plausibility probes' as one type of case study, by which is meant what is now more commonly termed a pilot study. This obviously has overlaps with the single/multiple case study distinction, as it implies that more cases will then be selected for study once the pilot study has been completed, and lessons have been learnt from it.

Whether or not the focus of the case study is on theory is also a key concern. A focus on theory is conveyed by Eckstein in his 'disciplined-configurative' type, by Cunningham in the term 'intensive', by Edwards in the 'theoretical-heuristic' and 'theory-testing' distinctions, by Levy in the 'idiographic' type (and also, to an extent, in the 'hypothesis-generating' and 'hypothesis-testing' types), and by Yin in his 'explanatory or causal' category.

Alternatively, a focus which is explicitly not on theory is classified by both Edwards and Yin as 'descriptive', and by Eckstein as 'configurative-idiographic'.

Other elements are emphasised in their classifications by just one of the authors included. For Scholz and Tietje, the holistic/embedded distinction is partly about the use of qualitative and/or quantitative methods. Cunningham links case study to another research design when he uses 'action research' as one of his categories (this linkage is further discussed and exemplified in Chapter 6). Edwards brings in a further research design when he links both of his 'theoretical-heuristic' and 'theory-testing' categories to grounded theory (which is also discussed in Chapter 6). Gerring's classification is unusual in emphasising the relation of the case to the population from which it is chosen.

Other distinctions do not appear in any of the eight classifications considered here. The most notable of these is probably the distinction between teaching and research case studies, which is discussed in the next section.

It is worth mentioning here the contributions to this discussion of another two authors. First, Mitchell (1984, p. 239) introduces a typical/telling case dichotomy (cf. Gerring's use of typical and influential) in this context:

> A good case study… enables the analyst to establish theoretically valid connections between events and phenomena which previously were ineluctable. From this point of view, the search for a 'typical' case for analytical exposition is likely to be less fruitful than the search for a 'telling' case, in which the particular circumstances surrounding a case serve to make previously obscure theoretical relationships suddenly apparent.

Second, Simons (2009, pp. 21–22), after noting Stake's distinction between intrinsic, instrumental and collective cases, and the theory-led or theory-generated categorisation, also draws attention to evaluation and ethnographic case studies. These last two categories reflect, on the one hand, the purposes to which case study research is often put, and on the other hand, particular traditions of case study research (both of which are discussed in more detail in Chapter 6).

While none of the nine typologies seems entirely satisfactory, therefore, and their use of alternative terms to mean the same thing (or, at least, much the same thing) is confusing, this analysis suggests that there are three major factors to bear in mind when considering examples of case studies:

- Whether they focus on a single case or involve a comparative study of two or more cases.
- Whether they confine themselves to description or engage with theory.
- Whether they are intended primarily to support teaching or research.

While the third of these factors is discussed next, the first two are considered in more detail in Chapter 8.

TEACHING AND RESEARCH CASE STUDIES

In some disciplines, case study is used as a teaching method as well as, or instead of, a research method. This is common, for example, in various disciplines in the health/medicine field (e.g. Bair 1980), in law (e.g. Caulley and Dowdy 1987) and social work, and in business/management studies (e.g. Forman 2006; Garvin 2003; Zhao 1996). Case studies are used, for example, to explore and exemplify particular medical conditions, legal precedents or business problems.

To take the example of business/management, Romm and Mahler (1991) offer 'a new approach to an old method', focusing on the use of case studies in teaching. They provide sets of guidelines for their usage, arguing that:

> By tailoring the use of cases to specific objectives and by matching these objectives with a diverse and imaginative case-related repertoire of methodologies, we can turn case analysis into a theoretically relevant, personally meaningful, and thoroughly enjoyable experience. (p. 300)

Contardo and Wensley (2004) also focus on the use of case studies in teaching and, in particular, on how the Harvard Business School has been both celebrated and constrained by its adherence to a particular form of the case method.

While recognising this broader usage, and accepting that teaching and research case studies may overlap, the focus in this book will be primarily on case study as a research method.

SUMMARY

In this chapter, we have:

- defined case study as involving the study of a particular case, or a number of cases, where the case will be complex and bounded, studied in its context, with the analysis undertaken seeking to be holistic
- indicated that different kinds of case study are recognised, notably whether they are single or multiple, and whether they are theoretical or descriptive
- shown that case study has been practised for at least a century, with its popularity and usage varying over time
- noted how case study is employed in a wide variety of disciplines, and that it is sometimes used for teaching as well as research purposes.

KEY READINGS

As will be clear from the discussion and references given so far, this is neither the first nor the only guide to case study research to be published. There are several introductory volumes which may usefully be consulted, including:

Gillham, B (2000) *Case Study Research Methods*. London, Continuum.
Stake, R (1995) *The Art of Case Study Research*. Thousand Oaks, CA, Sage.
Swanborn, P (2010) *Case Study Research: What, why and how?* London, Sage.
Thomas, G (2011a) *How to Do Your Case Study: A guide for students and researchers*. London, Sage.
Yin, R (2009) *Case Study Research: Design and methods* (4th edition). Thousand Oaks, CA, Sage.

Key Debates in Case Study Research

3

INTRODUCTION

Case study has attracted a lot of attention, both positive and negative. This chapter examines in detail the key debates, which have been going on for decades, around and about case study.

We start by considering alternative perspectives on what case study is and what it isn't. Is it a research method, an approach, a style, a strategy or a design, or perhaps all of these things? Case study is then considered in a comparative perspective in the light of other possible (and popular) forms of research, such as longitudinal, cross-sectional and experimental research. The position of case study with respect to qualitative and quantitative forms of research is also discussed.

The continuing debates around case study are then reviewed. Starting with the positive, the strengths and desirable qualities of case study research are identified. Taking the opposing perspective, its perceived weaknesses – particularly regarding the issues of generalisability, reliability and validity – and the responses that have been made to these, are discussed.

Finally, the criticism that case studies are so endemic and ill-defined that any and every piece of research could be termed a case study (or perhaps a multiple case study) is discussed.

ALTERNATIVE PERSPECTIVES ON CASE STUDY

The attention given to case study in the social research methods literature varies widely. Some texts ignore or barely mention it – clearly not considering it to be a major research method or design – while others give it considerable space. Thus, May

(2001) devotes only a page and a half to case study research, at the end of a chapter on participant observation, with which he links and compares it. Blaxter, Hughes and Tight (2006) give it just over three pages, presenting it as a research approach, alongside action research, experiments and surveys.

Those who discuss case study at greater length tend to present it in rather different lights. Punch (2005), for example, discusses case study as an approach to qualitative research design, allocating it seven pages, alongside ethnography, grounded theory and action research. He answers his own question 'what is a case study?' as follows:

> The basic idea is that one case (or perhaps a small number of cases) will be studied in detail, using whatever methods seem appropriate. While there may be a variety of specific purposes and research questions, the general objective is to develop as full an understanding of that case as possible. (p. 144)

He acknowledges that case study 'is more a strategy than a method' (p. 144), and accepts that:

> almost anything can serve as a case, and the case may be simple or complex. But... we can define a case as a phenomenon of some sort occurring in a bounded context. Thus, the case may be an individual, or a role, or a small group, or an organization, or a community, or a nation. It could also be a decision, or a policy, or a process, or an incident or event of some sort, and there are other possibilities as well. (p. 144)

Burns (2000) takes a similar approach to Punch, treating case studies as a qualitative method, alongside ethnographic research, unstructured interviewing, action research and historical research. Like each of them, case studies are granted a whole chapter, amounting to 22 pages. He makes a number of revealing observations:

> The case study has been unfortunately used as a 'catch-all' category for anything that does not fit into experimental, survey or historical methods. The term has also been used loosely as a synonym for ethnography, participant observation, naturalistic inquiry and fieldwork... The case study is rather a *portmanteau* term, but typically involves the observation of an individual unit, e.g. a student, a delinquent clique, a family group, a class, a school, a community, and event, or even an entire culture. (p. 459)

Bryman (2004) treats case study as a research design, but, unlike Punch and Burns, does not see it as being exclusively qualitative in nature. In his presentation, case study is contrasted with experimental, cross-sectional, longitudinal and comparative designs. Bryman notes that:

> The most common use of the term associates the case study with a location, such as a community or organization. The emphasis tends to be upon an intensive

examination of the setting. There is a tendency to associate case studies with qualitative research, but such an identification is not appropriate... case studies are frequently sites for the employment of *both* quantitative and qualitative research. (p. 49, emphasis in original)

Cohen, Manion and Morrison (2007) take another approach, seeing case study as a style of (educational) research, together with ethnographic, historical, action, experimental, internet-based and survey styles. They assert that case studies:

- will have temporal characteristics which help to define their nature
- have geographical parameters allowing for their definition
- will have boundaries which allow for definition
- may be defined by an individual in a particular context, at a point in time
- may be defined by the characteristics of the group
- may be defined by role or function
- may be shaped by organizational or institutional arrangements. (p. 254)

This set of characteristics seems both broad-ranging and rather repetitive.

Of course, there are many other social research methods texts which we might also examine, but this small sample already illustrates the range of alternative perspectives that are taken towards case study. Judging by these texts – summarised in Box 3.1 – we could view case study as a method, approach, style, strategy or design. And, whichever (and however many) of these it might be, it can be conceived in relation to a wide, but differing, range of other social research methods, approaches, styles, strategies or designs. These could include action research, comparative studies, cross-sectional studies, ethnography, experiments, grounded theory, historical studies, internet-based studies, interviews, longitudinal studies and surveys (these relations are considered further in the next section).

■ ■ ■ Box 3.1   Alternative Research Classifications of Case Study ■ ■ ■

Punch (2005): 'approaches to qualitative research design'

- Case studies
- Ethnography
- Grounded theory
- Action research

Burns (2000): 'qualitative methods'

- Ethnographic research
- Unstructured interviewing

- Action research
- Case studies
- Historical research

Bryman (2004): 'research designs'

- Experimental design
- Cross-sectional design
- Longitudinal design(s)
- Case study design
- Comparative design

Cohen Manion and Morrison (2007): 'styles of educational research'

- Naturalistic and ethnographic research
- Historical and documentary research
- Surveys, longitudinal, cross-sectional and trend studies
- Internet-based research and computer usage
- Case studies
- Ex post facto research
- Experiments, quasi-experiments, single-case research and meta-analysis
- Action research

But can we not be clearer about what case study is and isn't? In a carefully considered assessment, Verschuren (2003) sets out to 'clarify some ambiguities and misconceptions as to case study as a research methodology, and to define it more clearly as a research strategy' (p. 122). He notes differences among practitioners with respect to: '(a) the empirical *object* of a case study and the way we look at it; (b) the research methods that are used; and (c) the adequacy of the results to be obtained' (p. 122, emphasis in original). He argues that 'the main characteristic of a case study as a way of doing research is that it is a holistic rather than a reductionistic approach' (p. 128), with implications for both the object of observation and the methods used for generating research material.

We should not be surprised, of course, to find that case study has been interpreted in a variety of ways (see also the discussion of What is a Case Study? in Chapter 2). Similarly, we may readily accept that the terms method, approach, style, strategy and design – as they are used in the discussion of research – share overlapping meanings. Nevertheless, it will be helpful, for the discussion in the remainder of this chapter and throughout the book, to pin things down a little more firmly.

My own perspective, then, is that it is most sensible to view case study as a research design. As such, it represents a way of pursuing a particular research project or projects. Within this research design, as within others, particular methods may then be adopted in order to progress the research.

CASE STUDY AS A RESEARCH DESIGN

Where does case study sit in comparison with other research designs? We have already seen (in Box 3.1) that research designs, and the place of case study within them, have been variously categorised by different authors. There is, then, no single, definitive and widely accepted classification of research designs.

We will examine in more detail, however, one of the classifications already mentioned, that proposed by Bryman (2004). Bryman's classification has, to my mind, the considerable advantages of being both straightforward and neatly structured. He begins by explaining what he means by research design:

> A *research design* provides a framework for the collection and analysis of data. A choice of research design reflects decisions about the priority being given to a range of dimensions of the research process. These include the importance attached to: expressing causal connections between variables; generalizing to larger groups... understanding behavior... in its specific social context; having a temporal appreciation of social phenomena. (p. 27, emphasis in original)

Five research designs are then identified: experimental (the manipulation of one variable to measure its impact on another), cross-sectional ('the collection of data on *more than one case* and at *a single point in time*' [p. 41, emphasis in original]), longitudinal (the repeated collection of data on at least two different occasions), case study (which Bryman defines simply as 'the detailed and intensive analysis of a single case' [p. 48]) and comparative ('the study using more or less identical methods of two contrasting cases' [p. 53]).

In Bryman's terms, then, case study as a research design is less concerned with establishing causal connections, generalisation or temporal connections; it focuses instead on 'understanding behavior in its specific social context'. Or, to put it the other way around, if you are engaging in a research project with the intention of understanding some aspect of behaviour in its social setting, case study is an obvious and appropriate research design to employ.

Interestingly, case study would also be a possible approach (note that I am now using the term 'approach' rather than 'design' to indicate that an alternative overall design to case study is being employed) for at least three of the other four research designs suggested by Bryman. Indeed, this is clearly suggested by his use of the word 'case' in the sense of 'item' or 'individual' in the quotations given. Thus, a comparative design could proceed using a multiple case study approach, as might a cross-sectional design (though here a survey is probably a more obvious approach). A longitudinal design might involve returning to the same case study (or case studies) on a number of occasions.

The only one of Bryman's five designs where case study does not suggest itself as an approach is the experimental design, though even here the manipulation of the variable(s) involved could take place within cases (see the discussion of experiment as a research design that can be combined with case study in Chapter 6). What this discussion illustrates, of course, is the care needed in talking about, and distinguishing between, case study and cases. As was noted in Chapter 2, all research involves the study of cases in some form; case study is a research design which focuses on the detailed study of a particular case or cases.

THE QUALITATIVE/QUANTITATIVE DEBATE

[D]ifferent conceptions of the term 'case' are central to the enduring gulf between quantitative and qualitative social science… The view that quantitative researchers look at many cases, while qualitative researchers look at only one or a small number of cases, can be maintained only by allowing considerable slip-page in what is meant by 'case'… the tendency to conflate *qualitative research* and *case study* should be resisted. (Ragin 1992a, pp. 3–4)

As has already been stressed, when considering definitions of case study, some authors view case study as wholly or primarily qualitative in nature (and the classifications by Punch, 2005, of 'approaches to qualitative research design', and Burns, 2000, of 'quali-tative methods', summarised in Box 3.1, provide examples of this tendency). When looking at the origins and history of case study in Chapter 2, it also appeared that there had been much debate regarding the relationship between case study and statistical (i.e. quantitative) methods. It is important, therefore, to be clear about the position of case study with respect to the qualitative/quantitative debate.

As you are probably aware, much energy and paper has been expended on arguing the relative merits of qualitative and quantitative forms of research, and a great deal of this has not been particularly productive. Often, opponents in the debate have employed stereotypical or misleading representations of each other's assumptions and practices so as to be better able to critique and knock them down. Indeed, it is not uncommon to hear or read the view expressed that qualitative and quantitative research are based on fundamentally different views of the world and how it can, or should, be studied. If so, it would be very difficult – and, some would argue, completely out of the question – to employ both qualitative and quantitative methods in the same research study.

Thus, quantitative researchers may align themselves with the scientific method, portraying themselves as searchers for the objective truth about the world (social or physical) and how it works, and dismiss qualitative research as subjective, small-scale and lacking in rigour. Qualitative researchers, for their part, may highlight the richness and depth of their data and analysis, while accusing quantitative research of superficial-ity, arguing that everything – and certainly not the social world – cannot be reduced to mere numbers.

Often, of course, these preferences are linked to the skill sets of the research-ers concerned (e.g. some people feel at home with large data sets and multivariate analyses; others are much more comfortable talking to or observing other people in natural settings). They may also reflect their underlying world-views of knowledge and how it can be accessed or developed (i.e. their ontologies and epistemologies).

Nowadays, however, more pragmatically orientated researchers (of which, as you may have surmised, I am one) have distanced themselves from these debates, arguing that mixed methods research, making use of both qualitative and quantitative methods as appropriate, has much more to offer (e.g. Bryman 2004; Scott 2007; Tashakkori and Teddlie 1998). Indeed, I would go further in arguing that all researchers (or, at least, social researchers) should be able to use, and interpret, both qualitative and quantitative methods, at least to some level of understanding.

The same argument may be applied to case study research, which, though it is sometimes claimed by qualitative researchers (probably because of its typically small-scale, detailed focus), may make use of quantitative techniques as well as, or instead of, qualitative methods. It is both possible and acceptable, therefore, to pursue case study research using quantitative data and methods. Thus, for example, the *Sage Handbook of Case-based Methods* (Byrne and Ragin 2009) contains five chapters on quantitative approaches to case-based method and five on qualitative approaches.

Ragin (2000) himself has developed another way forward, through his application of fuzzy set methods to case study research. Fuzzy set methods are an approach which accepts that the researcher may not be able to categorise particular cases as belonging wholly to particular groups (e.g. if the case is a nation, and we are examining democracy, is the case wholly democratic?), but can give them an indicative percentage membership figure (e.g. 70% democratic). This then allows an approach to the cross-case analysis of multiple case studies which is both qualitative and quantitative.

DEBATES REGARDING CASE STUDY

Criticisms of, and debates about, case study are of long standing (see the discussion in Chapter 2 on The Origins and History of Case Study; for more recent, but now also historic, accounts, see: Atkinson and Delamont 1985; Mitchell 1983; Platt 1992). Hence, those in favour of, or using, case study as a research design often feel obliged to defend their choice. Here, for example, Mitchell provides a firm defence of case study, resting on the rigour with which it is carried out:

> [C]ase studies of whatever form are a reliable and respectable procedure of social analysis and... much criticism of their reliability and validity has been based on a misconception of the basis upon which the analyst may justifiably extrapolate from an individual case study to the social process in general... The validity of the extrapolation depends not on the typicality or representativeness of the case but upon the cogency of the theoretical reasoning. (Mitchell 1983, p. 207)

Note that Mitchell refers directly to the issues of both extrapolation (more commonly termed generalisation) and theoretical reasoning. As we will see, these come up repeatedly in discussions of case study.

Proponents of case study also often try to anticipate their critics by identifying and listing (at least some of) the criticisms that have been made of case study research, and then articulating responses to these. There is often a feeling of 'setting up paper tigers' about these exercises, with the supposed criticisms presented in an unduly favourable way which lends itself to a pointed riposte; one can, at times, be overly defensive.

One recent analysis along these lines, provided by Flyvbjerg (2004), is worth considering in some detail as an exemplar of its kind:

> [T]he problems with the conventional wisdom about case-study research can be summarized in five misunderstandings or oversimplifications about the nature of such research:
>
> 1. General, theoretical (context-independent) knowledge is more valuable than concrete, practical (context-dependent) knowledge.
> 2. One cannot generalize on the basis of an individual case: therefore, the case study cannot contribute to scientific development.
> 3. The case study is most useful for generating hypotheses, that is, in the first stage of a total research process, while other methods are more suitable for hypothesis testing and theory-building.
> 4. The case study contains a bias towards verification, that is, a tendency to confirm the researcher's preconceived notions.
> 5. It is often difficult to summarize and develop general propositions and theories on the basis of specific case studies.
>
> These five misunderstandings indicate that it is theory, reliability and validity that are at issue; in other words, the very status of the case study as a scientific method. (Flyvbjerg, 2004, p. 391; see also Ruddin 2006)

Flyvbjerg then proceeds to challenge each of these 'misunderstandings' in turn. On his first point, he argues that in social research 'we have only specific cases and context-dependent knowledge' (2004, p. 392). We may accept that this statement is literally true: all research, as we have argued, involves the study of cases, while few social researchers would argue nowadays that they were seeking 'objective' knowledge. Yet, Flyvbjerg's counter-point imposes a particular view of 'reality', denying the perspective of others who are searching for universal laws or explanations.

On his second point, Flyvbjerg contends that it depends upon the case and how it is chosen, an argument that, in Flyvbjerg's view, also disposes of the third misunderstanding, with attention given to the selection of extreme, critical or even paradigmatic cases for study. This may seem a rather trite response. Is it really always possible to select cases that are particularly pertinent for study, and can one always know that this is the case before studying them?

In this respect, however, Flyvbjerg would appear to have the support of both Yin (2003), who offers a series of rationales for studying a single case, and Stake, who goes so far as to state that 'The real business of case study is particularization, not generalization'

(1995, p. 8). By contrast, Mitchell (1983), as evidenced in the earlier quotation, was also concerned about generalising – but only in a theoretical sense – from the particular case being studied.

On his fourth point, Flyvbjerg contends that this criticism is true for all methods of social research, and thus does not apply specifically to case study. This is an argument that I have a lot of sympathy for; all too often, the motivation for undertaking research is to prove that the researcher's hypothesis, opinion or gut feeling is correct.

On his fifth point, which seems to overlap with his second, Flyvbjerg argues that:

> The problems in summarizing case studies, however, are due more often to the properties of the reality studied than to the case study as a research method. Often it is not desirable to summarize and generalize case studies. Good studies should be read as narratives in their entirety. (2004, p. 402)

This, to me, seems to be asking a lot, both of one's readers and one's critics. One has to doubt, therefore, if Flyvbjerg and his (real or imagined) critics could ever be reconciled; they would appear to be taking widely diverging perspectives on what is of most important and significance in social research.

Concern over the status of case study has been the stimulus for a series of conferences and edited texts during the last three decades (e.g. Feagin, Orum and Sjoberg 1991; Gomm, Mammersily and Foster 2000a; Ragin and Becker 1992). This move to not just defending, but arguing for, case study as a useful and important research design has also been reflected in its recent growth in popularity among social researchers (David 2006).

Feagin, Orum and Sjoberg (1991) start from the premise that 'social scientists need to make much more use of the case study approach to studying social life' (p. vii). They then outline how issues of reliability and validity can be handled (by conducting team research and triangulating data sources), and assert the strengths of case study in providing a close reading set within its context.

Ragin (1992a) opens a second edited text – in an examination of 'what is a case?' – by arguing that the response to criticisms of case study is implicit in its practice:

> Implicit in most social scientific notions of case analysis is the idea that the objects of investigation are similar enough and separate enough to permit treating them as comparable instances of the same general phenomenon... Social scientists who conduct case studies argue that their cases are typical or exemplary or extreme or theoretically decisive in some other way. Thus, even in case-study research the principle of repetition is often implicated in statements concerning the relation between the chosen case and other cases. (pp. 1–2)

In other words, as Flyvbjerg (2004) also argues, and as most social researchers making use of case study recognise, it is the selection of the case or cases to study that is paramount. Even if the case chosen for study may not always be exemplary, the reasons for its selection must be explained and justified in order for the completed case study to be of interest and use to other researchers (the practicalities of this are discussed in the section on Sampling and Selection Issues in Chapter 8).

Gomm, Hammersley and Foster (2000b) argue that 'while *some* case study research may be able to avoid 'the problem of generalization' because the case(s) studied have sufficient intrinsic relevance, this is not true of most of it' (p. 102, emphasis in original). They then articulate effective strategies for drawing general conclusions, involving theoretical inference and empirical generalisation, either to a larger population or within cases.

On the issue of theory, Hammersley, Gomm and Foster (2000) note that two main rationales are advanced by case study practitioners: that theoretical/relations may be perceived directly within the case (cf. Mitchell, 1983, argument), or through the application of some form of comparative method; with the former, in their view, necessarily relying upon the latter. They conclude that a number of problems remain:

> Some of these are practical in character, for example the fact that effective use of comparative analysis probably requires the investigation of a relatively large number of cases. Others are more fundamental, for example to do with whether we can reasonably assume deterministic laws of human behaviour. (p. 252)

But they seem confident that these problems may be resolved with some more work. Previously, Hammersley (1992) had offered another possible way forward for case study, in suggesting that:

> 'case study' be defined as one case selection strategy among others; the others being experiment and survey... Compared with the survey, there is a trade-off between generalisability of findings to finite populations on the one hand and detail and accuracy of information on the other. Compared with the experiment, case study involves a trade-off between control of variables and level of reactivity. (pp. 184, 196)

However, while this appears to be an admirably clear and reasonable – and arguably undeniable – rationalisation, it doesn't seem to take the debate any further forward. In a somewhat similar vein, Verschuren (2003) argues that single case studies should be downgraded and termed 'case research'; however, simple changes of label, which will not, in any event, be universally agreed and acted upon, do not really address the underlying issues.

George and Bennett (2005) offer a robust defence and elucidation of the case study method from the perspective of political science. They argue that:

> Case studies are generally strong precisely where statistical methods and formal models are weak. We identify four strong advantages of case study methods that make them valuable in testing hypotheses and particularly useful for theory development: their potential for achieving high conceptual validity; their strong

procedures for fostering new hypotheses; their value as a useful means to closely examine the hypothesized role of causal mechanisms in the context of individual cases; and their capacity for addressing causal complexity. (p. 19)

In a balanced way, they do then identify trade-offs, limitations and potential pitfalls:

Recurrent trade-offs include the problem of case selection; the trade-off between parsimony and richness; and the related tension between achieving high internal validity and good historical explanations of particular cases versus making generalizations that apply to broad populations. The inherent limitations include a relative inability to render judgments on the frequency or representativeness of particular cases and a weak capability for estimating the average 'causal effect' of variables for a sample. Potential limitations can include indeterminacy and lack of independence of cases. (p. 22)

In other words, the potential trade-offs, limitations and pitfalls appear to be as significant as the strengths of case study. The same, however, could be said of other research designs; and, as researchers, we have to make the best of the designs we have.

The debate over case study as a research design continues, of course, and you will find detailed reprises of, and responses to, it throughout this book.

STRENGTHS AND DESIRABLE QUALITIES OF CASE STUDY

These debates enable us to construct a shortlist of the strengths and weaknesses of case study as a research design (see Box 3.2). To strengths and weaknesses, I have added a third shortlist of desirable qualities: that is, qualities which case study research − like other forms of research − should strive to achieve, but may in practice fall short of. In this section we will discuss the strengths and desirable qualities, while the following section will focus − at somewhat greater length − on both the perceived weaknesses and the responses that have been made to them.

Box 3.2   Strengths, Weaknesses and Desirable Qualities of Case Studies

Strengths

- in-depth/detailed/particular
- holistic
- typical/exemplary
- critical/extreme
- feasible/bounded

Weaknesses

- generalisability
- reliability
- validity

Desirable Qualities

- rigour
- theoretical framing
- triangulation/comparison

As Box 3.2 indicates, in my judgement case study arguably has rather more key strengths than it has key weaknesses. To start with, case studies are in-depth, detailed and particular; they allow a close focus on the case, which the researcher thoroughly studies. Second, and relatedly, the research is holistic, aimed at understanding everything – or, at least, as much as possible – about the particularity of the case in question. These characteristics are in contrast to much other research, which tends to focus on a limited range of variables or factors and inevitably oversimplifies, and does not get into the depth of, what is going on.

Third, the case being studied may be typical or exemplary, and these qualities can provide, as we have already seen, one answer to the charge of lack of generalisability. For, if the case is typical or exemplary, and this can be verified and demonstrated, then the likelihood of the findings from it being generalisable increase significantly (though the researcher might still need to perform two or more such typical case studies to be convinced and convincing). Or, alternatively, if the case being studied is critical or extreme, the need to argue generalisability diminishes, for it is the very particularity of the case – its unusual nature – that is important.

Finally, a very important advantage of case study research from the point of view of the small-scale researcher is that it is bounded and therefore much more feasible. When there are limits – of time and other resources – on what the researcher can afford to spend on a particular piece of research, it is highly pragmatic to be able to tightly and precisely define what is going to be researched.

Of course, at the same time, the researcher will still wish and seek to complete a piece of research that is useful and meaningful, but that should also be feasible. Research cannot always change the world (it rarely does so, even if 'the world' is conceived as being just that small piece of it of particular interest to the researcher at a particular moment in time), but it can always aim to be of interest beyond the researcher and the case concerned.

Box 3.2 suggests, in its identification of three desirable qualities for case study (and other forms of) research, how a useful and meaningful case study might be achieved (this is discussed in more detail in Chapter 4). First, the case study needs to be approached and carried out rigorously (see Chapters 8 and 9 for detailed guidance on how to do this). Second, the case study should have a theoretical framework, enabling the development of a fuller understanding of how it works (this is also discussed in more detail in Chapter 8). And, third, it is highly desirable that the findings from the case study are triangulated in some way, for example by comparison with other similar case studies or other kinds of evidence.

Other researchers have come up with similar lists to those in Box 3.2. Thus, writing some 40 years ago, Adelman, Jenkins and Kemmis (1976) produced a list of what they termed the 'possible advantages' of case study:

a) Case study data… is 'strong in reality' but difficult to organize…
b) Case studies allow generalizations either about an instance or from an instance to a class…
c) Case studies recognize the complexity and 'embeddedness' of social truths…
d) Case studies, considered as products, may form an archive of descriptive material sufficiently rich to admit subsequent reinterpretation…
e) Case studies are 'a step to action'… Their insights may be directly interpreted and put to use…
f) Case studies present research or evaluation data in a more publicly accessible form than other kinds of research report. (pp. 148–149)

More recently, Simons (2009) provided the following summary of the strengths of case study:

• Case study using qualitative methods in particular enables the experience and complexity of programmes and policies to be studied in depth…
• Case study can document multiple perspectives, explore contested viewpoints, demonstrate the influence of key actors and interactions between them in telling a story…
• Case study is useful for exploring and understanding the process and dynamics of change…
• Case study is flexible, that is, neither time-dependent nor constrained by method…
• Case studies written in accessible language, including vignettes and cameos of people in the case, direct observations of events, incidents and settings, allow audiences… to vicariously experience what was observed…
• Case study has the potential to engage participants in the research process. (p. 23)

These lists both confirm and add to the strengths identified in Box 3.2, taking a more outwardly looking perspective on the broader purposes of undertaking case study research.

PERCEIVED WEAKNESSES OF CASE STUDY AND RESPONSES TO THESE

Box 3.2 identifies three key weaknesses of case study: generalisability, reliability and validity (or rather the perceived lack of these qualities). These weaknesses, particularly the perceived lack of generalisability, are persistent criticisms, and case study practitioners would do well to show awareness of them and respond appropriately. One appropriate response, of course, would be to emphasise the strengths of case study. Another, adopted in this section, is to explore and better understand the criticisms, and discuss how they might be addressed. We shall look first at generalisability, then at reliability and validity, and finally at some other issues that are raised less often.

These issues, as we have already indicated, have been widely and hotly debated with respect to case study. It is important to stress, therefore, that they are issues which need to be considered for all research designs. Indeed, like most such criteria, they originate from quantitative and scientific research, raising the issue of whether qualitative and social scientific forms of research can, or should, be judged in the same way. While, as I have argued, case study research may be quantitative, qualitative or both, these issues nevertheless have particular purchase because quantitative research is typically larger-scale, while case study research is expressly small-scale, so is always liable to be criticised in these ways.

Generalisability

The relationship between the singular and the general has long been the subject of discussion in case study research; indeed, it would probably be fair to say that it has been the most discussed issue of all (e.g. Bassey 1981; Kennedy 1979). It is an underlying problem with the case study design that needs to be recognised. Of course, if the case being studied has been chosen for its particularity or extreme characteristics, this may not be an important issue: the case is of interest because it is unusual, perhaps unique. Otherwise, however, unless the researcher can demonstrate that the case being studied is typical, generalising from the findings is problematic.

One common response to the generalisability issue has been to argue for the accumulation of single case studies on the same topic to allow for the identification of similarities and differences. This is, indeed, how case studies have long been used in certain disciplines. For example, writing in the 1980s, Tripp (1985) argued that:

> we must find ways of utilising the cumulated wisdom of the case studies we have available… We also need to build archives of the cases similar to those of the legal system, and we need to develop more formally organised and broadly based networks through which teachers and researchers can communicate amongst themselves. (p. 41)

Greene and David (1984) took a similar stance, stating that 'generalizing from multiple case studies – within the structure provided by a multiple case study design – has a sound basis in (inductive) logic' (p. 82). More recently, Jensen and Rodgers (2001) also appear to agree, arguing that meta-analysis (i.e. the collection and reanalysis of collections of case studies addressing the same topic; meta-analysis is discussed further in Chapter 7, where a range of existing meta-analyses of case studies are identified and discussed) may be used to cumulate what they refer to as 'the intellectual gold' of case study research.

So the multiple case study design offers one obvious and acceptable strategy for generalising from case study findings. But what if you do not have the results of multiple case studies available, and it would be impractical for you to go beyond a single case study design (or just a limited number)? Is it still possible to then argue for generalisability?

Evers and Wu (2006) argue that it is possible to generalise from single cases, but suggest that this is not easy or straightforward:

> Being able to generalise reasonably from a single case is a complex and difficult matter. But… the task is abetted by three important factors. First, cases possess considerably more structure than is commonly supposed… Second, researchers bring to a case much more knowledge than is often supposed… Finally, an ongoing trajectory of inquiry through time and changing circumstances makes it less likely that a stable match between patterns of researcher expectations and what is observed is sheer coincidence. (p. 524)

What they seem to be arguing here is that the researcher's experience is a key factor, which relates to their knowing how typical or not the case being studied is, their having carried out other, and perhaps similar, case studies before, and their having an informed awareness of other relevant research. It would not, by comparison, be advisable for a young, inexperienced, honours or postgraduate student, carrying out a case study for perhaps the first time, to seek to generalise from their findings.

Thomas (2011b) reminds us that generalisation is an issue throughout the social sciences, by no means confined to case study research. He reasons that: 'to argue that to seek *generalizable knowledge*, in whatever form – everyday or special – is to miss the point about what may be offered by certain kinds of inquiry, which is *exemplary knowledge*' (p. 33, emphasis in original). We study particular cases for their interest and what we can learn from them. Whether these findings can be applied to other cases may be beyond the scope of the study, and is at least partly the business of other researchers to determine.

Mjoset (2006) suggests a further, pragmatist, stance towards generalisation, going beyond the natural/social science dichotomy, and uses a case study of the Israeli/Palestinian conflict as an example. This is, though, what might be called a critical case: understanding the Israeli/Palestinian conflict is of widespread interest – as it directly affects millions of people and many more indirectly – particularly if it helps to lead to some sort of solution of it (this case study is discussed in more detail in Chapter 7).

Ruzzene (2012) offers a further response to the dilemma, arguing that 'the emphasis should be placed on the comparability of the study rather than on the typicality of the case' (p. 99). This again suggests a kind of multiple case study approach, even if the case studies are carried out by different researchers (and may not have been carried out yet). In other words, one might study a school class or a small business, producing findings which others who were interested in schools or businesses could explore to assess their relevance.

What all of these authors and examples have in common is the realisation that there is no easy answer to the issue of generalisation. Yet it has to be faced, and addressed, every time a case study is carried out. Are you undertaking a case study to compare it to other, similar or related, case studies, whether carried out by you or others? Are you undertaking a typical, exemplary or indicative case study, the findings from which should be more broadly applicable? Or are you undertaking a case study which is of interest for its very particularity or extreme nature?

It is, of course, possible – and probably quite common, particularly among novice researchers – that the researcher does not (yet) know the answers to these questions. But the questions still need to be recognised and addressed as well as they can be (the practical issues involved are discussed further in the section on Sampling and Selection Issues in Chapter 8).

Validity and Reliability

The concepts of validity – is the way in which you are collecting your data appropriate for answering the questions you wish to answer? – and reliability – would another researcher collecting the same data in the same way produce much the same results? – are clearly related to that of generalisability. Each addresses aspects of how other researchers, viewing your research results, would judge their quality and usefulness.

Kazdin (1981), working in the context of clinical psychology, notes that 'The case study has been discounted as a potential source of scientifically validated inferences, because threats to internal validity cannot be ruled out in the manner achieved in experimentation' (p. 183). However, he then identifies a set of procedures which can, at least partly, overcome these threats:

> Specific procedures that can be controlled by the clinical investigator can influence the strength of the case demonstration. First, the investigator can collect objective data in place of anecdotal report information. Clear measures are needed to attest to the fact that change has actually occurred. Second, client performance can be assessed on several occasions, perhaps before, during, and after treatment. The continuous assessment helps rule out important rival hypotheses related to testing, which a simple pre- and posttreatment assessment strategy does not accomplish. Third, the clinical investigator can accumulate cases that are treated and assessed in a similar fashion. Large groups are not necessarily needed but only the systematic accumulation of a number of clients. As the number and heterogeneity of clients increase and receive treatment at different points in time, history and maturation become less plausible as alternative rival hypotheses. (p. 190)

That Kazdin is working within a scientific framework is clear from his use of words like 'objective' and 'fact', and in his reliance on careful measurement (he is also clearly discussing quantitative case studies). His two other suggested strategies are similar to those advocated to enhance generalisation, and would also be helpful for qualitative and social researchers: the assessment of the case over time (the use of time series research designs in combination with case studies is discussed further in Chapter 6), and the accumulation of multiple case studies.

Riege (2003) considers which validity and reliability tests can most appropriately be used at each stage of case study research. He argues that:

> The validity and reliability of case study research is a key issue… A high degree of validity and reliability provides not only confidence in the data collected but, most significantly, trust in the successful application and use of the results… The four design tests of construct validity, internal validity, external validity and reliability are commonly applied to the theoretical paradigm of positivism. Similarly, however, they can be used for the realism paradigm, which includes case study research… In addition to using the four 'traditional' design tests, the application of four 'corresponding' design tests is recommended to enhance validity and reliability, that is credibility, trustworthiness (transferability), confirmability and dependability. (p. 84)

Riege here brings in the notion of paradigms, which can be expressed more simply as our ways of thinking about the world, contrasting the positivist paradigm (the foundation of conventional science, which argues that there is a real world which we can measure and understand) with what he calls realism (which others would call post-positivist, the belief that, while there is a real world out there, and we may try to comprehend it, we accept that we cannot fully do so). The earlier discussion of case study in the context of qualitative and quantitative forms of research would suggest, however, that case studies could be carried out within both the positivist and realist paradigms, and, indeed, in others as well (alternative paradigms, notably the positivist and interpretivist, are further discussed in the section on Alternative Methodological Approaches in Chapter 9).

Riege also introduces the notion of different forms or measures of validity, identifying three types (other authors identify more or different types, and/or give them different names):

- construct (whether the constructs which are being used to measure concepts of interest are appropriate)
- internal (the quality of the explanation of the phenomena examined)
- external (whether the findings can be extrapolated beyond the case studied; the equivalent of generalisation).

Most interestingly, however, he introduces four alternative, or parallel, ways of judging the quality of a piece of case study research: credibility, trustworthiness (transferability), confirmability and dependability (see also Lee, Mishna and Brennenstuhl 2010). These also have the benefit of being phrased in more common-sense language.

Such alternative criteria for judging the quality or worth of research have been taken up quite widely by qualitative researchers. Box 3.3 gives four different recent formulations, showing the alternative terms used by – or which may be applied to – positivist/post-positivist, interpretivist and/or constructivist, or quantitative and qualitative, forms of research. There are clearly many overlaps between these formulations.

■ ■ ■ Box 3.3   Alternative Criteria for Judging the Quality of Research ■ ■ ■

Denzin and Lincoln (2005b, p. 24)

- positivist/post-positivist paradigms – internal and external validity
- constructivist paradigm – trustworthiness, credibility, transferability, confirmability

Guba and Lincoln (2005, p. 196)

- positivism/post-positivism – conventional benchmarks of 'rigor': internal and external validity, reliability and objectivity
- constructivism – trustworthiness and authenticity, including catalyst for action

Farquhar (2012, pp. 100–110)

- classical approaches – construct validity, internal validity, reliability, generalizability
- interpretivist views – credibility, transferability, dependability, confirmability
- an ethnographic contribution – authenticity, plausibility, criticality

Denscombe (2014, pp. 297–300)

- quantitative research – validity, reliability, generalizability, objectivity
- qualitative research – credibility, dependability, transferability, confirmability

---

Taking Denscombe's formulation, he explains credibility as 'the extent to which qualitative researchers can demonstrate that their data are accurate and appropriate' (p. 297), perhaps through the use of techniques like respondent validation (asking your respondents to comment on and confirm your findings), grounded data (provided through extensive fieldwork) and triangulation. Dependability involves the researcher demonstrating that 'their research reflects procedures and decisions that other researchers can 'see' and evaluate in terms of how far they constitute *reputable procedures and reasonable decisions*' (p. 298, emphasis in original).

Transferability has to do with the researcher supplying 'information enabling others to infer the *relevance and applicability of the findings* (to other people, settings, case studies, organizations, etc.)' (p. 299, emphasis in original). And confirmability involves recognising the role of the self in qualitative research and keeping an open mind, by, for example, not neglecting data that do not fit the preferred analysis and checking rival explanations.

Interestingly, Farquhar also brings in an ethnographic contribution, which she derives from Golden-Biddle and Locke (1993). Their concern was with how ethnographic writing was convincing (or not), identifying three elements of convincingness: authenticity, plausibility and criticality. These elements could, of course, be seen as analogues for credibility, dependability and transferability.

There are, then, other languages available to case study researchers – particularly, perhaps, those approaching their case studies from a qualitative perspective – with which to evaluate and justify the quality of their research and findings. Most researchers, though, have sought to remain true to the older, more conventional ideas, derived from quantitative/positivist research, of validity and reliability when assessing the results of case study (and other forms of) research.

Thus, Gibbert, Ruigrok and Wicki (2008) offer a meta-analysis of 159 articles based on case studies published during the period 1995–2000 in ten management journals, focusing on their methodological sophistication. They conclude that researchers have placed too much emphasis on external validity and need to pay more attention to internal and construct validity.

Diefenbach (2009), in an article pejoratively titled 'Are Case Studies More Than Sophisticated Storytelling?' identifies 16 criticisms of case study research, particularly when based on interviews. These criticisms relate to all aspects of research design, data collection and analysis, but focus in particular on validity and reliability issues. He concludes that: 'many qualitative case studies either do not go far beyond a mere description of particular aspects or the generalisations provided are not based on a very sound methodological basis' (p. 892).

One of the strongest contemporary advocates of case study, Yin (2013), offers rather more hope in this respect. He discusses a range of different approaches that have been taken towards addressing validity and generalisation in case study evaluations, including alternative explanations, triangulation, logic models (which represent 'the key steps or events within an intervention and then between the intervention and its outcomes', p. 324) for validity, and analytic generalisation and theory. In the particular context of case study evaluations, he recommends paying more attention to the questions posed for the case study, being clearer about what it is that makes the case study complex, and focusing carefully on the methods used.

As with generalisation, then, there is a need for case study researchers to be aware of, and to address, issues of validity and reliability posed by their research. You may choose to do this in a conventional positivist/post-positivist fashion, using the language of construct, external and internal validity and reliability. You may choose to locate your case study in a constructivist/interpretivist paradigm, and use the language of trustworthiness, credibility, transferability and confirmability. Or you can adopt the procedures suggested by other case study researchers, such as Yin.

Other Issues

Other authors have raised somewhat different issues regarding the perceived weaknesses of case study, though they could also be seen as the same issues approached in different ways, or concerns faced by specialised forms of case study.

Mahoney (2000), a political scientist, focuses on the issue of causal inference, i.e. how we infer what is causing something to happen. He discusses three strategies of causal inference in what he calls small-n analysis (i.e. studies of small numbers of cases):

- nominal comparison in cross-case analysis (which 'entails the use of categories that are mutually exclusive and collectively exhaustive', p. 390)
- ordinal comparison in cross-case analysis (which 'entails rank ordering cases into three or more categories based on the degree to which a given phenomenon is present', p. 399)
- within-case analysis.

The third of these strategies – which, unlike the first two, can be applied to single case studies – is broken down into three sub-strategies:

> The most general type of within-case analysis is *pattern matching*, a procedure in which the analyst assesses cross-case associations in the light of multiple within-case hypotheses. An important subtype of this procedure is *process chasing*, a technique in which the analyst attempts to locate the causal mechanisms linking a hypothesized explanatory variable to an outcome. Finally, a third technique – *causal narrative* – combines cross-case analysis and within-case analysis by comparing cases in terms of highly disaggregated sequences of processes and events that lead to outcomes. (p. 409, emphasis in original)

Noting that the application of these strategies can lead to rather different conclusions being drawn, he argues for greater care in selecting and applying them.

Elliott and Lukes (2008) consider the ethnographic case study (the combination of case study with ethnography as a research design is discussed further in Chapter 6) in the context of policy-making. They stress the importance of this context, arguing that 'questions about the level of confidence or warrant that can be placed in different sorts of research evidence and findings cannot be answered independently of forming a view about the appropriateness of the policy culture that shapes political decision-making' (p. 87). Or, in other words, the research design needs to be agreed between the different parties in the light of their beliefs and plans for using the research findings.

As these authors indicate, there are likely to be specific issues about the use of case study designs that are particular to their applications in given disciplines or sub-disciplines, or for certain sorts of projects. As with generalisation, validity and reliability, the case study researcher needs to be aware of, and respond to, these issues.

IS EVERYTHING A CASE?

Finally, let us return to the question of whether case studies are so endemic and ill-defined that every piece of research may be regarded as a case study, or, at least, as a multiple case study. Earlier in this chapter, Punch (2005, p. 144) was quoted as remarking that 'almost anything can serve as a case'. He is not alone in expressing this view. Thus, Stake, one of the key contemporary proponents of case study research, while noting that 'Custom has it that not everything is a case' (1995, p. 2; 2005, p. 444), also recognised that 'Here and there, researchers will call anything they please a case study' (2005, p. 445).

If you spend a little time searching an academic library catalogue or a bibliographic database, it will soon become apparent that the words 'case study' are very widely used in the titles of academic articles, monographs, reports and theses. These words crop up particularly frequently in sub-titles, where, having indicated what the focus of the study is, it is then described as a 'case study' of something or other (this issue is discussed further in the section on Writing on Case Study in Chapter 7).

This rather loose usage suggests two things. First, that, as Punch and Stake have noted, everything could be regarded as a case. Second, that case study is quite often adopted or identified as the research design when the researcher can think of no clearer or perhaps stronger way of describing it; calling a piece of research a case study and adding a brief reference to the case study literature may then seem to add credibility.

It is critically important, therefore, that we exercise care and discretion in using the label 'case study'. Overuse encourages disregard. We need to restrict the use of the term to research which explicitly employs a case study design and criticise those who use it too loosely. While, in one sense, everything is a case (i.e. all individual items may be seen as worthy of analysis), all research is not case study research.

SUMMARY

In this chapter, we have:

- considered alternative perspectives on case studies, arguing that it is best seen as a research design
- examined where case study sits in relation to other recognised research designs
- explored the relation of case study to qualitative and quantitative forms of research, concluding that it may make use of either or both

- reviewed its strengths and weaknesses, discussing how these impact on the choice (or not) of case study as the selected research design
- considered the issues of generalisability, reliability and validity as they impact upon case study research
- concluded that while everything may be a case, not all research is case study research.

KEY READINGS

The six articles and book chapters listed here, all of which have been referred to and discussed in this chapter, take critical or supportive perspectives towards case study as a research design. Looking at a number of them should give you a fuller idea of how case study is viewed in contemporary research.

Diefenbach, T (2009) Are Case Studies more than Sophisticated Storytelling? Methodological problems of qualitative empirical research mainly based on semi-structured interviews. *Quality and Quantity*, 43, pp. 875–894.

Flyvbjerg, B (2004) Five Misunderstandings about Case Study Research. pp. 390–404 in C Seale, G Gobo, J Gubrium, and D Silverman (eds) *Qualitative Research Practice*. London, Sage.

Gibbert, M, Ruigrok, W, and Wicki, B (2008) What Passes as a Rigorous Case Study? *Strategic Management Journal*, 29, 13, pp. 1465–1474.

Riege, A (2003) Validity and Reliability Tests in Case Study Research: A literature review with 'hands-on' applications for each research phase. *Qualitative Market Research*, 6, 2, pp. 75–86.

Verschuren, P (2003) Case Study as a Research Strategy: Some ambiguities and opportunities. *International Journal of Social Research Methodology*, 6, 2, pp. 121–139.

Yin, R (2013) Validity and Generalization in Future Case Study Evaluations. *Evaluation*, 19, 3, pp. 321–332.

PART B

USING CASE STUDY

4

The Value of Case Study

INTRODUCTION

This chapter argues that it would be helpful to start thinking of case study research in a somewhat different way: as small-scale research with meaning. This involves two changes of perspective.

First, we need to accept that case study research – particularly single case studies – is in essence small-scale research. In accepting this we, of course, recognise the limitations, but also the potential strengths, that small-scale research possesses.

Second, we need to place much more emphasis on the meaningfulness of the case study research we undertake. In other words, we don't simply undertake case study research because it is small-scale (though that may be a pragmatic factor); we do it because of its potential interest and/or usefulness. Small-scale research can help to unravel very complex issues and be highly influential.

This chapter has three main sections, considering:

- what makes a meaningful case study
- some examples of meaningful case studies
- small-scale research with meaning.

WHAT MAKES A MEANINGFUL CASE STUDY?

If we are to reconceptualise case study research as small-scale research with meaning, we need, of course, to be able to identify what makes a case study (or, more generally, a piece of small-scale research) meaningful. There is, unsurprisingly, some guidance on this available in the case study literature (see also the discussion of Assessing Your Work in Chapter 9).

Thus, Yin (2009, pp. 185–190) identifies five 'general characteristics of an exemplary case study':

- The Case Study Must be Significant
- The Case Study Must be 'Complete'
- The Case Study Must Consider Alternative Perspectives
- The Case Study Must Display Sufficient Evidence
- The Case Study Must be Composed in an Engaging Manner.

All of these characteristics are, of course, as Yin is well aware, couched in rather subjective language. What, for example, is significant, complete, sufficient or engaging, and who is to be the ultimate judge of this? But they do offer some useful guidance. Yet, if a case study was felt to fall down on one or more of them, it might still be judged 'useful', if perhaps not 'exemplary'. To be 'exemplary' is probably too high a target for most case study researchers, though one might still aim for it.

These characteristics are also, however, generic in nature and can be applied to any piece of research as much as to a case study (though, in the case of quantitative forms of research, the term 'significant' would have a specific statistical meaning and would be measurable). All research, for example, should surely aim to be 'composed in an engaging manner' and ought to 'consider alternative perspectives', even if it does not achieve these elements as well as it might.

Thomas (2011a, pp. 67–68) provides an alternative checklist. He stresses the broader notion of quality, which he suggests can be assessed through three questions:

1. How well has the case been chosen?
2. How well has the context for the study been explained and justified?
3. How well have the arguments been made? Have rival explanations for the same kinds of observations been explored?

Thomas's first two points can be thought of as incorporating most of Yin's five bullet points, while his third point restates Yin's third bullet point. Like Yin, his checklist is also both subjective (how do we judge well-ness?) and generic.

Both lists are also, of course, retrospective: the case study is being judged after it has been completed and presented, and presumably also at a point when additional research on it might be difficult to undertake. Both Yin's and Thomas's first points make this clear: one can only really judge whether a case study is 'significant' or 'well chosen' with hindsight. Researchers may do all that they can to try to ensure that their case study has these qualities before commencing it, but the proof, as they say, is 'in the pudding', and is only confirmed on completion and consumption.

Is it possible to do any better? One approach is to provide a much more detailed set of criteria. Kim, Price and Lau (2014), working in the context of healthcare informatics, offer an example of this. They identify 25 criteria for judging published case study research, broken down under the headings of planning and objectives, study design, data collection, analysis and quality. That could be said to be going a little over the top, and, for generic advice, it is probably better to keep things simpler.

Box 4.1 suggests some alternative criteria that may be taken into account in the form of four questions. I would not, of course, seek to claim that these criteria are any less subjective or generic than those of Thomas and Yin. Nor could I claim that they are wholly original, as there is inevitably some overlap with both of the lists already reviewed. But, hopefully, the criteria are expressed in reasonably accessible language and add something more to those offered by Thomas and Yin.

■ ■ ■ Box 4.1   What Makes a Meaningful Case Study? ■ ■ ■

- Can you understand what the researchers have done and why?
- Does their interpretation of their findings seem reasonable and defensible?
- Can you relate the case study to other research on the topic?
- Does the study suggest plausible change actions and/or further research directions?

We will now consider each of these criteria in a little more detail.

Can You Understand What the Researchers Have Done and Why?

This criterion has to do with whether the case study has been written up in an intelligible and accessible fashion, and whether it incorporates sufficient and convincing explanations for the methodological and other choices taken by the researcher(s). It has some overlap with Yin's fifth characteristic, 'the case study must be composed in an engaging manner', but takes the point further.

One of the most common criticisms of published research, particularly perhaps by those coming to it for the first time, is that it is often written in a seemingly deliberately difficult style, with overlong sentences and lots of specialist terms (or 'jargon' if you wish to be pejorative). Sometimes this is made worse by poor grammar and punctuation (on the part of native speakers as much as by those writing in a second or third language), and an overuse of abbreviations or acronyms. It can almost seem as if the authors do not want anyone to read and understand their work, or that they think no one else is capable of doing so, apart from themselves and a few close colleagues or acolytes.

Writing up research in a style that is accessible and engaging is important, though it undoubtedly takes time and practice (see, for example, Sword 2012). Where this has been done, however, the experience of reading an academic article, report or monograph can be so much easier and more enjoyable, and the reader is likely to be able to understand and engage with much more of what the author(s) is seeking to convey.

As the criterion implies, understanding links fairly directly with reasoning. If something is written clearly and intelligibly, it is a lot easier to follow the reasoning and make a judgement as to whether the researchers have carried out their research in an appropriate fashion. This is not to say that you would have made the same methodological choices – that is unlikely, and is no reason for critique in itself – rather that the choices made are justifiable.

There is another issue here, common to academic research, particularly when it is written up in article form, where there are usually limits on the numbers of words that can be included, and often also an expected format. This issue is exacerbated by the pressure on academics to publish as much as they can, which typically leads to one research project being sliced up, salami fashion, into as many articles as possible.

Thus, it can be difficult to glean sufficient information from a single article to form a reasoned judgement on a research project, whether it is a case study or some other design. It may be necessary, then, to look at a number of articles stemming from the same project to make an overall judgement, or to go back to the original research report (this may mean contacting the researcher(s) directly, but such reports are increasingly commonly available on academic websites).

Does Their Interpretation of Their Findings Seem Reasonable and Defensible?

This criterion has to do with the fullness and persuasiveness of the researchers' writing, and is similar to Thomas's third question: 'how well have the arguments been made?' There are two main elements to the criterion.

First, are all of the stages in the researchers' argument evidenced, and do they clearly lead from one to another? Beginning from the data they have gathered and/or used, can you see how this has been coded, selected, analysed, marshalled and presented to support a particular interpretation of the evidence? Or are there some aspects which appear to be missing or overlooked, or which have been inadequately explained?

Second, while always accepting that you do not have to agree with it, how convincing do you find the researchers' argument? Have they, to use the term in at least two senses, made their case? Are there other possible interpretations of the data that you can think of, or that you are aware of (there almost always are)? Have these been considered, and, if so, is the researchers' rejection of them in favour of their preferred explanation convincing? How well have they defended their position?

A real example (without, for obvious reasons, attribution) might be helpful here. I can remember reading a doctoral thesis dealing with the staff experience of evolving quality assurance regimes in UK higher education. The author had interviewed a number of academic and administrative staff for their experience and opinions. The argument made was that developments in quality assurance were essential, but that academic staff were often guilty of obstructing or ignoring these, or only taking them on board in as minimal a fashion as possible. As I read the thesis – and this shows my allegiance to the academic rather than the administrative role – I wondered whether, using the data the author had collected, I could make an opposing argument, namely that the academic staff were heroically resisting the unwanted and unnecessary imposition of quality assurance regimes on their work. That this explanation was not considered, even if only briefly, by the author led me to have reservations about the soundness of their overall argument.

In the human and social worlds, matters are always multifaceted. There are always other explanations and counter-arguments, other sides to the story, indeed other (but related) stories altogether. As researchers, we need to recognise and respect these, even as we take them on. So, when assessing a case study, or other piece of research, what matters is not so much whether you agree with the researchers' position, but how good an argument you judge them to have made.

Can You Relate the Case Study to Other Research on the Topic?

There is, as the saying goes, really nothing new in the world, and this applies to research as much as anything else. While researchers may like to – indeed, in order to get published and read, they have to – claim that their research is original, startling and new, it is always grounded in, and building on, existing research undertaken by others. Its actual contribution to the sum of human knowledge may be very limited, perhaps applying a proven technique to another example, or verifying, and perhaps slightly extending, an existing theory in a new setting.

It is important, therefore, and particularly so if, as the reader, you are coming to a topic with limited existing knowledge, that researchers place their studies in the context of existing research and findings. Or, to put it another way, the report of the research should contain a literature review (see, for example, Hart 1998). Clearly, the format that the research report is in will place some limitations on this, particularly if it is a journal article, and it may not be placed in a section explicitly labelled 'literature review', or may be spread throughout the report, but it should still be there.

Literature reviews should, in the space available, serve a number of functions:

- They should identify (some of) the classic pieces of research on the topic concerned, by those sometimes referred to as the 'founding fathers' (the authors so acknowledged usually are men).
- They should summarise the current state of research on the topic, referring to (some of) the most recent research.
- They should indicate where there are differences of opinion in the research on the topic, and why these exist.
- They should also indicate the current researcher's opinions on the existing research.
- They should make clear how the current research builds upon the existing research, and what contribution it has to make to our better understanding of the topic.

Doing all of these things places the research being reported within its broader context and enables the reader to better judge where and how it fits.

In addition to reviewing the literature on the topic being researched, one would also expect to see some (albeit, perhaps, briefer) discussion of the literature on the methodology and methods being applied, particularly if the research was seeking to advance or take these forward in some way.

As well as there often being limits on the space that can be given to a literature review, there are also other factors which may restrict its scope, and thus usefulness. Chief among these is the tendency of many researchers to work in a narrow, specialist field – sometimes referred to as a 'silo' – and to have little to do with those working outside this field, or even those researching the same field but using different approaches. In other words, they may not see or be aware of (or even care about) the broader picture. This is something to bear in mind when assessing any case study report. It may well be that you are aware of relevant related research which is seemingly unknown to the author(s). It is also, of course, something to bear in mind when doing your own case study research.

Does the Study Suggest Plausible Change Actions and/or Further Research Directions?

It is a characteristic of researchers – even, or perhaps especially, those engaged in small-scale research – that they want to have an impact. They may want to be noticed, read, appreciated and cited; they may want to change the way in which things are done, and have a broader impact socially or economically. While it is almost certainly wildly unrealistic to expect to 'change the world', as some – often younger, less experienced or more naïve – researchers may do, some will nevertheless achieve this.

But, for those engaged in case study research, the aims and outcomes are likely to be much more modest. There is nothing to be ashamed of in this, however, and some, albeit limited, impact on practice or research may still be aimed for. And this is something that should be addressed in the report of the case study, even when, as often happens, the aims have not been entirely achieved.

Case studies are commonly carried out in organisations, or parts of organisations, where the authors/researchers may work (if so, they are commonly termed 'insider researchers') or have been called in to conduct their research. In such circumstances, they may focus on assessing a particular practice or process, and then seeking to improve it. Students undertaking what are often termed 'professional' doctorates frequently do this kind of research.

Such case studies have close links with, and may also often be termed, action research (the combination of case study and action research is discussed in Chapter 6). If they are genuine action research, they will typically go through, and report upon, a number of successive cycles of research, implementation and evaluation, ending only when a suitably improved practice or process has been achieved. Alternatively, such case studies may be called small-scale evaluative case studies (the link between case study and evaluation designs is also discussed further in Chapter 6), a popular form of research in many professional disciplines.

Such case studies will typically close, following a summary of their findings, with a series of recommendations, which, if implemented, should improve practice. The other strategy, which may be pursued instead or in combination with recommendations, is to conclude with suggestions for future research, to be carried out by the current researcher or others. This is the more academic approach. It recognises that any given piece of research, but particularly small-scale research, cannot expect to provide the final, definitive answer on the topic being researched.

So, partly as a guide to other interested researchers, and partly as an *aide-mémoire* to themselves, reports of academic research usually end with an indication of what might be researched next. This is also something their readers will look for – otherwise, what was the point of doing the research, if it wasn't to lead on to something else? – and which may also suggest practical or research directions to them.

We will see how these four evaluative questions, intended to encapsulate what makes a meaningful case study – Can you understand what the researchers have done and why? Does their interpretation of their findings seem reasonable and defensible? Can you relate the case study to other research on the topic? Does the study suggest plausible change actions and/or further research directions? – can be used and articulated in the next section, where some examples of published case studies are considered in detail.

SOME EXAMPLES OF MEANINGFUL CASE STUDY RESEARCH

The purpose of this section is to identify, describe and assess – in terms of the four questions identified in the previous section – some examples of existing case study research which may be judged as being meaningful. This should be useful to you in practically demonstrating how to read, interrogate, summarise, evaluate and critique published research, and in seeking to get the 'best use' out of it.

It is important at this point to issue a caveat. In selecting the case studies that are discussed in this section, I am most definitely not stating or implying that these are the best case studies that have ever been conceived, carried out and published. I think they are good, useful and meaningful examples, which also illustrate some of the diversity of forms and disciplinary range taken by case study research designs, but there are many, many other examples I could have chosen.

Four of the five case studies that are reviewed in this section share the characteristic of being at the simpler end of the single case/multiple case study spectrum; that is, they each deal with only one case or a very limited number of cases. As such, they offer good examples of what might be attempted and achieved in small-scale research projects. The fifth case study considered is somewhat more complex, but is based on a number of studies carried out by the authors over a period of time.

All five examples also share a further characteristic, which is particularly appropriate for their inclusion and discussion in this book; namely, that they all show some interest in case study as a research design, and in making a contribution to its application and further development, as well as in adding to knowledge on the particular topic under study. Indeed, in some of the examples the focus of the article referred to is more on case study design than on the findings of the case study research.

Chapter 7 includes a briefer discussion of a broader range of published case studies, including some that challenge our understanding of what is meant by case study.

Bygstad and Munkvold (2011)

This article, by two Norwegian information systems researchers, focuses on the involvement of informants in longitudinal, interpretive case study research. The case study is longitudinal in that it involved data collection over a prolonged period of time (18 months in all). It adopts an interpretive epistemology, rather than a positivistic stance (the meaning of these terms is discussed further in Chapter 9), as the researchers contend that knowledge and understanding are developed through collaborative interpretation of the data collected. The authors note that:

> Interpretive case studies can be distinguished from positivist case study research by the focus on close interaction between researcher and participants throughout the case study process, viewing the case members as active participants in the construction of the case narrative. However, while the interpretivist perspective ascribes an active role to the case study informants, in practice the extent of this involvement is normally confined to the data collection process and discussion of early versions of the case narrative. In few cases is the involvement of the informants reported to continue further to the final stages of analytical abstraction of the case study data, where the aim is to develop the overall patterns and explanations. In this paper we explore the question of how the informants may be involved in the co-construction of the case narrative and theory building in interpretive research. (p. 32)

They indicate that this is an unusual approach in information systems research. It is also fairly demanding in terms of time and commitment. The case being examined was an international airline developing an e-business solution. Data were collected through two workshops, 20 interviews with central stakeholders and information systems developers, and organisational documents. The researchers proceeded in accordance with the principles of longitudinal process research:

- Engaging with the research site at several times during the study, to collect data reflecting changes over time.
- Participant observation, to understand the actors' language and problem solving, and to make sense of different situations.
- Collecting systematically different types of data, to secure validity. (pp. 36–37)

Feedback was gathered from informants at three stages:

> First, the documented chronology of events and the illustrated socio-technical network from the workshops were sent to the participants for comments and corrections. Then, at the end of the case study there was a long review session with technical and business stakeholders to discuss the final report. And lastly, the research papers that were published were sent to the two project managers and two business line managers for comments. (p. 37)

The researchers employed a process called the 'ladder of analytical abstraction' for analysing the data collected, which also involved three stages: (1) summarising interviews and technical documents; (2) identifying themes and trends; (3) identifying patterns and explanations. While this process is given a particular name, it is, in essence, a very popular approach for analysing qualitative data, more commonly called thematic analysis (see, for example, Braun and Clarke 2006).

Bygstad and Munkvold identify four conditions that are required for their approach to case study research to be successful: 'It requires a longitudinal case study design... some of the informants must be knowledgeable on how the case connects to other structures... the researcher and the informants should share some basic objectives and terminology... the informants need to engage in reflection-in-action' (p. 42). By 'reflection-in-action' they mean the ability to be able to reflect upon an action as you are doing it. Clearly, this approach to research needs not only an informed and willing set of participants, but also that they are well educated professionals.

Bygstad and Munkvold also indicate how informants' feedback might best be used at different stages of the research project:

> In the data collection phase, informants' feedback can increase the quality of the case documentation through factual verification and the generation of new data... In the case study report, informants' feedback may enrich the case narrative and increase the internal validity of the study... In the dissemination phase, the role of the informants is more discursive, contributing to increase the relevance of findings, the external validity, by assessing the conclusions and implications of scientific publications in a practitioner context. (p. 43)

Their approach seems particularly suited to anyone wishing to examine the adoption of a new or revised process of operation in an organisation – whatever its nature: private sector, for-profit, public sector, voluntary sector – and who has the time and commitment to engage with informants over a prolonged period in order to do so. This is the size of project that might suit a doctoral researcher, and could lead to useful and interesting results, both in research terms and for the organisation involved.

If done for academic research and credit, however, it would be important for the researcher to draw up an agreement at the start regarding what was involved, mutual expectations and responsibilities, who the results of the research belonged to and how they could be used. Organisations have been known to withdraw access and cooperation, and to block researchers' use of data for publication.

We may now consider this study (as we will for each of the five case studies discussed in this section) in terms of the four questions suggested for assessing whether a case study is meaningful or not:

1. *Can you understand what the researchers have done and why?* The article clearly outlines the researchers' aim of carrying out a longitudinal, interpretive case study, focusing on the issue of informant collaboration. In terms of data collection, the use of interviews, workshops, documents and feedback is described.
2. *Does their interpretation of their findings seem reasonable and defensible?* The researchers' findings relate to the practice of this kind of case study design rather than to what the research found in the organisation investigated. They offer useful guidelines on informant collaboration in research.
3. *Can you relate the case study to other research on the topic?* The authors, through their referencing, link their work to other research, including their own, both on the research topic, e-business solutions, and on case study design.
4. *Does the study suggest plausible change actions and/or further research directions?* The authors suggest the need for further research into the use of informant collaboration in other research designs, such as ethnographic studies, action research and critical studies (all of which, as Chapter 6 makes clear, have been used in combination with case study research designs).

In all, then, this is clearly an example of a meaningful case study. It is readable, interesting and makes a valuable contribution, both to the area researched and to the use of case study as a research design.

Watson (2009)

Watson, a UK academic based in a business school but taking a sociological approach, looks at the notion of managerial identity, making use of the concepts of narrative (a concept also employed by Bygstad and Munkvold), identity work and the social construction of reality. The main source of data he uses is somewhat unusual: the two-volume private autobiography by Leonard Hilton, a former senior manager in a telecommunications business. Watson explains how he analysed this data source:

> First, the two massive volumes were carefully read over a two-month period and a much-condensed version extracted. As this process was occurring, a list was compiled of categories and themes which seemed theoretically relevant to the researcher's interest in narrative and identity work (with no formal technique of 'qualitative data analysis' being used). The material was then reorganized under these headings and this was read and re-read alongside readings of the academic literature to produce the conceptualizations and analyses presented here... In this way, theorization and empirical analysis proceeded in a mutually supportive manner. (pp. 433–434)

Watson then justifies the choice of this particular case for study:

> [T]he warrant for selecting Leonard Hilton as a case-study is precisely not that he is in any way a *typical* manager or relater of life stories. He is an *extreme* case of an identity-worker with a powerful attachment to narrative thinking and advanced narrative skills. This means that, having been provided with an unusually 'strong case' of an individual who makes and uses narratives in their identity work, we can examine the *processes* that come into play when people do narrative-based identity work more generally. (p. 434, emphasis in original)

In the remainder of an over-average length article (28 printed pages), Watson proceeds to provide this examination, making extensive use of quotations from Hilton's autobiography. He ends the article by stressing 'Here, we have a case in which, to an unusually high degree, an individual puts "being a manager" at the heart of his expressed self-identity and, certainly, we can learn a lot about how this comes about by examining his activities with his organization. However, we learn a vast amount more by looking at his whole life, his life history, his full autobiography' (p. 450).

This article is a good example of the potential value and usefulness of single case studies, whether they are seen as typical or, as here, unusual or extreme. Having access to an extensive unpublished autobiography is unusual, but there are many other ways in which relevant data for such studies may be gathered. This example also indicates the potential usefulness for case study research of data that already exists – often referred to as secondary data – and does not need to be collected or created, because someone else has already done that. Using secondary data, where it exists and is accessible, can be a very sensible research strategy when time and other resources are severely constrained.

In terms of the four suggested criteria:

1. *Can you understand what the researchers have done and why?* Watson clearly sets out his research as an extreme case study, analysing an unpublished autobiography, and making use of the concepts of narrative, identity work and the social construction of reality.
2. *Does their interpretation of their findings seem reasonable and defensible?* Watson's underlying argument that you can learn much more by looking at an individual's whole life story, rather than just the particular role of interest, is well evidenced.
3. *Can you relate the case study to other research on the topic?* The article is extensively referenced, both to publications, including his own, on the practice of management, and on the use of autobiography and case study.
4. *Does the study suggest plausible change actions and/or further research directions?* Watson's conclusion concerns the need for more studies of this kind, focusing on whole individuals and their life stories.

This meaningful case study is particularly useful for suggesting alternative forms of data collection and analysis from the more conventional approaches. There are many, published and unpublished, documents which are available for analysis, dealing with almost any topic that might be researched.

Johnston (1985)

The third of the five case studies to be considered in this section is over 30 years old. While much more research will, of course, have been done on the topic on which this article focuses in that period, this does not diminish the interest of this particular case study, which could be regarded as a pioneering example of its kind. Johnston was a US-based educational psychologist.

Johnston's focus is on reading disability, and its causes among adults, and he presents and considers three case studies of American men. He explains the choice of a case study design in the following way:

> Case studies were used on the assumption that there can be substantial individual differences in experience and in important dimensions of behavior (both overt and covert) which are as critical as the commonalities between individuals. (p. 155)

Data were collected during eight individual 'instruction' sessions, each lasting between 45 minutes and two hours, with each man. The sessions 'involved interactive assessment, spontaneous and elicited introspection and retrospection, and elicited think-aloud reports and oral reading performance' (p. 156). The analysis is organised in terms of the identified themes of conceptual problems, strategies, anxiety, attributions, goals and motivation.

Johnston argues strongly for 'a multifaceted yet integrated picture of adult reading failure' (p. 174). He concludes that:

> Most current explanations of reading difficulties focus on the level of operations, devoid of context, goals, motives, or history. While some work has focused on the context of reading failure rather than mental operations, there has been little effort to integrate these two dimensions. The consequent explanations of reading failure are sterile and have resulted in more or less terminal diagnoses of reading failure. Until we can integrate the depth of human feeling and thinking into our understanding of reading difficulties, we will have only a shadow of an explanation of the problem and ill-directed attempts at solutions. (p. 175)

This is, then, a fairly conventional case study design, involving three cases selected purposively because of their varied nature. While only three cases were involved, the many and sometimes lengthy sessions amounted to a substantial amount of work, although this work was directed primarily towards treatment rather than research.

In terms of the four criteria:

1. *Can you understand what the researchers have done and why?* Johnston clearly sets out the rationale for his study, and the structured and varied ways in which data were collected.
2. *Does their interpretation of their findings seem reasonable and defensible?* Johnston's position is somewhat similar to that of Watson in the previous example, although the contexts and topics are very different. He argues cogently that a broader, holistic understanding of the individuals involved is needed if a better grasp on reading failure is to be achieved, hence the selection of a case study design.

3. *Can you relate the case study to other research on the topic?* Johnston provides an extensive bibliography of research into reading disability up until the time of publication.
4. *Does the study suggest plausible change actions and/or further research directions?* Johnston's integrative approach provides an alternative way forward for research on the topic.

That this is a meaningful case study is apparent, and this is also made clear by the many citations to Johnston's work by others since its publication.

Kyburz-Graber (2004)

The fourth case study to be considered in this section is by Kyburz-Graber, a Swiss academic, and focuses on sustainable development in secondary and higher education. She presents an explanatory-causal case study of a high school in Zurich, involving students, teachers and the researchers, arguing that:

> Case-study research is a method which goes beyond the mere thick description of a situation. It can be fully recognized as a scientific method if certain quality criteria which follow the general criteria of objectivity, reliability and validity are fulfilled:
>
> - a theoretical basis including research questions is described;
> - triangulation is ensured by using multiple sources of evidence (data collection and interpretation);
> - a chain of evidence is designed with traceable reasons and arguments;
> - the case-study research is fully documented; and
> - the case-study report is compiled through an iterative review and rewriting process. (p. 58)

Clearly, then, Kyburz-Graber is inclined towards the positivist/post-positivist end of the epistemological spectrum, and is greatly concerned to conduct her case study in a careful, considered, defensible and robust fashion. She examines her case study using the criteria that she has set out, demonstrating that it stands up well to scrutiny.

So far as sustainable development education is concerned, Kyburz-Graber concludes that:

> educational institutions, most of them very experienced in the tradition of structured and guided teaching and learning, are fundamentally ill-equipped to cope with issues of sustainable development, because of their unstructured and complex features and their need for cooperative problem-solving. We thus conclude that educational institutions can hardly expect to play a significant role in societal processes of sustainable development, unless they start to reflect upon and significantly change their teaching and learning culture and the roles of students in decision-making. (p. 63)

While this conclusion could be read as rather depressing from the perspective of sustainable development, it might also serve to provide the stimulus needed to bring about the kinds of changes identified as essential.

So far as case study is concerned, Kyburz-Graber argues for a careful, rigorous and stringent approach in accordance with the criteria outlined. While one might question the use of terms such as 'scientific method' and 'objectivity' in this respect, the argument is well made that case study research designs need to be carefully planned and rigorously carried out if they are to persuade others.

1. *Can you understand what the researchers have done and why?* Kyburz-Graber clearly sets out the processes involved in both carrying out the case study (interviews followed by thematic analysis) and evaluating its rigour (against the quality criteria she identifies).
2. *Does their interpretation of their findings seem reasonable and defensible?* Kyburz-Graber offers conclusions relating to both the application of case study design and the findings of her particular case study.
3. *Can you relate the case study to other research on the topic?* She provides plentiful references to other sources discussing both case study and education for sustainable development.
4. *Does the study suggest plausible change actions and/or further research directions?* Kyburz-Graber argues for further research on the topic and the adoption of greater rigour in case study research design.

This, then, is a fourth example of a meaningful case study, which contributes to our understanding of both case study as a research design and the topic being studied, education for sustainable development.

Payne et al (2007)

Payne and her four co-authors were researchers based in four different UK institutions. They:

> explore issues in case study research design, recruitment and data collection drawing on three studies conducted between 2000 and 2005 in six community hospitals, five adult hospice bereavement services and eight childhood bereavement services in the United Kingdom. Quantitative and qualitative data were collected using interviews, focus groups, observations, documentary analysis, standardized measures and questionnaires. (p. 236)

The three case studies examined the involvement of community hospitals in end-of-life care, and the bereavement support provided by adult hospice and childhood services. This is undeniably a far from straightforward context:

[N]ursing interventions may form part of a complex pathway of care and medical treatment which may be difficult or impossible to disentangle into their constituent parts. End-of-life care in the United Kingdom (UK) represents a good example of this complexity, where health and social services may be provided by statutory, non-statutory and commercial providers. (p. 237)

They 'chose case study methods as the most appropriate research design for examining process and outcome issues in UK community hospitals and bereavement services' (p. 239), since the 'lack of previous research meant that we were not able to construct adequate theoretical frameworks and so hypothesis-driven deductive designs were out of the question' (p. 240). In this context, case study designs have other advantages:

The real-world nature of much of nursing research means that it is impossible or unethical to deny patients access to existing services, and therefore randomized control designs are often not feasible. Case study methods are not constrained by these considerations and have the advantage that they enable complex and multifaceted services to be understood in context. (p. 242)

Payne et al also point out that case study designs lend themselves well to collaborative research, and that they can be empowering for participants. They do, however, adopt a pragmatic approach, accepting that the choice of research design is driven to a large extent by what is feasible in the context being researched.

Each of the three case studies began with a national postal questionnaire survey of known providers (i.e. community hospitals, adult hospice bereavement services, childhood bereavement services), which also provided the sampling frame for the selection of case studies, with each study focusing on between five and eight organisational cases. The case studies themselves involved a mix of interviews and focus groups with the different stakeholders involved, and documentary analysis.

Payne et al conclude that:

case study methods may be a useful design for practice-based nursing research and to evaluate developing services. There is often an interdependence of nursing interventions with the care provided by other healthcare professionals, especially doctors. In such cases, it is often difficult and perhaps inappropriate to disentangle nurses' work from that of others, and therefore there are advantages to understanding the totality of the service through case study designs. The apparent sensitivity and credibility of case study methods for investigating realistic clinical contexts may be appealing to nurses, as the nuanced understandings they produce reflect the highly contextual environments of clinical practice. Moreover, case study methods may be empowering for participants because they value their experiences and reveal how their work contributes to team work within organizations. They can therefore be both affirming and also challenging, as they may expose conflicts and tensions. (p. 244)

Turning again to the four evaluative questions posed:

1. *Can you understand what the researchers have done and why?* Payne et al summarise
    the approach adopted in each of the three linked case study research projects they
    undertook, with references provided to further publications for those readers
    requiring more details.
2. *Does their interpretation of their findings seem reasonable and defensible?* Payne et al's focus
    in this article is primarily on assessing and arguing the usefulness of the case study
    design for research in the healthcare context, rather than with the findings from their
    studies. The usefulness of the case study design in this context is well exemplified.
3. *Can you relate the case study to other research on the topic?* Extensive references are
    provided, linking the study to other research into end-of-life care and the use of
    the case study design.
4. *Does the study suggest plausible change actions and/or further research directions?* The
    article argues for greater use of case study designs in researching the complex
    world of health care.

Four of the five examples considered in this section are, as indicated, relatively small-
scale. One of these (Watson) involved the study of a single individual, while two others
focused on single organisations (Bygstad and Munkvold, Kyburz-Graber), and one on
three individuals (Johnston). Though small-scale in nature, significant amounts of data
were collected and analysed. The fifth example was somewhat more ambitious, with
Payne et al reflecting on the use of the case study design in three related research projects, each of which had focused on five to eight cases.

All five examples displayed an interest in case study as a research design as well as in
the topic under consideration (which were as varied as e-business solutions, end-of-life
care, managerial identity, reading disability and education for sustainable development).
While all five examples were chiefly qualitative in nature, two of them (Johnston, Payne
et al) also involved significant quantitative elements.

SMALL-SCALE RESEARCH WITH MEANING

I began this chapter by arguing that it is possible to assess the usefulness or meaningfulness
of case studies by seeking the answers to four questions:

*   Can you understand what the researchers have done and why?
*   Does their interpretation of their findings seem reasonable and defensible?
*   Can you relate the case study to other research on the topic?
*   Does the study suggest plausible change actions and/or further research directions?

These questions were then employed to assess five varied examples of published case
study research, which were chosen because they were judged to be useful or meaningful.

The same set of questions can, of course, be used to assess other examples (and not only of case study research), as well as your own research.

Case study research, if it is done properly and with due care, is small-scale research with meaning.

There is nothing inherently right or wrong about the level or scale at which research is carried out, which often is simply a matter of the time and other resources available. Large-scale research may seem to offer great advantages, notably in its representativeness and generalisability, but it also needs to be carried out properly and with due care. Small-scale research may be judged by these same criteria, and has the advantages of being more feasible and accessible. It can also, over time, be scaled up through repetition and extension.

The key factor about research, then, is not its scale, but how well and carefully is has been carried out and reported. This applies to all research, not just case study research, but it is, perhaps, particularly important for case study (and other small-scale) research, given the way in which it has often been regarded by large-scale, quantitative researchers. This applies both to the case study research you carry out yourself and to the published case study research you read.

Case study research should be presented in a way that is readily intelligible and accessible. As a researcher, you need to set out what you have done as clearly as you can, showing the different stages the research has gone through, and explaining why you took these steps. It is also helpful to clarify why you opted for a case study design, and what sort of case study design it is.

The findings and conclusions of case study research need to be set out clearly as well, together with the reasoning that led the researcher to them. You don't have to agree with them, if you are reading someone else's work – or your readers do not have to agree with you, if they are reading your report – but the reasoning has to be articulated to show that there is a justifiable and defensible argument. These findings might also, as in the case of some of the examples considered in the previous section, indicate how useful the case study design proved to be, and how it might be modified in the future.

Case study research should be appropriately referenced, so that the reader can assess what related research there has been, and how the research project fits into this, through its citations. These should include references to case study as a research design, as well as to the particular topic being studied.

Finally, if case study research is to have some impact – and be seen as having that impact – it needs to spell out what that actual or intended impact is. This goes beyond the conclusions from the study itself. It might have to do with, in academic terms, the further research directions that are suggested to follow up and extend its findings, or, in more practical terms, what the conclusions suggest for changing or improving practice related to the topic studied.

If it is to have any point, research needs to be meaningful: make your case study research have meaning.

SUMMARY

In this chapter, we have:

- identified a series of questions with which to assess the meaningfulness of case study research
- used these questions to discuss five examples of published case study research considered to be meaningful
- argued that case study research should be reconceptualised as small-scale research with meaning.

KEY READINGS

Both of these publications contain reprints of dozens of published articles on case study research. These illustrate something of the huge range of disciplinary and design variations adopted in case study research.

David, M (ed.) (2006) *Case Study Research* (4 volumes). London, Sage.
Tight, M (ed.) (2015) *Case Studies* (4 volumes). London, Sage.

The Use of Case Study in Different Disciplines

INTRODUCTION

As indicated in Chapter 2, case study is widely used in a range of disciplines, in the social sciences and beyond, both for research (the focus of this book) and teaching purposes. After reviewing the disciplines that are involved, this chapter considers writing on case study research from each of them. This examination indicates the breadth and flexibility of case study as a research design and the ways in which it has been applied by and in different parts of the academy.

This analysis should allow the reader who is interested in one or more disciplinary areas to focus on them. How has case study been applied in those disciplines, and what research, literature and approaches can be built upon in conducting new case study research?

In addition, the chapter should provide ideas to those who are more open to applying practices from elsewhere within their own disciplines. Inter- or trans-disciplinary borrowing has a long history, in case study research and more generally, and may lead to useful innovations or developments. There is much to be learnt from across disciplinary boundaries; taking on board alternative perspectives is both more interesting and more challenging.

WHICH DISCIPLINES USE CASE STUDY?

Swanborn (2010, p. 11), as quoted in Chapter 2, identifies several disciplines as being important in the development of case study, including the health sciences, clinical psychotherapy and law; cultural anthropology; sociology; political science; psychology and psychoanalysis; and policy fields such as social work and youth support. As well as being strong in the social sciences, therefore, by this analysis case study is a recognised research design in a number of professional and some science disciplines.

Scholz and Tietje (2002, p. 4) identify a similarly broad scope of usage:

the use of case studies is becoming an increasingly respected research strategy in the following areas:

- policy and public administration research
- community sociology
- management studies
- branches of psychology and medicine, particularly neuropsychology
- educational sciences
- planning sciences
- civil engineering
- environmental sciences.

Most of the time, the case study approach is chosen in research fields where the biographic, authentic and historic dynamics and perspectives of real social or natural systems are considered.

Scholz and Tietje, therefore, largely confirm Swanborn's view on the widespread application of case study research, adding a number of other disciplines to the list, including the key fields of education and management.

In my reading and research for this book, I have found instances of case study being applied and/or discussed in the disciplines, sub-disciplines or fields of accounting, anthropology, banking, computer science, counselling, criminology, development, economics, education, environmental studies, geography, health, human resource development/management, information systems, international business, law, library and information studies, marketing, medicine, nursing, operations management, pharmacy, philosophy, planning, politics, psychoanalysis, psychology, public administration, purchasing, second language learning, small business, social work, sociology, statistics and urban studies.

I may, of course, have missed others: it is difficult to keep track of developments across all disciplines, sub-disciplines and fields, especially as these are themselves subject to change and development. While in some of these disciplines or fields case study is relatively rarely used, in others it is a popular and established research design. Indeed, the only disciplines where case study does not seem to be widely applied, at least not explicitly, are the hard sciences. Yet, even here, of course, the investigation of particular cases (e.g. planets in astronomy, species in biological sciences, elements in chemistry, forces in physics) of interest is common, but those involved do not usually call it case study or refer to the case study research literature.

For the purposes of organising the remainder of the chapter, I have divided the disciplines and fields that regularly employ case study as a research design into five main groups:

- business and management
- education
- health
- other professional disciplines
- other disciplines.

This reflects the popularity of case study designs in the business and management, education and health disciplines, and other professional or applied disciplines, and its more measured use in what might be termed the pure disciplines. There are, of course, many overlaps between these groups, and between the disciplines and sub-disciplines located within them.

Some general conclusions from across the disciplines are drawn together at the end of the chapter.

BUSINESS AND MANAGEMENT

Business and management is a broad and growing field in contemporary higher education. Indeed, it is typically one of the largest, if not the largest, department or school in the university, recruiting the largest numbers of students: undergraduate and postgraduate, home and international, full-time and part-time.

It is scarcely surprising, therefore, to find that the greatest number of published articles and books on case study – particularly in more recent decades – come from this field. This concentration is heightened by the widespread use of case study throughout business and management not only as a research design (the focus of the discussion here, and of the whole of this book; see Farquhar 2012), but also as a teaching tool (see, for example, Contardo and Wensley 2004; Forman 2006; Garvin 2003; Romm and Mahler 1991; Zhao 1996).

In this section, we will discuss examples of case study research from the following disciplines or sub-disciplines within business and management: accounting, international business, marketing, operations management, public administration, purchasing and logistics, and small business. It is also, however, applied in many other sub-fields, such as human resource management (Haunschild and Eikhof 2009) and supply chain management (Seuring 2008). We will start by examining some generic examples of case study research in business and management that do not locate themselves within a particular discipline or sub-discipline.

Generic Studies

Lee (1989a) examines organisational case studies as a means of bridging the perceived divide between objectivist and subjectivist schools of thought (cf. the discussion of the qualitative/quantitative debate in Chapter 3, and of positivist and interpretivist strategies in Chapter 9). He notes the then 'current re-emergence of subjectivist methods in the field of organizational research' (p. 118), and the four methodological concerns expressed by objectivists regarding organisational case studies: the difficulty of making controlled observations, of replicating the study, generalisability, and the non-quantified nature of many studies (these issues, which are common across the disciplines, are discussed in Chapter 3).

Lee argues that even predominantly qualitative case studies may, nevertheless, follow the three key conceptions of objectivist research: 'that research involves the management of theoretical propositions... that hypothetico-deductive logic can be utilized to confirm or disconfirm the truth of the theoretical propositions, and... that the theoretical propositions, when properly managed, satisfy the four requirements [i.e. the methodological concerns previously identified]' (pp. 127–128).

Addressing these four methodological concerns directly, Lee goes on to argue that 'it is possible to make controlled observations in a case study, where the case study is conducted as a *natural experiment*' (p. 132, emphasis in original) (the combination of case study and experiment in a research design is discussed further in Chapter 6). While such a case study may not be literally replicable, replicability can be addressed through comparing the results of related experiments/studies. The issue of generalisability requires the conduct of more than one case study. The fourth concern, of non-quantifiability, he counters by arguing that it is the logical nature of the research presented which is key, rather than its quantification (though quantification would be an alternative response).

Writing over a decade later, Meyer (2001) provides an overview and critique of the use of case study designs in business and management, illustrated with an example from her own research. She takes a similar position to Lee, arguing that greater care needs to be taken in the conduct of case study research:

> As opposed to other qualitative or quantitative research strategies, such as grounded theory or surveys, there are virtually no specific requirements guiding case research... This is both the strength and the weakness of this approach. It is a strength because it allows tailoring the design and data collection procedures to the research questions. On the other hand, this approach has resulted in many poor case studies, leaving it open to criticism, especially from the quantitative field of research... that the case study is a rather loose design implies that there are a number of choices that need to be addressed in a principled way. (pp. 329–330)

She concludes that 'there is a particular need in case studies to be explicit about the methodological choices one makes' (p. 349).

Writing at the same time as Meyer, Weerd-Nederhof (2001) offers a similar overview, also using her own (PhD) research as an exemplar, but focusing specifically on qualitative forms of research. She offers a step-by-step guide to design and practice, drawing on other authors, but concludes that 'Carrying out qualitative case study research... is first and foremost a matter of learning by doing (while taking into account all useful advice that one can get of course). The next most useful thing is to learn from other people's practical experiences (to avoid the big mistakes)' (p. 535). Her article should be a reassuring guide to other individual researchers planning or conducting a case study, particularly in the business and management disciplines, for their doctoral degree.

Accounting

Case study as a research design has been extensively applied in accounting. In an early contribution, Hagg (1979) discusses the advantages and criticisms of case study designs, before offering several suggestions for improving their practice. He concludes:

> Case methods could play an important role in accounting research. In an area where there is a lack of theory, real difficulties in defining context, an acknowledged importance of patterns of historical development and continued questioning as to the normative or descriptive basis of the discipline, more explicit consideration needs to be given to the advantages that case approaches to research and inquiry can offer.

Scapens (1990) considers the role of case studies in management accounting practice. He argues that:

> Case studies offer us the possibility of understanding the nature of management accounting in practice; both in terms of the techniques, procedures, systems, etc. which are used and the way in which they are used. In undertaking case studies we need to be careful to distinguish the formal accounting systems which senior managers believe are used and the ways in which they are actually used. (p. 264)

Data collection would take place through fieldwork, yielding descriptive, illustrative, experimental, exploratory or explanatory case studies. He discusses their links to neo-classical economics and more recent social theory, outlines the practice of case study research, and concludes: 'In comparison with the more traditional forms of accounting research, it is important to recognize that case studies are concerned with explanation, rather than prediction' (p. 278).

In a follow-up comment on Scapens' article, however, Llewellyn (1992, p. 29) argues that his position 'has a number of ambiguities and apparent contradictions', and that it leaves unclear when 'sociologically informed case study research' is to be preferred. Otley and Berry (1994, p. 46) also joined this debate, arguing that:

> Case studies appear to have a number of potential roles to play, but the central role seems to be that of exploration. The idea of an exploratory case goes beyond that of mere description (an idea which is itself problematic) towards explanation.

Otley and Berry also recognise critical, illustrative and (where access is limited) 'accidental' cases. They provide a summary and reflection on four case studies that they have been involved with, noting that 'we have not generated much new theory, but have rather explored the nature of theory in respect to the four case studies' (p. 55).

Modell (2005) focuses on the use of case studies in triangulating the results of surveys in management accounting research, noting the different validity concerns (see the discussion of validity in Chapter 3) of theory testing and theory development approaches. He notes that:

> Where a theory testing logic dominates, triangulation efforts tend towards external and construct validation through the development of hypotheses and/or measurement instrument applied in survey-based research. This is a suitable approach where prior theorizing provides reasonably well-established constructs and a solid understanding of causal relationships... By contrast, the studies primarily aiming at theory development originate from failures to corroborate particular theoretical models or hypotheses and use triangulation as a means of extending established theory based on the examination of alternative or complementary causal relationships. Such internal validation efforts typically take the form of ex post probing of survey results. (p. 250)

In a more recent contribution, Cooper and Morgan (2008) argue for the usefulness of case study for developing, and reflecting on, professional knowledge in accounting, helping to make it more relevant:

> The case study research approach is useful where the researcher is investigating:
> - complex and dynamic phenomena where many variables (including variables that are not quantifiable) are involved;
> - actual practices, including the details of significant activities that may be ordinary, unusual or infrequent (e.g. changes in accounting regulation); and
> - phenomena in which the context is crucial because the context affects the phenomena being studied (and where the phenomena may also interact with and influence its context). (p. 160)

They note that one of the strengths of case study is that 'Cases can be selected to understand discontinuity and disequilibrium' (p. 161). They argue that 'case studies, while contributing to practice, can also be valuable for theoretical work in identifying new problems to be investigated and testing theories of reasoning, decision making, and justification in complex and value-laden contexts' (p. 165). They offer examples of extreme or deviant, maximum variation, critical and paradigmatic case studies from accounting, and consider the use of case studies in the management accounting, auditing and financial accounting sub-disciplines.

International Business

Piekkari, Welch and Paavilainen (2009) examine evidence on the use of case study research in the field of international business. They focus on the outputs of such research, analysing 135 articles published in four core international business journals – *International Business Review, Journal of International Business Studies, Journal of World Business, Management International Review* – between 1995 and 2005, and a further 22 published between 1975 and 1994.

Case studies accounted for 10.5% of the 1,287 articles published in the four journals between 1995 and 2005, and for 4.7% of the 459 published between 1975 and 1994: 'Overall, we found that a convention prevailed in IB [international business] journals: exploratory, interview-based multiple case studies based on positivistic assumptions and conducted at a single point in time' (p. 577). In other words, only a restricted range of case study designs were being applied, or at least published in the journals examined. Not surprisingly, Piekkari, Welch and Paavilainen argue for greater variety in the use of case study approaches.

Ghauri and Firth (2009) emphasise the benefits of using computer-aided qualitative data analysis software, such as NVivo, for analysing the data collected in case study research. For them:

> the use of NVivo can help researchers systematize and order data, enabling a more thorough and reliable analysis. If qualitative case study research is to become more accepted and publishable, its transparency must be improved. The use of a standardized type of data analysis software may go some way towards helping researchers achieve this goal. (p. 29)

Vissak (2010), an Estonian-based researcher, reviews the usefulness and limitations of case study as a design for international business research, and offers suggestions for making it more effective. She notes that:

> Case studies are quite often used in the area of international business, and they are appropriate for several purposes, including theory generation, testing, refutation, refining, and prediction. The case study method can be applied in small countries and new topic areas, for studying complex phenomena and incremental processes, answering 'how' and 'why (not)' questions. This method allows collecting additional data at any time, and using different additional sources. (p. 382)

In other words, they offer a great deal of flexibility to the small-scale researcher.

Marketing

Bonoma (1985) provides an overview of what he terms case research in the marketing field, and offers guidance in its practice. He concludes that:

Case research does offer significant opportunities to the marketer and the marketing community. First, it allows investigation of a number of important marketing problems which to date have been ignored in theory building and analysis – often because of their complexity or ecological-rootedness. Second, the clinical judgment obtained from case research may feed back not only into the research project itself, but to the classroom, to consulting, and to other, deductive theory-testing efforts as well. More generally... case and other qualitative research can move marketing scholars closer to marketing managers, while laying a clinical foundation for advancing marketing knowledge in new and significant areas. (p. 206)

Note the (false) association of case study with qualitative research.

Johnston, Leach and Liu (1999) consider the use of case studies in theory testing in business-to-business research. They argue for the development of a systematic case methodology to do so, which they term the confirmatory case method:

Central to this confirmatory case method are three elements. First, the research must begin with hypotheses developed by theory. Second, the research design must be logical and systematic. Third, findings must be independently evaluated. By designing research projects around these aspects, case studies become theory-based, systematic, rigorous, and more objective. (p. 201)

They are by no means alone, of course, in calling for a more systematic approach to case study research; Lee (1989a), for example, in the earlier discussion of generic studies, was making much the same point. Taking the point further, Riege (2003) argues that the 'rigorously analytical method of case study research... seems to be especially appropriate for two areas: the study of network systems and international business-to-business marketing' (p. 75). He has a particular interest in the validity and reliability of case study research (see the discussion of these issues in Chapter 3).

Halinen and Tornroos (2005) examine the use of case studies in analysing contemporary business networks. They argue that:

In business network research, we attempt to gain a rich view of connected business actors, activities and events. A trade-off always exists between what is attainable and what is feasible concerning boundary setting, complexity, temporality and comparability across cases. As network researchers, we need to find a feasible ground for research to grasp both the richness of chosen cases and the comparative elements needed. (p. 1296)

Beverland and Lindgren (2010) consider 'what makes a good case study?' through a positivist review of 105 articles based on qualitative case research (there were also 16 quantitative case studies, which were not reviewed) published in the journal *Industrial Marketing Management* between 1971 and 2006 (cf. Piekkari, Welch and Paavilainen's,

2009, analysis of four international business journals, discussed in the section on International Business; meta-analyses of case study research, which both of these studies are, are considered further in Chapter 7). They conclude that:

> there has been a steady improvement in how authors address research quality in qualitative cases. Although, it is unlikely that one dominant design will ever emerge, authors are attempting (within ever tighter page limits) to provide enough information for readers to judge quality, without diminishing the quality of the story. (p. 61)

In the same special issue of *Industrial Marketing Management*, Dubois and Gibbert (2010) focus on the interplay between theory, method and empirical phenomena in case study research. They argue that:

> there is a gamut of approaches possible to case research in industrial marketing, each with its specific links to theory and empirical phenomena, and that this is promising for the development of research in the field, as long as it helps reduce, rather than increase, the complexity of the case studied. (p. 129)

Operations Management

McCutcheon and Meredith (1993) provide an introduction to case study as a field-work method (cf. Scapens 1990 in accounting) for those researching in the operations management field. They present case study as an 'objective, in-depth examination of a contemporary phenomenon where the investigator has little control over events' (p. 240). While one might question the use of the term 'objective', the remainder of the characterisation seems apposite. McCutcheon and Meredith suggest that in data collection:

> Observations and interviews may be supplemented with documents, historical records, organization charts, production statistics and other sources that either provide a clearer understanding or corroborate other data. Given enough background theory, a standardized survey might also be conducted within the case organization. (p. 243)

Case study, as a research design, is clearly seen as having both strengths and weaknesses, with rigour and standardisation (or the lack of these) again seen as key factors:

> This methodology's flexibility, while valuable, limits the development of common standards and practices. A case study's research contribution is largely determined by its design quality and by the researcher's analysis. Design quality depends primarily upon the researcher's rigor in dealing with validity and reliability issues. (p. 245)

McCutcheon and Meredith conclude by providing a list of the 'true' case studies published in five operations management journals in the period 1981–1991, 48 in total, of which they provide a brief analysis.

In another article, Voss, Tsikriktsis and Frohlich (2002) also review the use of case research in operations management, but with a particular focus on theory development and testing. They suggest that: 'Field research with case studies is an iterative approach, which frequently involves multiple methods of data collection, multiple researchers and an evolution of concepts and constructs' (p. 210).

Public Administration

Barzelay (1993) seeks to demonstrate how the single case study can 'produce empirical generalizations regarding administrative rationality, professional treatment, and normative reasoning' (p. 305) in public administration research. Jensen and Rodgers (2001) take a rather different stance, showing how meta-analysis can be used to cumulate what they term the 'intellectual gold' of case study research. They argue that 'public administration is well suited to case studies because they satisfy the recognized need for conditional findings and in-depth understanding of cause and effect relationships that other methodologies find difficult to achieve' (p. 235).

Jensen and Rodgers offer an interesting typology of case studies: snapshot, longitudinal, pre-post, patchwork and comparative (cf. the discussion of Types of Case Study in Chapter 2). For Jensen and Rodgers, 'the generalizability of individual case studies – the foremost concern underlying any form of case study research – can be tested by cumulating evidence from individual case studies into a meta-analysis' (p. 239; see Chapter 7 for further discussion of this technique).

Purchasing and Logistics

Ellram (1996) provides a thorough overview of case study applications in the field of purchasing and logistics, dealing with misconceptions, design issues and data analysis. She argues:

> Not just 'anyone' can use a case study research methodology. Its execution requires careful planning and execution. It requires the ability to step back from the data, analyze data objectively, creatively develop explanations and search for patterns, and rigorously attempt to find holes or problems in the patterns suggested. One of the keys in gaining credibility for case study research and qualitative studies is to make the case study research procedures and process explicit. (p. 114)

Once again, explicitness, rigour and 'objectivity' are held up as the keys to successful case study research. Ellram helpfully suggests a series of potential topics suitable for case study research and, in lengthy appendices, shows what the nuts and bolts of a case study investigation look like.

Small Business

Chetty (1996) reports on the use of the case study method in researching small and medium-sized firms, discussing its application in an export performance study. A number of insights were gained that, she argues, 'would not have emerged through a large survey' (p. 81).

Perren and Ram (2004) offer a mapping of the paradigms that small business case study researchers employ. They hope that their analysis will aid paradigmatic awareness and in so doing help researchers to 'move beyond the paradigmatic islands that currently appear to exist in this area, move beyond crude "belt-and-braces" attempts at pluralism and provide some shared space in which to debate' (p. 95). Researchers often feel more comfortable on their isolated islands, however, and/or working in their insulated silos, to use another commonly employed metaphor.

De Massis and Kotlar (2014) offer guidelines for researchers, reviewers and editors on the use of case studies in family business research. They argue that:

> case study research offers family business scholars significant opportunities to contribute to the family business literature by advancing the theoretical understanding of family firms… as the family business field continues to mature, case study research provides family business scholars with growing opportunities to contribute to the mainstream management literature. (pp. 27–28)

Among the suggestions made and conclusions drawn by case study researchers in business and management, two in particular stand out time and again. First, on the plus side, case study is an extremely flexible approach, widely suited to exploring many different aspects of business and management. Second – and whether this is on the plus or minus side depends on your own perspective – and partly because of its very flexibility, there is a need to exercise considerable care in conducting case study research and to be explicit about the choices you have (inevitably) had to make.

EDUCATION

Good (1942) offers an early analysis of the procedures involved in educational case study. He contrasts case study with case work, which is concerned with the corrective work that needs to be done to the case, and case method, which refers to the use of case studies for teaching purposes.

Writing some 45 years later, Wilson and Gudmundsdottir (1987) note that 'our experiences as researchers developing a series of case studies about novice teachers have made it clear that the dominant characterization of case studies in recent literature is incomplete', and focus on 'the conceptual issues involved in defining what we mean by a "case"' (p. 42). Going through a process akin to the hermeneutical circle (a cyclical process of questioning and revision), they note particular problems with the bounding of cases:

The type of research we have described begins with the roughest notions of case boundaries. Through the progressive elucidation and articulation of theoretical constructs and models, limits are gradually drawn around the empirical cases in question... our struggle with our data has made us wiser. Researchers cannot assume that boundaries of cases are tangible, readily apparent, or static. In our research, theory and empiricism have worked in tandem, contributing equally to the definitive marking of cases. (p. 52)

The issue of bounding cases is discussed further in Chapter 8.

Bassey (1981, 1983, 2001) has paid repeated attention over the years to issues of generalisation in pedagogical case studies. He begins by noting that:

Recent British writings on the nature of educational research seem to agree on two expectations: (a) that educational research should result in generalisations which will coalesce into educational theory, and (b) that educational research should contribute in some way to improvement of educational practice. (1981, p. 73)

However, echoing a long-standing debate in educational research, he queried whether these two expectations were compatible, arguing that:

the study of single events is a more profitable form of research (judged by the criterion of usefulness to teachers) than searches for generalisations... the merit of study of single events lies not in the extent to which it can be generalised, but in the extent to which a teacher reading it can relate it to his own teaching. (1981, p. 73)

Wilson (1979) comes to a similar conclusion about the usefulness of case study evaluations of policy and practice.

By 2001, Bassey had changed his mind, and was arguing the merits of 'fuzzy' generalisations, that is generalisations that may hold, but not necessarily in all circumstances. Such generalisations are accompanied, where possible, by 'best estimates of trustworthiness'. Hammersley (2001) critiques this notion, however, arguing that all generalisations are conditional, querying the need for a form of generalisation specific to case study research, and questioning 'the idea that generalisations of any kind, including those based on research, can tell us what *will* happen in the particular situations in which we must act as practitioners' (p. 224, emphasis in original).

Stenhouse (1979; see also Stenhouse 1978) argues that case studies have a great deal to offer those interested in studying comparative education. He notes that:

Criticism of the experimental sample paradigm in educational research has led to a resurgence of interest in case study. I am mounting a like criticism of the tradition in comparative education of studying and writing about the systems of other countries, and asking that we develop in our field a better grounded representation of day-to-day educational reality resting on the careful study of particular cases. The accumulation of cases may yield some generalisations in due course; but these will never supplant the need for shrewd practical understanding which can only feed on the descriptive representation of practice. (p. 10)

Donmoyer and Galloway (2010) take a similar stance to Stenhouse in considering the utility of case study designs in the neo-scientific era, when large-scale randomised trials are seen as the gold standard for driving evidence-based practice. In examining the use of quantitative techniques within or alongside case study, they conclude that:

current attempts to place quantitative measures front and center in case study design, although not totally inappropriate, often overestimate what quantitative measures can reveal in case study contexts. In addition, our study highlights some rather substantial, and possibly insurmountable, problems associated with using large-scale studies to test and validate hypotheses generated by case study research. Finally, the study also reminds us of what is lost in terms of nuanced understanding of interacting contextual variables when case studies are used merely as sources of hypotheses for larger studies with large sample sizes. (p. 24)

While this perspective lends support to the widely held view that case study research is, or should be, wholly or predominantly qualitative in nature, it is important to bear in mind that what matters is the appropriateness and usage of methods within case study, whether they be qualitative, quantitative or mixed (see also the discussion of the qualitative/quantitative debate in Chapter 3).

Examining a different area of case study research in education, Foster, Gomm and Hammersley (2000, p. 227) note that 'much case-study research investigating educational inequalities draws evaluative conclusions and that it should not do so'. They argue instead that 'Case study research should concentrate on providing value-relevant factual information, and make explicit the value assumptions on which that relevance depends' (p. 228). Lakomski (1987, p. 147) makes the related point that 'case studies which base the accuracy of their findings on participants' interpretations or understandings claim more than they can validly justify', linking this to an inadequate understanding of the nature of knowledge.

Snyder (2012) offers what she terms a 'case study of a case study', which may be considered as an illustrative example of the use of the design within educational studies (or the social sciences in general). She presents what she claims is a robust qualitative research methodology developed from 'a study which tracked the transformative journeys of four career-changing women from STEM [i.e. science, technology, engineering and mathematics] fields into secondary education', using 'archived writing, journaling, participant-generated photography, interviews, member-checking, and reflexive analytical memos' (p. 1).

Canen (1999) reports on a contrary experience, indicative of the risks that researchers can run in focusing on a single case for data collection. While conducting ethnographic case study research in a UK teacher education institution, she ran into opposition from a senior administrator:

> When I wrote a clarification document to the administration reminding it of the commitments agreed to… I received an answer accusing me of *discourtesy, lack of ethical awareness and of distorting opinions* expressed… The letter spelt out that I should pursue no contacts between me and students or members of staff of the institution from then on. The fieldwork ended. (p. 53, emphasis in original)

This example demonstrates the key importance of access to any empirical research (this is discussed further in the section on The Role of Access in Chapter 8).

Different Educational Areas, Sectors or Levels

Examples of the use of the case study design can be found in all areas, sectors or levels of educational research, though most of the studies referred to so far have been concerned with school, and particularly secondary, education. Thus, Sleeter (2009) provides a case study of an individual teacher's curriculum decisions, and Wells et al (1995) investigate the effects of reducing ability grouping or tracking in racially mixed schools.

In special needs education, Ghesquiere, Maes and Vandenberghe (2004, p. 171) discuss the 'use of qualitative case studies to describe and understand the complex reality of the innovations taking place in our schools'.

In educational technology, Khan (2008) compared the use of case studies with other sources of knowledge, practitioner and disciplinary, in the design of an educational computer simulation, concluding that 'the case study was the source of 16 out of 23 design decisions and therefore was the most significant influence on the design of the simulation' (p. 423). Williams van Rooij and Zirkle (2016) provide a case study of the collaborative development of an online learning programme for disabled learners.

In higher education, Harland (2014) notes the ubiquity of the use of case study design for undertaking small-scale research on a one-year course he teaches on academic development. He identifies four questions that participants find particularly challenging: '(1) What is the potential of case study? (2) What forms of data are acceptable? (3) When does analysis stop? (4) What makes a quality case study?' (p. 1115; these questions are, of course, all picked up elsewhere in this book, particularly in Chapters 8 and 9). Parker et al (2009) look at the impact of student involvement in community service learning as part of an undergraduate health unit.

Healey et al (2010) report on a single institution case study of students' perceptions of academics' research role. The study made use of quantitative and qualitative data collected through a questionnaire survey and small group interviews. They conclude that 'active learning through enquiry is as relevant a way of linking research and teaching in less-research intensive universities as it is in more research-intensive ones' (p. 243).

Corcoran, Walker and Wals (2004; see also Jones, Trier and Richards 2008; Kyburz-Graber 2004), consider the use of case study methodology to research sustainability in higher education, reviewing 54 journal articles. Similarly to Harland, they identify four areas of concern:

> The first of these areas is *purpose*. From our analysis it became clear that many case studies did not have a clear purpose and, when they did, failed to show how the study adequately addressed this purpose... The second area is the *role* of the players. It is important that all the actors, representing potentially diverging interests, be involved in the study and their role in the innovation be explained... The third area concerns the *tension* between the universal and the contextual. Every school or institution is different and the ways in which sustainability issues are dealt with in one institution are very contextual. Therefore, it is important that a study addresses how practice and learning from one institution can become transformative beyond the context in which the case was developed, both within and across institutions. The fourth area is *challenge*. A study is more transformative when it challenges the reader and/or sets challenges for the writer. (pp. 14–15, emphasis in original)

Once again, as in the business and management field, the need to aim for high standards in conducting and reporting case study research is stressed.

HEALTH

Case studies are widely used in healthcare research, both generally and in research focused more specifically on aspects of, for example, medicine, nursing or physiotherapy. A number of guides to the use of the case study design in healthcare research have been published (e.g. Crowe et al 2011; Kim, Price and Lau 2014).

Looking at the more generic studies first, there are many, comparable or contrasting, examples that might be examined. For example:

- Fletcher et al (2009) report on the use of qualitative case studies, involving interviews with students in two sample schools, for exploring how schools might influence drug use.
- Flicker (2008), on the basis of a case study of a community health education project, questions who benefits from such research and to what extent.
- Yin (1999), in one of his many publications on case study research, offers guidance for improving the quality of case studies in health services research.
- Wilson, Huttly and Fenn (2006) provide a case study of sample design in a complex, longitudinal project focusing on children's lives in less developed countries.
- Abbato (2015) reports on the use of case study in the evaluation of a mobile dementia education and support service in rural Australia, which involved interviews with stakeholders and documentary analysis of client data.

In each of these examples, there is a clear focus on using the research to improve people's lives. This is a general characteristic of case study research, indeed of almost all research, in health care. Most of this research is, however, carried out within a particular discipline or sub-discipline. Research in the disciplines of medicine, nursing and physiotherapy, and in the overlapping disciplines of psychiatry, psychoanalysis and psychotherapy, will now be examined.

Medicine

Lukoff, Edwards and Miller (1998) suggest that case studies can provide valuable insight and data in studying alternative medical therapies. This is partly because of their specialist historical usage within the fields of medicine and health: 'From Hippocrates to recent times, the case history, a narrative form, has been the cornerstone of all literature concerned with the healing arts' (p. 44). Case studies are, of course, widely used in medical training (e.g. Bair 1980; Griffiths 2009).

While Lukoff, Edwards and Miller accept that case study is not always highly regarded as a scientific method, they argue that 'Even in the most challenging circumstances, the validity of case study research can be improved when researchers follow the guidelines for case study research published in several texts on this method' (p. 46). They reference the works of Stake and Yin in particular. Yet again, standardisation of practice and care in delivery are identified as key for successful case studies.

Schneider (1999) discusses what he terms 'multiple-case depth research', incorporating multiple case design and depth therapeutic principles, as a means of addressing key questions:

> (1) which therapies, under what conditions, help or hinder which kinds of clients; (2) what are the respective benefits of symptom alleviation versus personality change; (3) what factors outside of therapy – such as family relationships, social networks, and economic circumstances – both affect and are affected by therapy; (4) what is the impact of time on therapeutic outcome; and (5) what is perceived suffering, health? (p. 1538)

Clearly, Schneider has little doubt about the usefulness of case study designs, appropriately applied, in medical research.

Blencowe et al (2015) go further in applying case study in the context of the gold standard of medical research, the randomised controlled trial (RCT), albeit only at the pilot research stage. Eight qualitative case studies of gastric bypass surgery were undertaken, involving video data capture, non-participant observation and interviews with the surgeons involved. They conclude that:

> Randomised controlled trials in surgery can be difficult to design and conduct, and one of the reasons for this is that surgical interventions are complex. Case studies provide a way of exploring this complexity to make sense of how surgical interventions are described and standardised in trials. Successful completion of

case studies within the operating theatre has developed methods that can be transferred to intervention design and delivery within the broader context of surgical RCTs. They enable the components and steps of interventions to be established, including those which are considered as crucial, and the extent to which standardisation may be required. This has the potential to influence the way in which surgical interventions are designed and delivered within RCTs. (p. 8)

Here, case studies are being used to help design the randomised controlled trials upon which so much medical research relies, in much the same way that interviews are often used in mixed methods research designs (these are discussed further in Chapter 9) to help determine the questions to be asked in surveys.

Nursing

Anthony and Jack (2009) report on an analysis of 42 case study research papers in nursing (another example of meta-analysis, which is discussed further in Chapter 7), with a particular focus on qualitative case study methodology (QCSM). They conclude that:

> First, judicious selection and diligent application of literature review methods promotes superior development of nursing science. Secondly, QCSM is becoming entrenched in the nursing research lexicon as a well-accepted methodology to address the phenomenon of human care and other complex issues germane to the discipline worldwide. Thirdly, outcomes arising from increased knowledge about and use of QCSM not only contribute to nursing science, but also can make significant contributions to health and well-being. Finally, differences and conflicts among methodological experts notwithstanding, the use of QCSM in nursing science is growing and warrants continued analysis and appraisal for the promotion of nursing knowledge development to address increasingly complex challenges in nursing, health and health care. (p. 1177)

That is about as glowing a recommendation for case study research as its most enthusiastic proponents could hope for. Case study research is clearly better accepted and in more widespread use in nursing than in medical research.

Bryar (1999), Casey and Houghton (2010) and Woods (1997) all provide accessible guides to the use of case study in nursing research, with Woods concluding that:

> One of the key benefits of the case study approach is that it takes into account the naturalistic setting of the phenomenon being observed, without losing the contextual detail that has a significant effect on the subjects and their behavior. The case study approach to research should be seen as being complementary to other research approaches in common use. It has a great deal to offer the nurse researcher in that it aids in increasing understanding of how nursing is practised. (p. 55)

Walshe (2011) advocates the use of case study research for evaluating complex interventions in palliative care. She notes that 'Researchers seeking to use case study strategies need to consider three main issues in order to develop and improve the evaluation of complex evaluations: case selection, longitudinal design, and the use of rival hypotheses' (p. 780). The mention of longitudinal design is important, affirming the necessity for time series studies to assess the worth of interventions in health care (the combination of case study and time series research designs is further discussed in Chapter 6).

Physiotherapy

Ritchie (2001) considers the use of qualitative methods – in particular, what she terms 'case series research', that is carrying out a series of qualitative case studies – to enhance the findings of quantitative research:

> The value of the series is that some commonalities may be observed across the cases which can, with appropriate rigorous analysis, be shown to reveal important implications for making decisions on treatment in the clinical situation. What makes this level of evidence different is that the implications arising from the case series are derived inductively, that is, through observing a series of examples or applications, leading to finding an explanation for patterns arising across these examples. (p. 131)

She concludes that 'well done case series research has the potential to add considerably to the assembling of evidence for better clinical interventions' (p. 134). Thus, multiple case studies, as well as time series studies, are useful in assessing health interventions.

Case study designs are widely used in physiotherapy, as in other areas of health research, but the great majority of such studies simply offer descriptive analyses of completed case studies, examining aspects of practice, management or training (e.g. Adams and Tyson 2000; Cowell and Phillips 2002; Ogulata, Koyuncu and Karakas 2008; Young 2013), rather than suggesting developments in research design.

Psychiatry/Psychoanalysis/Psychotherapy

Psychiatry, psychoanalysis and psychotherapy are closely related disciplines where case studies have had a long and particular usage (see also the discussion of the use of case studies in the related discipline of psychology in a later section of this chapter). Here, as in other branches of health care, the individual clinical case study is a cornerstone to the working of the profession (McLeod 2010). Leitenberg (1973) outlines and illustrates the range of single-case experimental designs available.

As in other fields, however, there are some doubts expressed about the usefulness of case studies for research. Thus, Jones and Windholz (1990, p. 987) note that 'some demonstration of the research utility of formalized case studies is needed to establish the applicability of clinical evidence in the testing of psychoanalytic constructs'.

They apply the Q-technique to illustrate how psychoanalytic case studies may be made amenable for quantitative analysis.

Jones and Windholz developed a 100-item 'Psychotherapy Process Q-set... to provide a basic language and rating procedure for the comprehensive description, in clinically relevant terms, of the therapist–patient interaction in a form suitable for quantitative comparison and analysis' (pp. 988–989). They explain their strategy in the following way:

[The] Q-set captures a wide range of phenomena in the domain of analytic process, including transference manifestations, resistance, and reconstruction, as well as the analyst's activity (e.g., clarification, interpretation) and the patient's affective states, such as anxiety, depression, or other symptomatic behavior. A coding manual details instructions for Q-sorting and provides the items and their definitions, along with examples in order to minimize potentially varying interpretations of the items. (p. 990)

Using a particular clinical case, Jones and Windholz demonstrate how this technique can be used to provide quantitative summaries of the case.

Elliott (2002) takes an alternative approach, in exploring what he terms hermeneutic single case efficacy design, an approach to evaluating treatment causality in therapy cases which uses a mixture of qualitative and quantitative methods. His concluding comment illustrates just how closely interwoven the relationship between researcher and researched may be in small-scale research, particularly when it is designed to effect change:

[T]he development of explanations of therapy outcome is a fundamentally interpretive process, involving a 'double hermeneutic' of client (engaged in a process of self-interpretation) and researcher (engaged in a process of interpreting the interpreter). The double hermeneutic suggests that the client is actually a coinvestigator, who acts always as an active self-interpreter and self-changer. As researchers, we follow along behind, performing a second, belated act of interpretation, carefully sifting through the multitude of sometimes contradictory signs and indicators provided by the client. (p. 20)

Edwards, Dattilio and Bromley (2004) examine the relationship between case-based research and evidence-based practice in the context of psychological treatments. They argue that:

A limitation of multivariate studies is that the statistical procedures they use deduce the properties of a population from those of a sample; they cannot deduce from a sample the properties of individual cases. Yet this is what practitioners need to know... Case-based research can provide a therapist with more differentiated knowledge with respect to aspects of clients' motivations, attitudes, or beliefs that are likely to affect engagement with treatment and with respect to how to respond effectively to the details of clients' emotions, thoughts, and behavior as the treatment unfolds. (p. 595)

Clearly, in offering therapy to individuals, case-based (or individual) knowledge is key.

In a similar vein, Etherington and Bridges (2011; this article is discussed in more detail in Chapter 7) describe the use of a narrative case study approach in counselling, focusing on case reviews and the ending of counselling programmes. They found the process of narrative case study to be 'empowering for those who take part in it' (p. 21).

Gottman (1973) argues for the use of time series case study designs, as have other researchers working in other areas of health care (this combined research design is discussed in more detail in Chapter 6):

> Time-series analysis permits the study of a single subject over time and the study of effect patterns of an intervention over time. It also allows the therapist to use information as feedback for making decisions, a useful tool in the evaluation of psychotherapy. (pp. 104–105)

On similar lines, Jones et al (1993; this article is discussed in detail in Chapter 7) articulate what they term a 'paradigm' for single-case research, involving time series study of long-term psychotherapy.

Many more studies could be referenced in this section, demonstrating how knowledge and usage of the case study research design has built up over the years in these related disciplines. For example:

- Kazdin (1981) discusses the procedures that may be adopted in order 'to maximize the likelihood that internally valid conclusions may be drawn' (p. 183) from case studies.
- Hilliard (1993) discusses the use of single-case methodology in psychotherapy process and outcome research, distinguishing between single-case experiments, single-case qualitative analyses and case studies.
- Dugard, File and Todman (2012) focus on the use of randomisation tests in single-case and small-n experimental research.

Clearly, case study research has much to offer professional disciplines where the focus of practice is on the individual.

OTHER PROFESSIONAL DISCIPLINES

In addition to the major fields of business and management, education and health, there are numerous other professional or applied disciplines that make use of case study as a research design. Here we will discuss examples from development, information systems, law, library and information studies, and social work. As with business and management, in a number of these professions case studies take a particular form or forms, including their use as a teaching method as well as a research design (the focus of this book).

This is not an exclusive list of the professional disciplines in which case study designs have been applied. They have also been used, for example, in counselling (Lundervold and Belwood 2000), second language learning (Casanave 2003) and software engineering (Runesson and Host 2009).

Development

Vellema, Ton, de Roo and van Wijk (2013; this article is discussed in more detail in Chapter 7) use case studies to analyse company–non-governmental organisation partnerships in development initiatives in Uganda and Rwanda. They argue that 'Case studies of these partnering processes can help to refine the theoretical underpinning of the anticipated developmental impact of VCPs [value chain partnerships] and the rationale for adopting them' (p. 305). They employ both within-case and comparative case analysis, and conclude that the analysis:

> shows the value of case studies for contextualizing and delimiting the specific contribution that partnerships make to promoting change. We consider this to be an important step towards developing more refined theories of partnering. (p. 316)

Woolcock (2013) also uses case studies to explore complex development interventions, here focusing on their external validity. In discussing the usefulness of case studies in this context, he emphasises three key points:

> ...the distinctiveness of case studies as a method of analysis in social science beyond the familiar qualitative/quantitative divide; the capacity of case studies to elicit causal claims and generate testable hypotheses; and (related) the focus of case studies on exploring and explaining mechanisms (i.e. identifying how, for whom and under what conditions outcomes are observed – or 'getting inside the black box'). The rising quality of the analytic foundations of case study research has been one of the underappreciated (at least in mainstream social science) methodological advances of the last twenty years. (p. 241)

Indeed, it would be difficult to imagine the evaluation of development initiatives not using case study research designs, as each such initiative is, in essence, a case, bounded (limited to or targeted on) a particular group, region or nation.

Information Systems

Cavaye (1996) provides an overview of the various kinds of case study research that may be fruitfully applied to the field of information systems, giving examples from the published literature. She organises her review in terms of epistemology (interpretivist, positivist or combined), objective (description, discovery or testing, or combinations of these), whether quantitative or qualitative methods are used and whether the design is of a single case or multiple cases (there is more discussion of these issues in Chapter 9).

Dube and Pare (2003) look at how the information systems field has advanced in its use of case studies, focusing on the methodological rigour of positivist case studies. To carry out this review, they assess 183 articles published in seven major information systems journals, focusing on design issues, data collection and data analysis (cf. the studies by Beverland and Lindgren 2010 of articles on marketing, and by Piekkari, Welch and Paavilainen 2009 of international business journals; Meta-analysis is discussed further in Chapter 7).

Dube and Pare focused on the 10-year period 1990–1999. Of 261 articles identified that used case research methodology, 210 employed it as the primary research methodology, and 87% (183) of these were classified as having a positivist epistemology. Dube and Pare were, however, disappointed in their findings:

> [W]e found it astonishing that more than 4 out of 10 case study articles in our database made no attempt at describing the data collection process… only 9 percent of all case studies in our population provided clear and detailed information about how their data were analyzed. (2003, p. 626)

Clearly, then, in their assessment, there was a considerable distance to go to bring the practice of case studies, particularly (or perhaps even) positivist case studies, in the information systems area up to standard.

In an earlier, smaller-scale study, Doolin (1996; see Benbasat, Goldstein and Mead, 1987, for a similar earlier study) reviewed 50 articles using case study design in four journals over the period 1989–1993. Unlike Dube and Pare, however, Doolin compares positivist and (emerging) interpretive approaches to case study research, rather than just focusing on positivist approaches. He notes:

> Methodologies informed by a positivist research philosophy tend to treat case research as an exploratory tool for developing hypotheses in the construction of 'scientific' theory. By contrast, interpretive methodologies give a more central role to case research, utilising case studies to obtain a deeper understanding of the phenomenon and of the meaning of human behaviour. (p. 28)

This finding is not, of course, surprising, as it matches standard perceptions of positivist/quantitative and interpretivist/qualitative epistemologies (see the discussion of the qualitative/quantitative debate in Chapter 3, and of positivist and interpretivist strategies in Chapter 9).

Darke, Shanks and Broadbent (1998) offer guidelines for carrying out case study research (which they mistakenly present as an exclusively qualitative form of research) on information systems that combine rigour, relevance and pragmatism. Lee (1989b) provides a similar overview, suggesting how case study research can overcome the methodological problems of making controlled observations, making controlled deductions, allowing for replicability and allowing for generalisability. Hashim (2010) looks at the use of multiple case studies in theory building, using the example of information and communication technology implementation and management in Malaysia as an illustration.

Law

Caulley and Dowdy (1987) consider evaluation case histories as a parallel to legal case histories, which would assist in the development of the evaluation profession. They argue that 'Surely no profession makes more extensive use of case histories than does the Law' (p. 360). As to their format, they note that:

> Case histories are written by judges, usually aided by their law clerks… There is no mandatory format or formula for the writing of a legal opinion. However, most opinions do follow a certain structure which has evolved to present all the necessary elements of the decision in a logical, orderly fashion. These elements, in order of their usual presentation, are: (a) the procedural history of the particular action; (b) a statement of the facts of the case; (c) a statement of the legal issues to be decided by the court; (d) a discussion of legal principles as set forward in prior decisions and now applied to the facts of the present case; and (e) finally, the result reached. (p. 360)

Legal case histories are a particular, discipline-specific kind of case study, one which, while arguably research-based (and which might be termed a descriptive case study), is widely used in teaching. The development of similar case histories for evaluation, it is argued, would be useful guides to how to do evaluations, and would serve to accumulate knowledge and experience.

Other legal scholars have also carefully reviewed the usefulness of case studies. Thus, Linos (2015) discusses the selection and development of international law case studies, considering issues such as generality, causation, most different and most similar cases, critical and deviant cases, and comparison across and within cases. She concludes: 'By testing claims and moving from highly general theories to midrange theories that specify clearly under what conditions particular results obtain, scholars can do work that is both theoretically rich and more relevant to policy makers and practitioners' (p. 485).

Most uses of the term case study in a research context in legal studies, however, relate to descriptive analyses of particular cases (e.g. Brennan 1988–89; Sloane 2002; Urinboyev 2011).

Library and Information Studies

Fidel (1984) uses the case study method to identify broad patterns of online searching behaviour. Five experienced searchers were observed (and asked to think aloud while they searched) and then interviewed. The data recorded was then analysed using controlled comparison, with searches summarised in Venn diagrams.

Most applications of the case study design in library and information studies, how-ever, simply provide a descriptive evaluation of a particular innovation or practice (e.g. Battleson, Booth and Weintrop 2001; Funnell 2015), with little or no reference to the case study literature.

Social Work

Gilgun (1994) argues that:

> Case study research is a good fit with many forms of social work practice. Although disparaged as uncontrolled and uninterpretable, the case study has great potential for building social work knowledge for assessment, intervention and outcome. (p. 371)

In other words, case study research can be used in social work research and practice in much the same way as it is used in the health professions. Gilgun goes on to offer a series of guidelines for evaluating, interpreting and developing case studies.

Lee, Mishna and Brennenstuhl (2010) strongly agree with Gilgun, noting that:

> Case studies in social work have great value in building emergent knowledge, bridging the ongoing challenge of integrating research and practice, and ensuring quality client care in practice. Given the growing interest in evidence-based social work practice, a systematic evaluation of case studies based on varying levels of evidence is much needed. (p. 682)

They then offer guidance on how to critically evaluate case studies in social work, considering the issues of transferability/external validity, credibility/internal validity, confirmability/construct validity and dependability/reliability, as well as triangulation, sampling, sources of evidence and data analysis (these issues are all discussed further in Chapter 3).

OTHER DISCIPLINES

Case study is also employed as a research design in some of the 'pure' disciplines, particularly in the social sciences. We will discuss examples from geography and envi-ronmental studies, philosophy, political science, psychology and sociology.

Geography and Environmental Studies

Curtis et al (2000) focus on the issues of sampling and case selection (which are dis-cussed in more detail in Chapter 8), using as examples some of their own qualitative research into the geography of health. They evaluate six criteria proposed by Miles and Huberman (1994): (1) the sampling strategy should be relevant to the conceptual framework and the research questions addressed by the research; (2) the sample should be likely to generate rich information on the type of phenomena which need to be studied; (3) the sample should enhance the 'generalisability' of the findings; (4) the sample should produce believable descriptions/explanations; (5) the sampling strategy should be ethical; and (6) the sampling plan should be feasible. They conclude that:

> Consideration of these three study examples seems to emphasize the importance of the choices which are made in sample selection. It seems essential to be explicit about these, rather than leaving them hidden, and to consider the implications of the choice for the way that the qualitative study can be interpreted. (Curtis et al 2000, p. 1012)

The need to be explicit about sampling choices and their implications apply even when – and arguably particularly so – the sample is a single case.

Ford et al (2010) compare the use of case study and analogue (temporal or spatial) methodologies in climate change vulnerability research. They note that 'the majority of vulnerability case studies are conducted at the local (i.e., community) level. This is essential for identifying opportunities for local adaptation intervention and community planning, but case studies are also required at regional to national levels to identify opportunities for adaptation at broader scales' (p. 384). Grima et al (2016) also focus on the environment, in this case the use of market mechanisms to improve land management practices. They analyse 40 published case studies of 'payment for ecosystems service' schemes in Latin America.

Hopwood (2004) provides an example of a multi-method case study, using elements of phenomenology, ethnography and grounded theory (the use of both ethnography and grounded theory in combination with case study designs is further discussed in Chapter 6). Hopwood offers a checklist for the use of multiple methods in case study research:

a) Ensure that the theoretical and epistemological bases of research are in harmony, and use these to develop a complementary methodology.
b) Once specific research questions have been developed, consider how a reliable and valid interpretation of data may be elicited in answer to those particular questions. Explore and develop techniques, customizing accordingly.
c) Regard data collection and analysis as simultaneous, ongoing processes, and allow analysis to engage with data collection. A more robust interpretation results.
d) Exploit the potential of multiple-method designs to produce a range of response formats and content, but be aware of potential problems with triangulation across formats – 'imagine' the data and how to analyse them before they are collected.
e) Produce matrices for all techniques, detailing the substantive focus and response format for every (planned) item. This can be used to ensure balance and to incorporate opportunities for triangulation into the design. (p. 352)

Case study is also used in more applied or professional areas of geography and environmental studies, such as planning and urban studies (e.g. Franz, Tausz and Thiel 2015).

Philosophy

Ruzzene (2012) focuses on the issue of external validity (which is discussed in more detail in the section on Validity and Reliability in Chapter 3), challenging what he terms the 'traditional' view, namely that the case study method is weak in this respect:

> The traditional view treats the problem of external validity as a problem of representativeness. This has two major normative implications. First, its methodological precepts are all and only oriented to guide the selection of the 'right' case, understood as a typical one. Second, the traditional view ascribes the difficulty that case study research has in putting together a representative sample as the source of the method's incapacity, or the extreme weakness, in achieving external validity. But this reasoning goes wrong already at the first step, and this makes problematic its gloomy conclusion. External validity is *not*, I argue, essentially a problem of representativeness but rather one of inference and so a problem to which the representativeness of the case might offer (one) possible solution. (p. 106, emphasis in original)

Enhancing the comparability of the cases studied then becomes a key issue, for which the criteria discussed by Curtis et al (2000) in their examination of case selection in studying the geography of health (see previous sub-section) have clear relevance.

Political Science

Political science has been one of the more important 'pure' disciplines for developing case study research in recent times. It has witnessed intensive debate on, for example, rational deterrence theory and comparative case studies. Achen and Snidal (1989; see also Most and Starr 1982) concluded that:

> Case studies are an important complement to both theory-building and statistical investigations... they allow a close examination of historical sequences in the search for causal processes. The analyst is able to identify plausible causal variables, a task essential to theory construction and testing. Comparison of historical cases to theoretical predictions provides a sense of whether the theoretical story is compelling, and yields indispensable prior knowledge for more formal tests of explanatory adequacy. The method also generates novel empirical generalizations, which pose puzzles and challenges for theory to explain. (pp. 168–169)

Gerring (2006) offers what he calls a methodological primer for single-outcome studies, that is, those case studies which seek 'to investigate a bounded unit in an attempt to elucidate a single outcome occurring within that unit' (p. 707). He argues that:

> The analysis of a single outcome may be approached from three different angles. The first, which I refer to as *nested analysis*, employs cross-case analysis from a large sample in order to better understand the features of an individual outcome. The second, known most commonly as *most-similar analysis*, employs cross-case analysis within a small sample (e.g. two or three cases). The third, known generically as *within-case analysis*, draws on evidence from within the case of special interest. (p. 717, emphasis in original)

He warns, however, that 'Cross-case and within-case evidence often tell somewhat different stories and there is no easy way to adjudicate between them' (p. 728). Clearly, though, his preference is to analyse single cases comparatively with reference to other related cases.

Bennett and Elman (2006) provide an overview of recent developments in case study research in political science, noting – as others have done in other disciplines – the renaissance of qualitative methods. They conclude, in very balanced fashion, that:

> Case study methods have emerged, like all widely used observational methods in the social sciences, as a useful but limited and potentially fallible mode of inference. Because the relative advantages of case studies are different from and complementary to those of statistical and formal methods, one of the newest and most exciting trends in methodology is the increasing focus on combining methods from the different traditions in the same study or research program. (p. 473)

While we may not be as dismissive of the relative strengths of case studies when used on their own in research (see the discussion in Chapter 3), the use of case studies in combined research designs is the subject of the next chapter (Chapter 6).

Levy (2008) offers a typology of case studies (discussed in Chapter 2 – see Box 2.2), and then focuses on their design. He discusses selection bias, comparable case research designs, process tracing, crucial case designs and deviant case designs. He concludes that:

> …[the] shared epistemological ground among quantitative, formal, and case study researchers is far greater than some of the methodological differences that divide them. I also think that some of the differences that do exist have been exaggerated by some qualitative methodologists. This suggests that the impediments to incorporating multiple methods into research programs are few, while the benefits are many. (p. 15)

Odell (2001), in a discussion of the use of case study methods for researching international political economy (IPE), offers a similar typology to that of Levy, recognising 'the disciplined interpretive case study, the hypothesis-generating case study, the least-likely, most-likely, and deviant case studies' (p. 161). He reaches the conclusion that:

> qualitative case study methods offer appealing advantages and suffer from significant limitations relative to statistical methods, in IPE just as in other subject areas. The most general implication is familiar but still inescapable, in my opinion. Neither family is sufficient without the other. (p. 173)

Nicholson-Crotty and Meier (2002), in the context of research into policy in the United States, make the argument for the usefulness of single case studies. They argue that:

> research designs focusing on a single state are sometimes preferable to those employing data from all 50 states. Single state studies are appropriate when the researcher wishes to generalize to a unit of analysis other than the states themselves, when conditions in a given state provide a unique opportunity for the most rigorous test of a hypothesis, and when the measurement advantages of a single-state study outweigh the costs of limited generalization… it is soundness of theory and rigor of analysis, rather than the number of states, that makes research valid and important. (p. 411)

Many American states, after all, have the area and population of sizeable nations. Anckar (2007; see also Dion 1998), taking a broader perspective, considers the selection of cases in cross-national political research; here it is worth noting that many international studies compare other developed nations with American states (most often, it seems, California).

Crasnow (2011), in a discussion of methodological and causal pluralism, argues that:

> the debate about case studies research in political science does not provide support for conceptual causal pluralism, though it does appear to provide additional means to acquire important evidence for causal claims… [C]ase study research is important for providing information needed for good risk assessment and… the inference to use (as opposed to warrant) requires risk assessment… Pluralism about the aims of science – recognizing use as well as warrant as goals – makes clearer the need for methodological pluralism and supports an important role for case study research in political science. (p. 47)

Case study research, alongside or in combination with other research designs, therefore has a continuing role to play in political science research.

Psychology

Psychology is another discipline where case study has a particular meaning and application, here referring to the individual and their treatment (see also the earlier discussion in this chapter in the section on health of the related professional fields of psychiatry, psychoanalysis and psychotherapy). Writing some 50 years ago, Shapiro (1966) considers the single clinical/psychological case and whether it can produce useful findings. He reviews what he terms simple and complex descriptive studies, and simple experimental studies, on three topics, and concludes that:

> one is unlikely to make important advances in the experimental investigation of processes if he [sic] makes no use of individual-centered investigations... individual-centered research in clinical psychology can produce meaningful and replicable results. (p. 19)

The usefulness of case study research to psychology has been regularly addressed over the years. Thus, Hayes (1981) examined the use of time series experimentation in single case designs, while McCullough (1984, p. 398) sets out some proposed guidelines for their conduct:

> Pathological phenomena should be measured repeatedly and systematically throughout the process of case assessment, treatment implementation, termination, and follow-up. Also, treatment methodology should be carefully operationalized and treatment subjects be classified and matched according to the symptom checklist criteria... If these minimal requirements for N = 1 research are met, cognitive investigators may, in time, move toward the establishment of generally accepted guidelines for N = 1 applied cognitive research.

More recently, Stewart and Chambless (2010) have compared research reviews with case studies in an empirical study of psychologists in private practice. They found that the addition of a case study to reports of empirically supported treatments (arrived at using randomised controlled trials) made the psychologists more open to following up the results and engaging in associated training.

Sociology

Burrawoy (1998, p. 4) describes what he calls the extended case method, 'which deploys participant observation to locate everyday life in its extralocal and historical context'. He sees this as an element of reflexive science, an alternative to the 'traditional' positivist science. He locates the case method within reflexive science, which he characterises in the following fashion:

Reflexive science… takes context and situation as its points of departure. It thrives on context and seeks to reduce the effects of power-domination, silencing, objectification, and normalization. Reflexive science realizes itself with the elimination of power effects, with the emancipation of the lifeworld. Even as that utopian point may be receding, the extended case method measures the distance to be travelled. In highlighting the ethnographic worlds of the local, it challenges the postulated omnipotence of the global, whether it be international capital, neoliberal politics, space of flows, or mass culture. Reflexive science valorizes context, challenges reification, and thereby establishes the limits of positive methods. (p. 30)

From Burrawoy's perspective, therefore, the case method has huge potential in sociology.

Mjoset (2006; this article is discussed in more detail in Chapter 7) sets out to 'bring more nuance into the discussion of "case studies and generalization", and to make it more difficult for future discussion on this and related topics to rely on simplified applications of the two dichotomies general/specific and explanation/understanding' (p. 737). He introduces a case study of the state of Israel, which was intended to 'clarify why the Israeli–Palestinian conflict has become so deep and persistent' (p. 738). This involved considering 22 alternative theories. He argues for what he terms 'pragmatic generalization', and concludes that:

The best single-case studies, then, are those which rely on reasonably saturated (thick) sets of comparisons, that is, on quite mature local research frontiers for the problem addressed in the case study. The explanations provided in such single-case studies then contribute to contextual generalization. (p. 763)

McCarthy, Holland and Gillies (2003; this article is also discussed in more detail in Chapter 7) explore 'approaches to the analysis of interviews with nine individuals drawn from three case study "families"' (p. 1). They found that different 'approaches to the analysis yielded different forms of knowledge' (p. 19). This is an important finding, supporting the general contention that given data sets can be interrogated both in different ways and from different perspectives, and that the findings, while perhaps supportive or complimentary, need not be the same. There is, in other words, no single correct interpretation or story.

Thacher (2006) argues for the development of normative as well as explanatory case studies in social science:

Case study research is a central part of social science analysis, and its contributions to causal explanations and interpretive understanding are well known… [S]ocial science cases can legitimately make contributions to normative understanding as well, and… many already have. They do so by presenting us with unfamiliar situations that inspire tentative moral judgments, which may destabilize the web of normative conviction we bring to them when we examine the connections among its elements... [W]e examine these connections in a number of different ways – by examining the consistency of general principles with judgments about specific cases, by juxtaposing cases and reflecting on the analogies between them, or by describing the features of a case using thick ethical concepts. In this respect, the normative case study represents a viable method that social scientists can use to answer the calls for normative study that have become common in sociology and other fields. (p. 1669)

Such normative case studies would deal with our underlying ideals, obligations and values.

Case study research has also been employed in more applied areas of sociology, such as criminology (e.g. Chesney-Lind and Chagnon 2016).

CONCLUSIONS ACROSS THE DISCIPLINES

The analysis presented in this chapter reveals that there are many similarities in the ways that the different disciplines are approaching and using case study as a research design, as well as (and perhaps more expected) divergences in practice.

To take the similarities first. In addition to the general guides to the use of case study as a research design (of which this book is one), there are many discipline-focused reviews of, for example, the advantages and disadvantages of case study research, the different kinds of case study, practical guides on how to carry out case study research and suggestions for improving that practice. Examples discussed in this chapter include Hagg (1979; accounting), McCutcheon and Meredith (1993; operations management), Harland (2014; higher education) and Woods (1997; nursing). Often these are contextualised in the light of the perceived, or hoped for, increase in the popularity of case study research within the particular discipline.

It is also evident that the concerns frequently raised regarding the case study design about issues such as generalisation, rigour and validity (discussed in Chapter 3) are shared across the disciplines, with responses to these widely sought and articulated. Examples include the articles by Barzelay (1993; public administration), Woolcock (2013; development), Dube and Pare (2003; information systems) and Ruzzene (2012; philosophy). These responses commonly include the use of case studies alongside quantitative/statistical studies, to offer triangulation or detailed exemplification, and to make use of the best aspects of both approaches in conjunction with each other (combined research designs involving case study are discussed in more detail in Chapter 6). They also manifest themselves in frequent discussions of the use of case study research in theory development and/or testing.

Another similarity in disciplinary practice has been the use of meta-analyses – in two related senses – of what has already been done within the discipline, or subdiscipline, in case study research. First, studies have analysed the relevant articles published in selected journals to reveal where and how case studies have been applied, to offer a critique of practice to date, and to suggest ways forward for future research. Second, other studies have aggregated the data collected in case studies focused on the same topic or issue in seeking to generalise their findings. Those analysed in this chapter include the articles by Piekkari, Welch and Paavilainen (2009; international business), Beverland and Lindgren (2010; marketing), Corcoran, Walker and Wals (2004; higher education) and Jones and Windholz (1990; psychoanalysis). Meta-analysis of case studies is discussed further in Chapter 7.

In terms of differences, we have already commented (in Chapter 2) on the use of the case study approach for teaching as well as research in certain disciplines (e.g. business studies, law, psychotherapy). From the analysis presented, it is clear that the development and use of teaching case studies also has implications in these disciplines for how they employ case studies for research purposes: for example, the use of case histories in law, or of clinical cases in psychotherapy and medicine more generally.

The other clear way in which disciplines diverge in their employment of case study research is in the development of specialist case study research designs, such as the confirmatory case method (Johnston, Leach and Liu 1999; marketing), hermeneutic single case efficacy (Elliott 2002; psychotherapy), single outcome studies (Gerring 2006; political science) and the extended case method (Burrawoy 1998; sociology). This is not to say, however, that these specialist designs should, or will, be confined to the disciplines in which they originated, or that specialist designs that are given different labels do not share things in common.

This leads us nicely to a general conclusion from this multidisciplinary examination, namely that is very apparent that, in the matter of case study research (as with many other matters), we all have a lot to learn from the approaches, practices and strategies adopted and applied in other disciplines. It is much healthier academically to keep an open mind on what we might learn from elsewhere, and not to get too bunkered down in our particular disciplinary, or sub-disciplinary, silo.

SUMMARY

In this chapter, we have:

- identified the widespread use of the case study design for research in a diverse variety of disciplines and sub-disciplines
- explored how case study has been conceptualised and applied in business and management, education, health, other professional disciplines and in the so-called 'pure' disciplines
- considered the similarities and differences in the application of the case study research design in the varied disciplines and sub-disciplines identified
- concluded that, if we are interested in the use and development of the case study research design, we need to keep watch on what is happening across the disciplines as well as within our own discipline or sub-discipline.

KEY READINGS

David, M (ed.) (2006) *Case Study Research* (4 volumes). London, Sage.

Scholz, R, and Tietje, O (2002) *Embedded Case Study Methods: Integrating quantitative and qualitative knowledge.* Thousand Oaks, CA, Sage.

Stake, R (2005) Qualitative Case Studies. pp. 443–466 in N Denzin and Y Lincoln (eds) *The Sage Handbook of Qualitative Research* (3rd edition). Thousand Oaks, CA, Sage.

Tight, M (ed.) (2015) *Case Studies* (4 volumes). London, Sage.

Yin, R (2009) *Case Study Research: Design and methods* (4th edition). Thousand Oaks, CA, Sage.

Case Studies in Mixed/Combined Research Designs

INTRODUCTION

Chapter 5 demonstrated that case study is widely used as a research design in varied ways in a range of disciplines. It is also, as this chapter will show, commonly used in combination with a considerable number of other research designs. These combined uses both strengthen the appeal of case study and make clear its robustness as a research design.

This chapter starts with a general discussion of the use of case study in combined research designs. Examples of such combined designs – with action and other participatory forms of research, complexity science and network theory, constructionism and critical realism, content analysis, ethnography, evaluation, experiment, grounded theory, surveys, systems and time series designs – are then identified and explored. Finally, some general conclusions on the facility of combining case study with other research designs, and what this shows about case study itself as a design, are discussed.

The careful reader will have noted from the list in the previous paragraph that 'design' is being used here in a broad or flexible sense (see also the discussion of Case Study as a Research Design in Chapter 3). While most of the items in the list are arguably research designs, a few might be more accurately termed theories (e.g. network theory, though not grounded theory) or epistemologies (e.g. constructionism, critical realism). That they are all gathered together here under the label of 'research design' is a convenience.

USING CASE STUDY IN COMBINED RESEARCH DESIGNS

Of course, one of the questions that immediately arises is 'why use combined research designs?' After all, each research design – though we have to acknowledge that every research design is subject to varied interpretation and application by different researchers – has been carefully put together on the basis of certain assumptions, evaluated in practice and revised in order to meet particular needs. Is it legitimate, then, to mesh together designs that may be based upon very different assumptions and which are intended to be employed in different ways? Clearly, though, some researchers do just this, so they must believe that it is legitimate to do so.

Box 6.1 suggests a range of reasons that might explain and/or justify the use of a case study design in combination with another research design. They are mostly of a positive – e.g. exploiting the strengths of combined research designs, improving rigour and generalisability – or experimental nature – e.g. introducing a particular variant of case study design or a new hybrid research design. Underlying all of them is the two-fold recognition: first, that researchers are always looking for ways in which to enhance and improve their work; and, second, that some researchers (though probably only a minority) are also looking for ways in which to improve research designs.

■ ■ ■ **Box 6.1   Possible Reasons for Using Case Study in Combined Research Designs** ■ ■ ■

1   To combine the strengths of the two designs and/or minimise their weaknesses.
2   To enhance the rigour, reliability, validity and generalisability (or trustworthiness, credibility, transferability and confirmability) of the research.
3   To design a particular sequence into the research project, i.e. case study followed, or preceded, by another design.
4   To extend the case study research (single or multiple) across time or between places.
5   To develop a particular kind of case study design.
6   To link case study design with another research design perceived as sympathetic to it (i.e. having similar assumptions).
7   To link case study design with another research design perceived as very different from it to create a new hybrid design.
8   To incorporate a particular approach within case study research.

Of course, combined research designs are not only an issue for case study researchers. Pragmatic or mixed methods researchers – i.e. those who combine qualitative and quantitative methods (see also the discussion of The Qualitative/Quantitative Debate in Chapter 3) – to take one obvious example, readily combine research designs (Tashakkori and Teddlie 1998, 2010; Teddlie and Tashakkori 2009).

Often the use of the different designs is sequential in nature. Thus, qualitative methods (e.g. in-depth interviews) may be conducted first with a sample of respondents in order to work out the best questions to ask of a larger population in a subsequent quantitative survey. Or the reverse order may be employed, with respondents to a largely quantitative survey asked to indicate if they are willing to be interviewed, with a sample of those willing then contacted in order to get a more detailed understanding of the issues being researched.

This may also occur with combined case study research designs, as the third reason given in Box 6.1 suggests. Case studies using multiple methods of data collection may be used to establish the framework for much larger research studies. Or they may follow them, with particular individuals or organisations having been identified for in-depth case study research.

Using case study in a combined research design is, therefore, a reasonable and justifiable strategy to adopt, although – because of the greater scale of the research implied – it is probably not an approach best suited to the novice researcher.

EXAMPLES OF COMBINED RESEARCH DESIGNS

This section highlights and discusses examples of the use of case study in combination with other research designs. While it is based on the results of an extensive literature review, it is not comprehensive. Other researchers have, for example, examined the relationship between cluster analysis and case study (Uprichard 2009). Other examples and combinations of research designs may well have been missed. The selection of studies and approaches described is illustrative, therefore, and the exclusion of any particular study does not represent a judgement on its quality or otherwise.

Action and Other Participatory Forms of Research

Action research is a research design in which the research is explicitly designed and intended to achieve positive change – i.e. action – in whatever context and/or topic is being researched. It is typically carried out in a participatory fashion, with the researcher or researchers involved working closely with those in the context or organisation being researched, through all stages of the research process, from design through data collection to interpretation and dissemination. Action research also normally goes through two or more cycles, with the learning and benefits garnered from the first cycle feeding into the research work of the second cycle, and so on, until all parties are agreed that suitable changes have been achieved (see, for example, Koshy, Koshy and Waterman 2011; McAteer 2013; Reason and Bradbury 2006).

Thus, Bates (2008), a criminologist concerned to evaluate and improve her practice, starts her account with the premise that:

> When an educational practitioner, committed to the notion of an emancipatory curriculum, attempts to research her own practice as a curriculum designer, convenor and lead teacher in a university course, the first impulse is to turn to action research as the most appropriate methodology. It offers a disciplined approach to data gathering, analysing, theorising, reporting, planning and then engaging in further action; it is built around a set of assumptions and beliefs that are corroborated by empirical data about how students learn through their own action. (p. 97)

Indeed, action research is, as Bates suggests, well established in the teacher research literature. The problem, for her, was that the course she was interested in researching was of short duration, so did not allow time for the feedback loops and cyclical development involved in classical action research. Her reaction to this was to develop a modified form of action research, which she termed the *responsive case study*:

> …a methodology that allowed the participants to contribute what they perceived to be relevant data (generally these include observations, descriptions of action, reflections and analysis) to assist in the planning of the next offering of the tertiary course. Thus, a new cycle of action, observation, reflection and planning followed and any reports or conceptual findings were generated as a set of ongoing reports or as a summary of the whole endeavour at the conclusion. This would form the base for the next iteration of the course and the cycle would occur again with a new group of participant students. (p. 98)

Another way of categorising Bates' research would be as a series of short case studies, which together build up to an action research project.

Action research is not, however, the only form of participatory research design, though the actual distinctions between the different designs in use may not seem that great. In some examples, this may even be because the researchers concerned are unaware of action research, and thus come up with a new design label to cover much the same thing; or perhaps they are aware of it, but do not wish to use that label, with all the associations it might be seen as bringing (these are common occurrences in research, where researchers often operate in relatively narrow and self-contained silos and do not have or seek a broader perspective). In the following examples, I do not know the reasons why the research design was not identified as action research.

Schiele and Krummaker (2011) discuss what they term 'consortium benchmarking', where, in a business setting, academics and practitioners work together to benchmark best practices. The process involved four stages: preparation, a 'kick-off' workshop, benchmarking visits and a joint review of the lessons learned. They argue that:

> Consortium benchmarking is an innovative multi-case study approach in management research… Consortium benchmarking simultaneously includes at least five additional facets either not accounted for or neglected in multi-case research. Consortium benchmarking (1) includes the practitioner as co-researcher; (2) is team-based; (3) uses different sources of evidence; (4) focuses on best practices and (5) stimulates metadiscourses which are likely to produce knowledge relevant for both academics and practitioners. (p. 1142)

While there might seem to be some judicious over-claiming going on here, the authors do acknowledge that the approach has some limitations, including its time-consuming nature and the difficulties inherent in getting the cooperation of those one wishes to benchmark against.

Flicker (2008) describes an approach she calls community-based participatory research (or CBPR), a popular strategy in health research:

> CBPR presupposes that working with community members as co-researchers renders results more accessible, accountable, and relevant to people's lives, with the added promise of a greater effect on public policy. Advocates of CBPR suggest that the very process of meaningful participation can be transformative. Through active engagement, individuals and communities may become more empowered and better equipped to make sustainable personal and social change. (p. 71)

She then goes on to describe a case study of a Canadian project aimed at young people living with HIV. Both service providers and HIV-positive youths advised the project, which involved interviews with 34 HIV-positive youths, regular meetings for analysis and subsequent dissemination of the results.

Action and other participatory forms of research might be argued to belong together with case study designs. Both are typically small-scale, focusing on a particular issue or problem in a single institution, department or group. The desired end result of both research designs is the same: namely, change, improvement or action, along, of course, with better understanding of the issue or problem involved. The key distinction could be said to be one of emphasis, with action research and other participatory designs ostensibly having collaboration in the research between the researcher(s) and the researched at their core, which might not necessarily be so for a case study design.

This does raise the question, though, that if a research project meets the definition of both a case study and a piece of action research, what do you call it: either or both? Is one of these designs seen as being in some way generally stronger or more desirable than the other, or is it safer – as in the examples discussed in this section – to either claim both or give the combined design a new name? Here, much will likely depend upon the context and tradition in which the research study is being undertaken – who it is being done for and why, the researcher's/researchers' disciplinary background – and, ultimately, the personal preferences of the researcher(s).

Complexity Science and Network Theory

Complexity science or theory, while not strictly a research design, is a perspective which views 'organizations as dynamic, living, social systems' (Anderson et al 2005, p. 671), rather than as mechanical operations. Network theory adopts a similar approach in embracing the complexity of organisations (Borgatti and Halgin 2011; Moliterno and Mahony 2011).

Complexity science, therefore, is obviously a perspective that can be applied to the study of complex healthcare organisations. Along these lines, Anderson et al argue that:

We can extend traditional ideas about the execution of case studies by applying the blueprint of complexity science. This will lead to new research strategies for fruitfully using case studies in health care settings... [W]e present the case study as a research approach uniquely suited to carrying out a study designed from a blueprint of complexity theory. (2005, p. 672)

To do this they extend the case study design to take into account interdependencies among elements, to add sensitivity to dimensions of relationships, to focus on 'nonlinearities' (instances where large events have led to small outcomes), to look for and examine unexpected events closely, to focus on processes as well as events, to recognise dynamics, to describe patterns as well as events, to see patterns across levels, to understand that patterns change, to recognise that, in any given situation, different patterns might be successful, to shift foreground and background, to redefine observer roles and to learn the system's history. Clearly, all of this will make the case study design much more demanding, though one might also argue that a 'good' case study of a healthcare – or any other complex – organisation would take most of these points into account anyway.

Gummesson (2007) argues for the combination of case study design with network theory in researching management, as both recognise in their different ways the complexity of what is being studied. He recommends the further development of the quality and productivity of case study research, the recognition that phenomena are complex, fuzzy, ambiguous and unpredictable, and the use of network theory as a supplementary, supportive component to case study research.

Constructionism and Critical Realism

Constructionism (or constructivism) and critical realism represent alternative, though linked, epistemologies, or ways of knowing the world (Crotty 1998; Denzin and Lincoln 2005a; see also the discussion of Alternative Methodological Approaches in Chapter 9).

Järvensivu and Tornroos (2010), who have a particular interest in business-to-business relationships, develop a case study approach that builds upon what they term 'moderate' constructionism and abduction. They compare this approach with realist, critical realist and relativist perspectives. They argue that:

Case study research can adopt ontologically, epistemologically, and methodologically different positions that can be placed along a continuum ranging from naïve realism to naïve relativism. As an extreme form of positivism, naïve realism is based on the belief that there exists a reality that is apprehendable through objective, empirical observations. Naïve relativism, an extreme form of constructionism, in contrast suggests that there are multiple local and specific constructed realities; reality exists only in texts and interpretations. (p. 101)

For Järvensivu and Tornroos, 'Moderate constructionism defines truth as community-based and derived from empirical data' (p. 101), and is closely related to critical realism:

> [C]ritical realism (CR) and moderate constructionism (MC) are... fairly close to each other. They both acknowledge that research should proceed towards finding local, community-bounded, interacting forms of truth that are created and validated through dialogue in different communities. Although they basi-cally have the same ontological and epistemological grounds, MC is more concerned with acknowledging the possibility of multiple community-formed knowledge bases, whereas CR is concerned with moving closer to the one universal truth. (pp. 101–102)

They make the differences clearer in discussing how the interview process is approached:

> In the CR mindset, interviewing is a search-and-discovery mission concerned with maximizing the flow of valid and reliable information that resides inside the informant's mind, minimizing any distortions of what the informant knows, and controlling the interview process to eliminate possible sources of bias, error, and misunderstanding. In MC studies, active interviewing treats the interview as a social encounter in which knowledge is jointly constructed by the interviewer and the informant. (p. 102)

They then present a business network case study to demonstrate how a moderate constructionism case study can address issues of validity and transferability.

Easton (2010), in a related article in the same journal issue, focuses squarely on critical realism. He starts from the position that 'Case study research is, probably, the most popular research method used by industrial marketing researchers' (p. 118), and argues that 'A critical realist case approach is particularly well suited to relatively clearly bounded, but complex, phenomena such as organisations, interorganisational relation-ships or nets of connected organisations' (p. 123). He explains that:

> Critical realists propose an ontology that assumes that there exists a reality 'out there' independent of observers... critical realists accept that reality is socially constructed... the world is socially constructed but not entirely so. The 'real' world breaks through and sometimes destroys the complex stories that we create in order to understand and explain the situations we research. (p. 120)

The critical realist approach to case study research, then:

> involves developing a research question that identifies a research phenomenon of interest, in terms of discernible events, and asks what causes them to happen. The key entities involved, their powers, liabilities, necessary and contingent relation-ships are then provisionally identified. Research then proceeds by capturing data with respect to ongoing or past events asking at all times why they happened or

are happening and taking into account the problems and issues associated with interpreting the empirical data back to the real entities and their actions. The research process is one of continuous cycles of research and reflection. The final result is the identification of one or more mechanisms that can be regarded as having caused the events. (p. 128)

The iterative nature of the research process is similar to that in action research designs, but in the critical realist approach there is clearly a greater emphasis placed on looking for explanations. This does sound like a fairly sensible strategy for organisationally based case study research.

Content Analysis

Content analysis is 'a strict and systematic set of procedures for the rigorous analysis, examination and verification of the contents of written data' (Cohen, Manion and Morrison 2011, p. 563). While originally conceived as a means of applying quantitative analysis to qualitative data, there are now also qualitative variants (Krippendorff 2012; Schreier 2012).

Jauch, Osborn and Martin (1980) suggest the use of content analysis to interrogate existing case study records in organisational studies:

A structured content analysis of cases uses a content analysis schedule to draw relevant information from published case materials. Information from cases is coded on a content analysis schedule much as a respondent would complete a questionnaire. Only specific information sought by the researcher is coded. Multiple readings of the case and multiple case coders are used to develop a broad sample that can be partially checked for reliability and validity. Because the technique relies on content analysis and content analysis schedules, a detailed examination of these is needed. (p. 517)

This combined research design obviously relies on the existence and availability of suitable case study records in the area of interest to the researcher. It offers an approach analogous to what is now more commonly termed meta-analysis (discussed in more detail in Chapter 7).

Kohlbacher (2006) provides an overview of both case study research and qualitative content analysis, also in the context of organisational studies. He argues that the latter offers a useful method for analysing the text produced by the former: 'qualitative content analysis perfectly fits the credo of case study research: helping to understand complex social phenomena' (p. 25).

Ethnography

Ethnography is a research design of long standing, with its roots in anthropology and sociology (Brewer 2000; Bryman 2001). In its classic form, it is closely associated with periods of extended fieldwork, in which the researcher immerses themselves within and attempts to gain a better understanding of the society, group or aspect of society they are studying. It has also – like many classic research designs, case study included – encouraged broader and looser interpretations.

Visconti (2010) offers an ethnographic case study model in the context of business marketing research. He defines ethnographic case study (ECS) as:

> the application of the ontological, epistemological and methodological features of ethnography to a theoretically selected set of business cases. More precisely, the ECS framework mostly adheres to case study research in the way empirical cases are selected (i.e. the case study theoretical selection as opposed to random, statistical sampling) and, accordingly, to ethnography in the way field materials are later acquired, interpreted and reported (i.e. interpretative ethnography strictu sensu). In so doing, while focusing on one or a few selected business contexts, the ECS method maintains all the genuineness of ethnography, including the researcher's immersion, the strongly participated activities of observation, and the constructivist lecture of organizational milieu leading to negotiated, shared interpretations of data (the principle of 'derived etic'). (p. 29)

This suggests a very close, almost natural, combination of case study and ethnography designs, one which Visconti also sees as potentially incorporating elements of action and participatory research (see the earlier sub-section). It also, at least in Visconti's view, specifies an interpretivist rather than a post-positivist epistemological stance.

Baines and Cunningham (2013) (this article is discussed in more detail in Chapter 7) take a similar stance. They describe the use of what they call 'rapid ethnography', employing multiple methods of data collection by small research teams in studying selected cases in a range of countries.

Hopwood (2004) reflects on the development and application of a multiple-method case study in research into students' conceptions of geography, which married together elements of ethnography, grounded theory (see the later sub-section) and phenomenology (a research design where the focus is on the study of a particular phenomenon): 'While the framework may be termed "phenomenological", the data-collection techniques may equally be viewed as "ethnographic", and analytical processes were custom designed, borrowing from elements of "grounded theory"' (p. 348). Data collection was by way of conventional questionnaires and semi-structured interviews, supplemented by students' posters of their conceptions of geography. Rather than offering a considered model in the way that Visconti does, this study comes over as a pragmatic selection of techniques for data collection and analysis within a case study, informed by ethnography and other designs, but not driven by them.

Alvesson (2003) advocates self-ethnography (sometimes called auto-ethnography: see McKenna 2015) – literally an ethnography of oneself – as a means for researching an organisation with which one is familiar, indeed in which one works, in his instance a higher education institution. He presents this as an alternative to the problems associated with both interview-based studies and larger-scale ethnographies: 'The intention is... to draw attention to one's own cultural context, what goes on around oneself rather than putting oneself and one's experiences in the centre' (p. 175).

Clearly, self-ethnography offers considerable advantages to the researcher: they are already at the research site and likely know a great deal about it. This does, however, imply a concomitant disadvantage, namely that they perhaps think they know the 'answers' already. Interestingly, Alvesson does not refer to his design as case study, but as close-up research. While claiming not to be a fan of research methods texts, he nevertheless offers some guidelines for undertaking self-ethnography:

1. Routinely scan what turns up in everyday life for interesting options for thick descriptions.
2. When something happens, document it...
3. Acknowledge that data are constructions...
4. Rethink and possibly rewrite the account from an (self-)ironic position...
5. Coping with ethics and politics: getting input from the victims in order to balance one's ideas and biases with those of one's fellows...
6. Developing some tentative conclusions on the empirical material...
7. Engage in reflexive lopes: repeat parts of the process (3–6) after having got some new input. (pp. 190–191)

There is an issue here concerning how self-ethnography differs from reflection or other approaches where an individual's day-to-day experiences are used as research data. While Alvesson suggests a structure for the activity, it is fairly generic in nature.

Evaluation

Evaluation and case study may also be viewed as closely related research designs (Russell, Greenhalgh and Kushner 2015). In my own analysis of research in the field of higher education, I identified the small-scale evaluative case study as one of two prominent research designs (the other being the critical policy review: see Tight 2012). More generally, one of the most prolific writers on case study in recent years, Yin, has often written on case study evaluations (e.g. Yin 1992, 1997, 2013).

Thus, in 1992, Yin began by defining evaluations as 'a particular type of research intended to assess and explain the results of "demonstrations"' (p. 121), linking the latter to contemporary US government-funded initiatives (Wilson, 1979, takes a similar approach in the same context). He then goes on to argue the usefulness of case study research for carrying out evaluations:

> ...the ability directly to incorporate an investigation of the context satisfies an evaluation's need to monitor and assess both the intervention and the implementation process. Second, the case study is not limited to either qualitative or quantitative data, but can incorporate both varieties of evidence. Further... the case study method can serve evaluation needs directly by being able to assess outcomes and test hypotheses. (Yin 1992, p. 124)

He contrasts this position favourably with evaluations using three other designs: ethnography, grounded theory and quasi-experimental studies (all of which are discussed in this chapter). On this basis, Yin then offers a step-by step guide to undertaking case study evaluations:

1. Develop a hypothesized understanding of the programme being evaluated.
2. Immerse this understanding within previous research, wherever possible.
3. Tentatively define the main and subordinate units of analysis.
4. Establish a schedule and procedure for making interim and final reports.
5. Define and test instruments, protocols and field procedures.
6. Collect, analyze and synthesize data.
7. Create a case study database.
8. Analyze the evidence.
9. Compose the case study report. (pp. 134–136)

This would, of course – like Alvesson's guidelines for undertaking self-ethnography, discussed in the previous section – be a useful guide to the structure of most case study research.

Yin's later (2013) paper concentrates on the issues of validity and generalisability as they effect case study evaluations. For strengthening validity, he reviews the strategies of considering plausible rival explanations, triangulation and logic models, while for generalisation, analytic and conceptual approaches are explored.

Ellis (2003), in a nursing context, looks at the use of illuminative case study designs for evaluating continuing professional education. She concludes that:

> The RCT [randomised controlled trial] may be the gold standard of scientific research, but it is clear from this illuminative case study that a range of extraneous variables influence the outcome of Continuing Professional Development [CPD]... cognizance of the variables influencing CPD is imperative to the evaluation of continuing education, and... of the range of factors influencing CPD, the practice milieu plays a highly significant role. (p. 58)

For evaluation purposes, then, the case study approach can get in closer and deeper, and identify factors of importance that might otherwise be overlooked.

Koenig (2009), from a critical realist tradition (see the section on Constructionism and Critical Realism), sets out 'to explore the potential of a case study to test and generate theories in an evaluation context' (p. 10). He clearly sets out the problems and contradictions involved:

> Evaluation work has to reconcile contradictory demands. On one hand, it is important for it to provide practitioners with rapid responses to their questions and on the other hand, it is essential that the procedures employed guarantee, as far as possible, the validity of the knowledge produced. The complexity of social

situations, the way they fit into changing contexts and the diversity of the latter make any comparison difficult and threaten a project that strives to produce useful knowledge in a rigorous manner. (p. 26)

In certain circumstances, and with due care, however, he believes these difficulties can be overcome, and useful case study evaluations produced.

Experiment

The experiment is, of course, the classic scientific method: with the aim of understanding the relationship between different factors or variables, in a controlled environment (ideally, the laboratory), some change is introduced and its impact is carefully measured. This may seem a long way from a case study research design, but, nevertheless, some researchers have attempted to link the two designs, and not only in the more obvious disciplines of the applied sciences.

Thus, Lee (1989a), in the context of organisational research and with the aim of getting beyond the objectivist/subjectivist dichotomy, proposes constructing case studies as a form of natural experiment: 'Rather than inducing controls and treatments in the subject matter, the case researcher observes the controls and treatments which occur in the subject matter naturally' (p. 132). In other words, if the researcher has developed particular theories or hypotheses, they then look for examples within the case study organisation where the variables involved are in play, observe them and see whether their predictions are borne out. Clearly, this could be quite a time-consuming form of data collection, and it would also depend upon those within the organisation not being overly influenced by the presence of the observer.

Lundervold and Belwood (2000), in the context of counsellor education, argue that 'Single-case (N = 1) designs offer a scientifically credible means to objectively evaluate practice and conduct clinically relevant research in practice settings' (p. 92). They have the advantages, from their perspective, of being 'theory free', flexible, evidenced-based and useable in practice settings, and do not require extensive statistical engagement or skills. The links, both with the encouragement of practitioner research and the accumulation of evidence case by case, are clear here.

The use of single case designs in an experimental or quasi-experimental fashion is widely practised in the health disciplines (see the discussion in Chapter 5). For example, in psychiatry, psychoanalysis and psychotherapy there have been numerous studies using this kind of combined research design (e.g. Dugard, File and Todman 2012; Elliott 2002; Hilliard 1993; Jones et al 1993; Leitenberg 1973).

Grounded Theory

Grounded theory may, like action research, ethnography and other forms of chiefly qualitative research, seem to be something of a 'natural fit' with case study research designs. In essence, grounded theory is a research design in which the researcher collects some data on the topic of interest, interrogates it, comes up with some hypotheses or theories and then collects further data with the aim of testing or illuminating them. The cyclical process of data collection and interpretation may take place a number of times as the project expands, until the researcher feels that they can offer an explanation for what is going on within the topic of interest.

Of course, as with all research designs of any age, there are contested versions of what grounded theory is and how it should be practised (Glaser and Strauss 1967; Strauss and Corbin 1990), and more modern versions (e.g. Charmaz 2006) appear to be a lot more accommodating to the demands of intensive, small-scale research. There are also plenty of critiques, one of which, for example (Thomas and James 2006), argues fairly convincingly that grounded theory is neither grounded nor a theory.

Viewed as a research design, however, grounded theory still has much to offer, particularly, in the present context, when practised in combination with case study. For example, Taber (2000), in a science education context, uses grounded theory as a bridge between case studies and large-scale surveys. He summarises the processes involved in the following fashion:

> A limited number of co-learners acted as the sources for preparing case studies. The researcher's (theoretical sensitivity) to commonalities between the cases acted as the starting point for constructing a general model of how college students' understanding of chemical bonding develops. The model was modified in the light of additional data collected from other students. The research used a variety of techniques to collect slices of data including interviews, recording student dialogues, construct repertory tests, concept maps, samples of coursework and test scripts… In research of this nature there is a temptation to indefinitely continue collecting data to refine the model further. It is always possible that additional data will provide new insights. The principle of theoretical saturation acts as a guide. (p. 482)

The notion of 'saturation' is widely used in qualitative research as a rule-of-thumb guide as to when to stop collecting and/or analysing data. It suggests that when additional data and/or additional analysis no longer add new themes or interpretations regarding the topic in question, or do not pose any further related questions, that is a good sign to stop and wrap up the project. In practice, of course, the perception of saturation may be as much about the researcher's fatigue – when new themes or questions may be missed – or wish to get on.

Taber concludes that:

> Taken together, the principles of grounded theory provide a sound methodological strategy for the researcher who wishes to construct general models of practical applicability from within the interpretative paradigm. Through this process it is possible to move from case studies to general models which offer testable predictions. So grounded theory allows the researcher to bridge the divide between

authentic accounts of the individual case (rich in detail, but only able to offer 'insight into' or 'resonances with' other cases), and generalized accounts which offer meaningful advice for curriculum planners and classroom teachers. (p. 483)

In another example, Andrade (2009) combines case study and grounded theory designs in researching traditional social networks and new virtual networks among rural communities in Peru. He argues that 'Case study design and grounded theory complement each other and can be used in a combined fashion by interpretive researchers aiming at theory building' (p. 54). Case studies, on their own, in Andrade's view, are of limited use for theory building. The systemic processes adopted in grounded theory, working within an interpretive rather than a positivist framework, enable theory building to be undertaken.

Both Taber and Andrade, therefore, employ a mixed design of case study and grounded theory to take their research beyond the perceived limitations of case study, enabling generalisation for the former and theory building for the latter. However, other case study researchers have argued that different strategies – solely using case study designs – can achieve these ends (see the discussion of Generalisability in Chapter 3, and of Case Studies and Theory in Chapter 8).

Surveys

Surveys, like experiments, are one of the mainstays of quantitative and positivist research, although it is, of course, perfectly possible to develop and administer surveys that are partly or wholly qualitative in nature. They may, however, seem about as far away from a case study design as it is possible to venture in research terms, yet numbers of researchers have nevertheless sought to draw them closer together, and thereby exploit the strengths of both.

In a contribution which is now nearly 40 years old, McClintock, Brannon and Maynard-Moody (1979, p. 612) start from the recognition that:

The differences between case study and sample survey strategies in the analysis of organizations reflect a broader distinction in the social sciences between qualitative and quantitative methods. While there are underlying similarities in logic – for example, both approaches recognize the need to control for threats to internal validity – it is the differences of method that are often emphasized. Qualitative methods are described as 'thick', 'deep', and 'holistic'. By contrast quantitative approaches can be characterized as 'thin', 'narrow', but generalizable. These distinctions often extend to fundamental epistemological differences resulting in the mutual denial of validity to the data of the other approach... [I]f you prefer data that are real, deep, and hard... [o]ne answer is to invent research designs that incorporate qualitative and quantitative strategies.

They then present their design, which they term a method (or perhaps we might call it a mixed method), called the case cluster method:

The method essentially involves three features: (1) the definition, enumeration, and sampling of units of analysis within the case study that are theoretically meaningful and represent the phenomenology of informants; (2) stratified sampling of data sources based on theoretical grounds and on features of the case, crossed with a stratified sampling of units of analysis; and (3) the optional creation of a quantitative data set consisting of standardized codes for variables pertaining to each unit of analysis. Qualitative analyses are possible both for the entire case and at the level of the unit of analysis and, indeed, are strengthened by the use of different data sources for each unit of analysis. By forcing different perspectives on the same phenomenon the researcher will need to qualitatively portray divergent images that might emerge from each perspective. Because the single case is treated as a cluster of heterogeneous units of analysis the term case cluster is used to designate this method. (p. 613)

They provide three examples to demonstrate how the design works in practice, and how it differs from case studies, on the one hand, and sample surveys, on the other.

Woodside (2010), in a much more recent contribution, sets out to provide a research design that can meet the three objectives of generality, accuracy and complexity/coverage, again by combining elements of case study and survey research designs. Having reviewed the standard criticisms of both case studies and surveys, he argues against the continued use of particular research designs simply because they are familiar and trusted. He ends by offering nine recommendations:

1. Use theoretical sampling.
2. Collect multiple instances of data on each topic.
3. Create degrees of freedom tests to generalize single case data to theory.
4. Re-interview the same informant during and after observation.
5. Do multiple individual interviews of different informants.
6. Apply triangulation using multiple methods that go beyond interviewing and observing.
7. Adopt systems thinking.
8. Build and test simulation models of thinking and deciding.
9. Build and test system dynamics models. (p. 73)

He concludes that 'Planning on using research designs that include taking modest-to-substantial steps toward achieving accuracy, generality, and complexity is now possible and appropriate' (p. 74).

Systems Designs

Systems theorists regard organisations as systems: complex, compartmentalised, inter-connected within and without, adaptive, more than the sum of their parts, situated within their environment(s). Such systems may be depicted, often diagrammatically, as a set of nodes and linkages, with different functions, stakeholders and reporting responsibilities clearly identified. Such an approach to analysis is clearly suited to modern, large-scale organisations, whether in the private or public sector.

Anaf, Drummond and Sheppard (2007), working in the context of health care, note that:

> The combined use of case study and systems theory is not often seen in the literature. The use of both approaches enables the specifics of the case to consider the influence of broader systems and external environments, offering in-depth exploration as well as comparative analysis between cases in the context of the system. (p. 1309)

How, then, to combine the two designs? They assert:

> One must pragmatically consider how to combine systems theory with qualitative case study research while maintaining the characteristics that make each approach useful and rigorous. After all, both approaches are robust and defendable in their own right, and this aspect must not be diminished. One effective way of blending case study research with systems theory is to use the systems framework as a dominant methodology, with case study being used as the research strategy of choice. (p. 1311)

They offer as an example a study of the implementation of emergency department physiotherapy in an Australian hospital, concluding that 'Use of both approaches enables the specifics of the case to be considered as part of the whole system regarding how the wider system influences the case, as well as how the system within the case is important. Case studies enable comparison as well as complexity' (p. 1314). Clearly, then, this combined research design draws particular attention to the issues of the boundedness of the case being studied and its place within its environment (see also the discussion of The Case Study in Context in Chapter 8).

Carden (2009) describes the adoption of a systems approach to a multiple case study. The concern was how development projects impacted upon public policy, with 23 evaluative case studies completed in a range of countries. While the systems approach is not made explicit in his account, it is clear in the description of the careful and ordered processes undertaken in order to complete the research.

Time Series Designs

Time series designs offer another way of extending a case study or case studies. In healthcare settings, for example, such designs enable the assessment of the efficacy of interventions, and judgments to be made regarding causality: 'the n=1 case study method has a great deal to offer as a practice-friendly method for evaluating the effectiveness of new types of therapeutic intervention' (McLeod 2010, p. 134). Thus, in an early study, Gottman (1973) examines strategies in psychotherapy research. He concludes that:

Single-subject research in psychotherapy has advantages in outcome research, process research, measurement, and linking the practice of psychotherapy with the investigation of psychotherapy. Time-series analysis permits the study of a single subject over time and the study of effect patterns of an intervention over time. It allows the therapist to use information as feedback for making decisions, a useful tool in the evaluation of psychotherapy. (pp. 104–105)

Taking a rather different approach, Haydu (1998), a sociologist, is interested in using information from one historical period to illuminate another. Seeing the process as somewhat analogous to comparative studies of different nations or systems at the same time, he argues that:

We can remedy the deficiencies of conventional comparative methods by rethinking the connections between events in different time periods as reiterated problem solving. This heuristic device overcomes the limitations of interpretive comparisons by identifying and making use of continuities across periods, and it avoids certain pitfalls of variable-based comparisons by putting historical particulars to explanatory work. (p. 341)

Each time period is then treated as a case, with the emphasis placed on the sequence of events observed:

Methods that put sequences of events at the center of analysis, including narrative and path dependency, strike a better balance between historically insensitive causal generalization and idiographic historicism… Connecting events across periods in terms of sequenced problem solving has three additional virtues that distinguish it from narrative and path dependency. First, it provides a better sense than narrative accounts of the mechanisms that conduct causal influence over time. Second, it captures the creative as well as the constraining role of the past at each turning point, as path-dependent models do not… Third, it accomplishes these methodological goals in part by making social actors the historical pivots that link 'cases' of problem solving. Reconstructing the problem-solvers' understandings and choices – how *they* make use of the past – enables us to account for trajectories across multiple periods. (p. 367)

In this example, then, an identified instance of problem-solving is treated as a case, and this case may then be compared with others identified in different time periods, addressing the same or a similar problem. Effectively bounding each case is clearly going to be an issue for the researcher here, as most social or political problems are rarely (and simply) solved, but tend to be ongoing issues that can persist for long periods of time, despite repeated and well-meaning attempts to 'solve' them.

GENERAL CONCLUSIONS AND GUIDANCE

It is clear, from the examples discussed in this chapter, that the basic case study design has been successfully employed in combination with many other research designs. The reasons for doing so are many, but are generally positive or innovative in nature (see Box 6.1). These uses confirm that the basic case study design is both robust and adaptable, and suggest strongly that it has a long and viable future as part of the overall research design palette (see also Chapter 10).

It was suggested at the beginning of this chapter that such combined research designs were probably not best suited to novice researchers. This is chiefly due to their relative complexity. As a novice, it is usually a safer alternative to make use of a simpler research design – i.e. just a case study or just an ethnography, rather than both in combination. For those with more experience or looking for a challenge, however, the best advice would be to study a number of examples where combined research designs have been employed, and take guidance from these.

SUMMARY

In this chapter, we have:

- discussed the possible reasons for combining case study with other research designs
- explored a variety of combined research designs, embodying case study research, that have been employed in different disciplines and fields
- offered some guidance on using combined research designs.

KEY READINGS

Bryman, A (2004) *Social Research Methods* (2nd edition). Oxford, Oxford University Press.
Byrne, D, and Ragin, C (eds) (2009) *The Sage Handbook of Case-based Methods*. London, Sage.
David, M (ed.) (2006) *Case Study Research* (4 volumes). London, Sage.
Denzin, N, and Lincoln, Y (eds) (2005) *The Sage Handbook of Qualitative Research* (3rd edition). Thousand Oaks, CA, Sage.
Mills, A, Durepos, G, and Wiebe, E (eds) (2010) *Encyclopedia of Case Study Research* (2 volumes). Los Angeles, CA, Sage.
Tight, M (ed.) (2015) *Case Studies* (4 volumes). London, Sage.

Learning from Case Study

INTRODUCTION

This chapter offers suggestions on how you might learn from existing case studies. You will probably have picked up already, as you have read or looked through this book, that a vast number of case studies have been carried out and published, so – whatever your own topic and interests – there are likely to be some available that you could usefully learn from, and which would add significantly to the analysis of your own case study.

The chapter starts with a general discussion of writing on case study, how extensive it is and how it varies.

Other researchers have already carried out analyses of case study research on particular topics or in particular disciplines or sub-disciplines. Such studies are often referred to as meta-analyses or systematic reviews. A number of these are reviewed in the second main section.

We then consider the strategies you might adopt to search for published case study material that might be of relevance to your interests, and what to do with the case studies you find.

Several examples of published case study research from different disciplines are examined to illustrate some of the possibilities, and some 'contrary' examples, which might or might not be considered to be case studies, are also examined.

WRITING ON CASE STUDY

Table 7.1 gives some idea of the volume of published material available that deals with case study. It records the results of a search using Google Scholar and Scopus, two well-known academic search engines (though others could also have been used), carried out on 3/2/2016. It should be noted, of course, that neither of these search engines is either wholly accurate or comprehensive. In Google Scholar, some early items, in particular, may be mis-dated and, when there are large numbers of documents recorded, the algorithms used give only a rough estimate of the total numbers. Scopus, for its part, does not cover the same range of sources as Google Scholar, particularly for the most recent period. Thus, it can be seen that Scopus records less than half the number of articles that Google Scholar does in the most recent years, but rather more in the pre–1990 period.

Table 7.1 Articles* published with the exact phrase 'Case Study' in the title, according to Google Scholar and Scopus

Year	Google Scholar	Scopus
2016	2,150	1,249
2015	38,200	15,733
2014	44,000	17,543
2013	44,400	16,712
2012	44,000	15,202
2011	37,900	14,050
2010	30,400	12,539
2009	22,600	11,458
2008	19,200	9,661
2007	14,500	8,869
2006	13,400	7,901
2005	11,800	7,295
2004	9,120	5,737
2003	8,390	5,011
2002	6,820	4,625
2001	6,360	4,165
2000	5,980	4,052
1999	5,160	3,769
1998	4,810	3,723
1997	4,140	3,674
1996	3,840	3,407
1995	3,350	2,957
1994	3,090	2,853
1993	2,670	2,736
1992	2,530	2,484
1991	2,350	2,537
1990	2,330	2,493
Before 1990	17,900	42,212
Total	411,390	234,647

* Search carried out on 3/2/2016. Articles include other forms of publication, such as books, conference proceedings and online publications, but citations and patents have been excluded.

Nevertheless, the table gives a good idea of the overall volume and trends in writing on case study. It records the total numbers of 'articles' in each database that have the exact phrase 'case study' in their title. This should provide a useful picture of the changing popularity of case study in academic writing over the last two and a half decades. After all, if case study is the focus of the article, you would expect to see it explicitly mentioned in the title. Many other articles will, of course, mention case study without including the term in their titles, but their discussion and/or application of case study is likely to be more limited. A smaller number, of course, which have been overlooked in this analysis, will have the phrase 'case studies' in their titles.

Table 7.1 shows a consistent trend for an increasing number of articles to be published, year by year (albeit with the occasional 'blip') with the exact phrase 'case study' in their titles. Thus, while, according to Google Scholar, only 2,330 were published in 1990, the figure had more than doubled to 5,980 by 2000, then increased over five times to 30,400 by 2010, and reached 44,400 in 2013. Alternatively, according to Scopus, 2,493 articles were published with 'case study' in the title in 1990, rising to 4,052 in 2000, 12,539 in 2010, and 17,543 in 2014.

This growth is what you would expect of any topic of contemporary interest, as case study undoubtedly is. As both the size of the academic community and the number of outlets for publication have continued to expand, so the interest in, and the writing on, case study has mushroomed.

For case study in particular, however, these figures have to be interpreted carefully in the light of what they actually represent. Examining the long lists of articles produced by Google Scholar and Scopus, it is clear that the great majority of the articles identified that include the exact phrase 'case study' in their title are straightforward reports of case studies. Very few of them are discussions of case study as a research design (such discussion may feature only in passing, if at all, in such articles), unlike most of the articles referenced in this book.

For example, in 2012, about 12,000 of the 44,000 articles recorded by Google Scholar as having the exact phrase 'case study' in their titles, or more than one-quarter, had this term as part of a longer phrase, 'a case study of', and this often featured in the sub-title rather than the title. Many others used the phrase 'case study' as a title or sub-title, with the sub-title or title respectively then detailing what the case study was about or focused upon.

The bulk of writing on case study, therefore, consists of reports of case studies. While there is a wealth of writing which discusses the advantages and disadvantages, usage and variants, of case study as a research design – a good deal of which has been referred to in this book – this constitutes a relatively small proportion of the overall total.

If you are a researcher interested in carrying out a case study on a particular topic, you will be interested in accessing both sorts of literature: previous case studies that have focused on your topic, and discussions of the use of case study as a research design. This does present challenges, of course, given the size of the literature potentially available to you. In terms of reading about case study as a research design, this book, and the other books and articles it refers to, offers a helpful guide. The strategies you might adopt to identify published case studies that have examined your topic are discussed in the later section in this chapter on How to Find Relevant Case Studies.

EXISTING META-ANALYSES AND SYSTEMATIC REVIEWS

It has been made clear elsewhere in this book that one of the main criticisms made of case study concerns the difficulty of generalising from their findings. Possible responses to this include carrying out multiple case studies or drawing together the findings from all of the individual case studies that have explored a particular issue or topic. The latter approach, which Jensen and Rodgers (2001) refer to as 'cumulating the intellectual gold of case study research', is commonly referred to more generally as meta-analysis or systematic review.

Lipsey and Wilson (2001) define meta-analysis in the following terms:

Meta-analysis can be understood as a form of survey research in which research reports, rather than people, are surveyed. A coding form (survey protocol) is developed, a sample or population of research reports is gathered, and each research study is 'interviewed' by a coder who reads it carefully and codes the appropriate information about its characteristics and quantitative findings. The resulting data are then analysed using special adaptations of conventional statistical techniques to investigate and describe the pattern of findings in the selected set of studies... Meta-analysis represents each study's findings in the form of *effect sizes*. (pp. 1–3, emphasis in original)

In other words, it is a quantitative analysis of pre-existing research reports, which may contain either or both quantitative or qualitative data. If the latter, this will be coded and analysed in a quantitative form.

Littell, Corcoran and Pillai (2008) usefully distinguish meta-analysis from systematic review:

A *systematic review* aims to comprehensively locate and synthesize research that bears on a particular question, using organized, transparent, and replicable procedures at each step in the process... *Meta-analysis* is a set of statistical methods for combining quantitative results from multiple studies to produce an overall summary of empirical knowledge on a given topic. (pp. 1–2, emphasis in original)

Meta-analyses, therefore, are essentially quantitative in nature, while systematic reviews may be more qualitative.

A number of meta-analyses and systematic reviews of case study research were identified in Chapter 5 in the course of the discussion of the use of case study designs in different disciplines and subject areas. These are summarised in Box 7.1, together with some additional examples which have not previously been referred to. There will, of course, be others I have not identified.

■ ■ ■ Box 7.1   Examples of Meta-analyses and Systematic Reviews of Case Study Research   ■ ■ ■

Identified and discussed in Chapter 5

Piekkari, Welch and Paavilainen (2009) examined the use of case study research in the field of international business, analysing 135 articles (11% of the total) published in four core journals between 1995 and 2005, and a further 22 (5%) published between 1975 and 1994. They found that 'exploratory, interview-based multiple case studies based on positivistic assumptions and conducted at a single point in time' (p. 577) were dominant.

Beverland and Lindgren (2010) reviewed 105 articles based on qualitative case research published in the journal *Industrial Marketing Management* between 1971 and 2006, concluding that 'there has been a steady improvement in how authors address research quality in qualitative cases' (p. 61).

McCutcheon and Meredith (1993) provide a brief analysis of the 'true' case studies published in five operations management journals in the period 1981–1991, 48 in total. They found that 'The most common form of case study has been the exploratory or theory-building type, using the case study method alone. Explanatory or theory-testing case studies are the least common, perhaps because of the relative scarcity of testable… theories' (p. 249).

Corcoran, Walker and Wals (2004) consider the use of case study methodology to research sustainability in higher education, reviewing 54 journal articles, and reaching fairly critical conclusions.

Anthony and Jack (2009) report on an analysis of 42 case study research papers in nursing, noting that qualitative case study methodology 'is becoming entrenched in the nursing research lexicon as a well-accepted methodology to address the phenomenon of human care and other complex issues germane to the discipline worldwide' (p. 1177).

Dube and Pare (2003) assessed 183 articles published in seven major information systems journals over the 1990–1999 period, focusing on design issues, data collection and data analysis. They found that 'a large proportion of them have actually ignored the state of the art of case study research methods that have been readily available to them' (p. 599).

Doolin (1996) reviewed 50 articles using case study design in four journals over the period 1989–1993, comparing positivist and (emerging) interpretive approaches to case study research. He noted that positivist approaches 'tend to treat case research as an exploratory tool for developing hypotheses', while interpretive strategies 'give a more central role to case research, utilising case studies to obtain a deeper understanding of the phenomenon and of the meaning of human behaviour' (p. 28).

Other Examples

Solomon et al (2012) conducted an analysis of 20 case study articles published over 16 years, 1993–2008, that focused on school-wide positive behaviour support, finding that such strategies were 'moderately effective in reducing problem behavior in students' (p. 116).

Greenwald, Hedges and Laine (1994) reanalysed 38 case studies on school finance previously studied by Hanushek (1981, 1986, 1989, 1991). They used more up-to-date techniques to demonstrate that 'the production function studies of the relation between resource inputs and student outcomes examined by Hanushek do not support his conclusion that resource inputs are unrelated to outcomes' (p. 19). Their study was, therefore, not simply a meta-analysis of a series of case studies, but a reanalysis of an existing meta-analysis.

Oberlack (2010) conducted a meta-analysis of 17 case studies which examined the adaptability of institutions to climate change, concluding, perhaps rather unsurprisingly, that 'institutions seem to be a crucial instrument for members of society to enhance their adaptive capacity by coordinating individual and collective action, shaping the generation and use of resources and shaping the capacity for individual and social learning' (p. 15).

Stall-Meadows (1998) carried out a qualitative meta-analysis using a grounded theory approach of case studies completed for dissertations that focused on distance education pedagogy. For a variety of reasons, however, the analysis was limited to just four such dissertations, so the study is more a demonstration of the possibilities than a finished piece of work.

Box 7.1 shows a number of interesting things. First, many meta-analyses and systematic reviews of case study research have clearly already been carried out. Second, they tend to focus on either particular journals, or groups of journals, disciplinary areas or specific topics. Naturally enough, this helps to keep the study more focused and feasible. Third, they are frequently fairly critical, concerned as much with identifying the best ways forward as with 'cumulating the intellectual gold of case study research'.

Clearly, if you are able to identify a meta-analysis or a systematic review, or even a fairly extensive and well-organised literature review, that has been carried out recently into case studies focusing on a topic similar to the one you are planning or carrying out, this is likely to be of considerable interest and use. As well as giving you useful guidance on your own research practice, you will have much easier access to studies (both the meta-analysis and the component case studies) with which to compare and contrast your own case study.

But how to go about finding such existing published studies? That is the subject of the next section.

HOW TO FIND RELEVANT CASE STUDIES

Strategies which you might use to find case studies relevant to your research are summarised in Box 7.2. We will discuss each of these in turn in some more detail; some have, of course, already been discussed in this chapter and elsewhere in the book.

■ ■ ■　**Box 7.2　How to Find Relevant Case Studies**　■ ■ ■

- Using search engines, e.g. Google Scholar, Scopus
- Using existing meta-analyses, systematic reviews and literature reviews (including this book)
- Using articles, books and reports
- Using theses and dissertations

Using Search Engines

With the development of the internet, search engines offer what for most is probably the most obvious way of finding details on just about anything, including relevant case studies. Google Scholar and Scopus have been used in this way for this book, but there are many other search engines available, both academic (e.g. PsycINFO, PubMed) and general in nature. Search engines work by getting you to input one or more key words – and, if you wish, more details, such as dates, journal and author names – and then let you search their database(s) for matches in the title, abstract or content of articles, books, reports, etc.

The downside of search engines is their very efficiency and the size of the databases they have access to. As remarked already in this chapter, simply putting 'case study' or 'case studies' into a search engine as your chosen key words is going to yield many thousands of responses, the vast majority of which will not be of interest or relevance to you. So you will have to develop ways of using your chosen search engine(s) more intelligently and refining your search. This might involve, for example, any or all of the following:

- Searching using 'case study' and other key words. For example, if your interest is in case studies of the use of problem-based learning, you might input 'case study' and 'problem-based learning' as your key words. Or, if your research was on company mergers, you might input 'company mergers' along with 'case study'. Sometimes you will need to experiment with a range and variety of key words to find what you want.
- Limiting the search by date. You might, for example, only be interested in more recent material, and limit the search to anything published since 2000. Or you might be interested in a particular historical period, for example case studies published between 1970 and 1980 on a particular topic.
- You might also wish to limit your search to a particular country or area of the world, but this is not easy to do using search engines (though limiting by language is), so you will probably need to do this manually after your search has been completed.
- Confining your search to items having the chosen key words in their titles. This is likely to yield a much more focused list of results, omitting many items that only make a passing reference to your topic of interest somewhere in their text.
- Some search engines contain information on the number of times an article has been cited by other authors. This will allow you to focus on the most highly cited articles, which are likely to include those that have been most influential.

It is also useful, as was done in the section on Writing on Case Study earlier in this chapter, to make use of more than one search engine. Different search engines have different coverages, strengths and weaknesses, so using more than one helps to ensure that you do not miss key articles.

Using Existing Meta-analyses, Systematic Reviews and Literature Reviews

We have already referred to and identified a number of these sources earlier in this chapter (see Box 7.1). Clearly, if you can find a meta-analysis, systematic review or straightforward literature review of relevance to your topic, this is likely to be extremely useful to you, particularly if it is reasonably up to date, and even if its focus is not simply on published case studies on your topic. Using 'meta-analysis', or one of the other terms, together with your topic as key words in a search engine, should help you to identify any of relevance that exist.

Using Articles, Books and Reports

Once you have identified particular articles, books, reports or other materials of relevance, one obvious strategy is to check through the items they reference to identify what might be of relevance to you. This will, of course, only lead you to older items, but can be a good way of identifying key publications on your topic, as these are likely to be frequently referenced (and discussed in the literature review section – if there is one – of the article, book or report). Once you have identified key authors, you can also – if they are still active – search their own personal websites to see what else they have published, including more recently, on the topic.

It is quite likely that in this process you will identify particular journals which regularly publish items of relevance and interest to you. It then makes sense to carry out a systematic search of those journals' websites, both to check if there are other relevant items which you have missed, and to see what the most recent material on your topic is (which may have only just been published online).

Using Theses and Dissertations

If your research is being carried out in an academic context, you are likely to want to check out theses and dissertations as well. These are now increasingly available in electronic form over the internet. ProQuest is one search engine which you may find of use; it has a particularly good coverage of theses produced in the United States and Canada, but has a reasonable international coverage as well. There are also a range of open access search engines and others restricted to theses produced in a particular country or institution.

Identifying one or more recent and relevant theses is likely to be extremely useful, because theses and dissertations usually include a fairly extensive and up-to-date literature review. These will be useful for checking how thorough your existing searches have been, and for identifying very specialist or local material you would have had difficulty in tracking down. Theses are also useful, if they include a case study of your particular topic, for reading about methodology and theory as well as the topic itself.

In practice, of course, it would make good sense to use more than one of these strategies – using search engines; existing meta-analyses, systematic reviews and literature reviews; articles, books and reports; theses and dissertations – to identify case studies of relevance to your research. Each of the strategies has its own strengths and weaknesses, which you can combine and overcome if you use two or more strategies together, but be prepared for a lot of the same material to be identified by different strategies. Once this happens repeatedly, you should be able to feel confident that you have identified much of the material of relevance to you.

USING EXISTING CASE STUDIES

Possible ways in which you might use existing case studies in your research are outlined in Box 7.3. We will explore each of these in turn.

Box 7.3   Using Existing Case Studies

- To inform your research design, choice of methodology and methods
- To inform your theoretical framework
- To compare your practice with
- To compare your findings and conclusions with
- To enable you to generalise further
- Reading non-case study research of relevance to the topic

To Inform Your Research Design, Choice of Methodology and Methods

The need to read about research design, methodology and method as well as your topic has to be stressed, particularly, again, if you are undertaking your research in an academic setting. You need to read about these aspects – for which this book, and the sources it recommends, should be helpful – in order to ensure that you are carrying out your research as appropriately and well as you can.

As indicated previously, however, only a relative handful of existing publications on case study are likely to be useful in this respect, as the majority of publications focus on the case study itself.

To Inform Your Theoretical Framework

Similarly, you need to read about theory to help place your research in its wider context: trying to explain why things are the way they are, and how they might be changed or improved. You may only be carrying out a single case study, and may even have no intention to do any more research beyond that, but to get the most out of the exercise you should aim to place your study in as broad a context as possible.

Again, however, as with research design, choice of methodology and methods, most publications on case study will not be useful in this respect, as their focus will be on the findings of the case study itself, and there may be little or no theoretical engagement.

To Compare Your Practice with

Reading about research design, methodology, methods and theory is not simply something you do before carrying out your study in order to determine how and in which context you are going to do it. You can also do this during and after your study, to compare how your practice of case study research progressed.

Bear in mind, however, that published sources usually present an overly positive and unidirectional account of research undertaken. In the vast majority of academic publications, whatever has been done appears to have been successful, the research described appears to have been a seamless and faultless process, and it reads as if this was preordained from the start. You may, though, come across some publications which tell it more like it was, 'warts and all'. So don't be too dispirited if it seems that your progress was not as smooth as some others.

To Compare Your Findings and Conclusions with

Perhaps the most obvious way in which to use other case studies of relevance to your topic, however, is to compare your findings with their results. Did similar case studies carried out in analogous settings come to much the same conclusions as yours did or are there significant differences in results?

If the former is the answer, then this is reassuring news, suggesting that you have carried out your research reasonably well, and that you have something to add to the developing research and literature on your topic, though perhaps not a huge amount.

If the latter is the answer, don't panic! So long as you are confident that you have pursued your research as carefully and openly as you could, this suggests that the case studies you are comparing yours with are not as analogous as you formerly thought. Do some more investigation, and see if you can work out what is different or particular about your case study. You may have chosen, perhaps without realising it, an extreme case to study. It might just be that you have come up with some really original findings which will make a significant contribution to your area of research.

To Enable You to Generalise Further

Then, of course, and underlying much of the discussion throughout this book, there is the question of generalisation (a topic which is discussed in more detail in Chapter 3). The difficulties of generalising from single case studies are widely recognised and accepted. If, however, your case study is one of a number carried out on the same topic in similar settings, you should be able to use their cumulative findings to argue their greater relevance and applicability.

This is a good reason for doing another case study on a topic that has already been addressed, in that it can help to build up the evidence base.

Reading Non-case Study Research of Relevance to the Topic

Finally, it makes sense to read research of relevance to your topic which has not used a case study design, as well as that which has. This should be useful to give you an idea of alternative ways of researching your topic, their advantages and disadvantages, and enabling you to develop a more considered justification of why you opted for a case study design. More broadly, it will also provide you with more findings with which to compare your own.

EXAMPLES OF CASE STUDY RESEARCH

In this section, we will examine several published examples of case study research. This will both demonstrate the great variety of approaches to research using the case study design across the disciplines, and the ways in which existing research may be assessed and used. The examples discussed here may be usefully added, contrasted and compared to the five examples of 'meaningful case study research' examined in Chapter 4.

Of course, with so many published case studies available, it would have been possible to choose any number of interesting and good quality studies to illustrate this section. The selection that has been made is, then, a convenience sample. It does not imply either that these are the best examples ever of case study research, although I clearly think that they are good examples or I would not have selected them, or that those studies that have not been selected are poor or deficient in some way.

Baines and Cunningham (2013)

This article, by Canadian and UK-based social work academics, reports on the authors' experience of carrying out nine intensive case studies of non-profit social services agencies in four countries (New Zealand, Australia, Canada and Scotland), using a data collection approach they term 'rapid ethnography':

> Rapid ethnography is a form of multi-method ethnography involving data collection from numerous sources over a relatively short period of time including interviews, participant observations, document review and sometimes surveys and focus groups. The goal of this method is to produce a multi-layered, textured analysis of a slice of life in an organization, environment or some part of society, intertwining the structure and consciousness with the larger socio-political context shaping social relations. (p. 74)

Unlike conventional ethnography (see also the discussion of the use of this research design together with case study in Chapter 6), this technique 'involves at least two researchers in all aspects of data collection' (p. 75). In this study one researcher is based in the country and one is from outside. Baines and Cunningham argue that rapid ethnography is 'an effective method for questions about pressing social problems that require relatively immediate solutions as well as contributions to a larger body of knowledge', and is 'appropriate to questions involving the intersection of policy and practice (such as the impacts of funding regimes and new managerial modes...), as well as to questions seeking to extend theory in any number of directions' (p. 77).

Baines and Cunningham use one of the nine case studies, which was of a faith-based agency, to illustrate their approach. They found that 'the shorter timeline... the pre-interviews and conversations we hold with participants ahead of time and our capacity to compare with international data seems to mean that we are folded quickly into the study site' (p. 79), and that 'undertaking multiple... case studies permitted us to uncover new and often unanticipated findings, collectively analyse them, fold them into data collection, dialogue and apply international comparisons' (pp. 80–81), though the insularity of the particular case study considered posed some challenges.

This, then, is an interesting example of the use of particular data collection techniques within a case study design. It involved multiple case studies, carried out internationally, and multiple forms of data collection, so it clearly required a small team of experienced and committed researchers to undertake the research successfully. Nevertheless, there are elements of this approach that would be replicable in a smaller-scale research project.

Etherington and Bridges (2011)

This article, by two British researchers, presents an in-depth, small-scale narrative inquiry into clients' experiences of counselling, with a focus on reviews of the progress made and the ending of the counselling. Six clients who had been helped by one community counselling agency, which dealt with people who had experienced abuse, were interviewed. Etherington and Bridges carefully outline their narrative approach to case study research:

[O]ur approach to case study research acknowledges researcher reflexivity as a main instrument for gathering, interpreting and re-presenting the 'data' (i.e. stories of lived experience), and views knowledge and knower as interdependent and embedded within history, context, culture, language, experience, and understandings. A narrative researcher begins from a 'curious, not knowing' position and focuses on questions that help the storyteller address cultural context... Narrative research seeks out how people make meanings of their experiences, and recognises that meanings are multiple and context dependent. (p. 12)

For ethical reasons, the researchers did not approach clients who had already ended their counselling sessions, but contacted new clients to ask if they would be willing to participate in the project after they had finished being counselled. Once the interviews were completed, Etherington and Bridges engaged in a complex and iterative process of data analysis:

> Initially I [i.e. Etherington, the first author] worked with each person's narrative on its own terms, treating them as knowledge in their own right, seeking out the stories, thinking with the stories as much as about them, noticing how the stories were told, the metaphors used, and emotional responses, thoughts and ideas: making meaning of them as I checked and amended the transcript against the audio-recording... I returned the amended transcripts to the participants asking them to highlight the most important stories from their point of view. The second author... also worked with the transcribed narratives; both of us comparing what was being said against our own understandings, trying not to fill in any gaps with 'grand narratives', but rather inquiring about how pieces of the stories made sense together. Following our independent work on the transcripts we met to jointly consider what seemed most significant, both of us drawing on our theoretical and practice knowledge, personal experience, resonances, and the meanings participants constructed as they told their stories, as evidenced in the transcripts... When all of the interviews/conversations were completed we took up a position from where we could look across the stories, exploring similarities, contradictions, ambiguities and differences – between the participants and between our ideas and theirs. (p. 13)

Three of the six participants' experiences are then discussed and exemplified in some detail. The researchers conclude their article with some very practical findings regarding the review process:

> The findings of this study suggest that reviews can be a useful tool for both counsellors and clients; and that their usefulness might depend upon their design and the manner in which they are implemented. The usefulness of the review process seems to be in: focusing the client on their aims and encouraging them to complete the tasks they need to achieve before counselling ends; enabling them to develop their ability to ask for what they want, i.e. to continue or to finish; and to monitor the relationship with their counsellor and their progress. (p. 20)

This is clearly small-scale research: just six people who had received counselling from one centre were interviewed. Nonetheless, the research had meaning: for the researchers and the researched, for the counselling centre involved, and, beyond that, for all those interested in the practice, experience and usefulness of counselling.

Though two researchers were involved, enabling discussion and the sharing of understandings, this project was of a size that could have been handled by a single researcher, with appropriate knowledge and contacts within the counselling profession. Beyond counselling, it would be relatively easy to think of similar sized projects focusing on other kinds of organisation and practices.

Garaway (1996)

Garaway, a researcher working in Israel, investigated the use of a simplified script to enhance literacy in seven locations, urban and rural, in India, applying, following Yin, 'a multiple-case, replication design, with each individual case embedded; that is, containing multiple units of analysis' (p. 203). She reports that by using this design, 'with criterion-referenced tests, surveys, focus-group interviews, document analyses and observations, the evaluation conducted on the script attempted to capture the reliability characteristics of a well-defined quantitative study and also some of the validity characteristics of a qualitative study' (p. 207).

She developed both student and case site profiles, then engaged in cross-case comparisons, and managed to summarise her findings in single pages and charts. She concludes that:

> cross-cultural evaluations, particularly in developing nations, tend to present extreme challenges in terms of uncontrolled-for variables. Traditional control methods are generally inadequate or inappropriate for controlling the number and type of factors encountered. This choice of design... was an attempt to address the demands of such a situation and provided a sound organizational framework. While such a design admittedly presents challenges in terms of tests of validity and reliability, it can provide an evaluator with an organizational frame for collecting and sorting of a wide variety of data. This organizational frame can in turn serve as a vehicle for examining a phenomenon in an ordered yet culturally flexible manner across a variety of cultural settings. (p. 210)

This is an interesting example of a complex case study design being applied in a challenging situation by a single investigator. It also shows how both qualitative and quantitative data collection and analysis strategies may be built into a case study design. In essence, Garaway was concerned to collect as much data as possible by whatever means were available and appropriate, which is a very healthy approach for a small-scale researcher to adopt.

Jones et al (1993)

Jones and his three colleagues, based in the United States, offer a 'paradigm' for single-case research in psychotherapy:

A patient diagnosed as having major depressive disorder was seen in an intensive, twice-weekly psychodynamic psychotherapy for 2½ years. Each session was videotaped, and assessments of patient change were obtained at regular intervals. A time-series analysis was used to model fluctuations in the therapy process to take into account time and the effect of previous events on subsequent changes, thereby preserving the context-determined meaning for therapist and patient actions. A bidirectional analysis of causal effects shows that the influence processes between therapist and patient are mutual and reciprocal and suggests that the effect of the patient on the therapist and on the process has not been made sufficiently explicit in previous models of process and change. (p. 381)

Interestingly, for a single-case study, the data collected was primarily quantitative. The patient, in particular, but also the psychotherapist, completed assessment instruments at regular intervals. The analysis then focuses on changes in these measures over time and the relationships between them, finding that both patient and psychotherapist influence each other. While Jones et al acknowledge that their findings are not generalisable, they argue that they suggest ways forward for researching the impacts of psychotherapy.

This case study is particularly interesting for two reasons. First, it illustrates how a single case study can produce extremely interesting and suggestive results. Second, it demonstrates that even small-scale case study research may be pursued through quantitative techniques, which are just as capable of producing rich, detailed data as are qualitative approaches.

McCarthy, Holland and Gillies (2003)

McCarthy, Holland and Gillies – three sociology researchers based in the UK – concern themselves with the family lives of young people. Their data consists of interviews with nine individuals from three case study families, and their focus lies in 'how to make sense of differences and of standpoints within this set of interviews, and questions that arise in approaching the analysis of clusters of interviews from within the same "family" units' (p. 2).

They examine their data using, successively, objectivist, interpretationist and reflexive approaches, and then, more briefly, from the standpoints of generation and gender. They note that:

each twisting of the analytic kaleidoscope brings different issues into focus, even when only nine interviews are being explored. We were struck by the way the various approaches to the analysis yielded different forms of knowledge. When we looked at individual accounts within families we saw multiple perspectives, and when we looked at the related family accounts we were able to discern commonality. We identified similarities within the standpoints of gender and generation, and again found that these were cross cut by further differences which seemed to reflect ethnicity and class. Indeed, we could argue that the overall effect of shifting our analytic focus in these different approaches has been to emphasize a key theoretical point, revealing in all its complexity how issues of individual histories, shared family lives and standpoints of gender, generation, class and ethnicity are all interwoven in these related but individual accounts. (p. 19)

The overriding conclusion, then, is one of the complexity of individual and social relations. This has an important message for all case study, and other, researchers: the importance not just of what others might term triangulation, but also of interrogating the data collected from different perspectives or positions.

Mjoset (2006)

Mjoset, a Norwegian sociologist, presents a single case study of the Israel/Palestine conflict, employing what he calls a pragmatic strategy of generalisation. The study was based on existing documents and studies. His interest was in why this conflict has become so deep-seated and persistent, for which he had to assess at least 22 differing theories, on topics such as colonialism, international relations and settler states. He argues that 'pragmatist researchers find ways of accumulating knowledge that transcend the engrained dichotomies explanation/understanding, generalization/specification… a researcher with a pragmatist attitude will seek the grounded knowledge necessary to answer her or his research questions in the relevant *local research frontiers*' (pp. 755–756, emphasis in original).

He explains the nature of local research frontiers, and the processes involved in the research, as follows:

[A]s empirical researchers, we observe with reference to several theories embedded in a smaller set of local research frontiers. My project relied on several more or less well-formulated local research frontiers that mediate between theories and observation. Although I did a single-case analysis, it relied on observations also from many other cases, observations that were synthesized in local, problem-related research frontiers that connect several 'literatures'. (p. 757)

In this way, he argues, he is able to produce a single case study which, as well as offering a reasoned explanation of the Israel/Palestine conflict, also suggests how we might progress thinking around similar conflicts:

[T]he results of my study may also be fed back into a research frontier on deep and persistent conflicts in the contemporary world, making that frontier more manifest. Who knows, within this skeleton of categories, we might be able to deal with Northern Ireland, Algeria, Chechnya and other contemporary deep-rooted, persistent conflicts. Here, systematic explanatory accounts of the case of Israel lead to another set of generalizations than those in the state formation literature. (p. 761)

Of course, as pragmatists we might well argue that the Israel/Palestine conflict is of such importance, not just regionally but internationally, that a single case study of it is more than justified, whether or not there is any potential for generalisation. But if a single case study like this allows the development of middle-range theories that might have some application to other similar cases, then it is even more worthwhile.

Nonthaleerak and Hendry (2008)

Nonthaleerak and Hendry, based in business schools in Thailand and the UK respectively, present an analysis of nine case study companies in Thailand, focusing on their use of the six sigma methodology, a quality improvement initiative widely used in industry. Data collection was through 43 semi-structured interviews. They note that:

> Case study research was chosen given the need to gather in-depth, rich data on the phenomenon of six sigma implementation... The advantages of the case study approach ... include the 'exploratory depth' of understanding that can be achieved... Exploratory research is appropriate here as very little is known in the academic literature about the six sigma phenomenon. A multi-case study approach is needed to overcome the shortcomings of much of the previous research reported in the literature, which has concentrated on a single organization... [T]he multi-case study approach allows a more direct comparison between the similarities and differences of the implementation practices in the different contexts considered. It also enables more generic conclusions to be reached. (p. 284)

The analysis proceeded through 'the identification of core categories within the interview data and the build-up of a logical chain of evidence... Data triangulation was used in the analysis by interviewing at least two levels of management and belt professionals [this is six sigma terminology for staff with a certain level of experience with the technique] in each company' (p. 285). The findings showed mixed success in the use of the six sigma method, and explored the possible reasons for this.

In this example, the cases were the companies investigated, employing a multiple case study approach. While a deliberate attempt was made to include varied companies, both manufacturing and non-manufacturing, in the sample, it could not be said to be representative. However, the use of a multiple case study approach adds strength to the findings.

Oke and Gopalakrishnan (2009)

Oke and Gopalakrishnan, two researchers based in the United States, examine the management of disruptions in the supply chain of a large retailer. They justify the use of a single case study approach in the following way:

A case study offers the opportunity to study a phenomenon in its own natural setting where complex links and underlying meanings can be explored, while also enabling the researcher to study whole supply chains. It is also appropriate where existing knowledge is limited because it generates in-depth contextual information which may result in a superior level of understanding. (pp. 169–170)

While only a single case was examined, this was a sizeable case: 'The retailer is North America's leading retailer of food, supplies, accessories, pets and professional services for the lifetime needs of pets... The retailer operates more than 700 superstores in the United States and Canada, with over $3 billion in sales in 2003' (p. 170). Data collection was through interviews with senior informants at the company's headquarters and distribution centre.

Oke and Gopalakrishnan found 'the simple classification of supply chain risks as high-likelihood, low-impact and low-likelihood high-impact to be highly relevant' (p. 174). They acknowledge the issue of generalisation, but argue that the value of the single case study lies in developing theories and hypotheses, which can then be tested by other means:

[T]he purpose of the empirical case study analysis in this study is not one of generalization but one of theoretical replication for which propositions have been developed in a theory-building approach... [T]he propositions developed from this study are broad, relating to classifications of risks and mitigation strategies that can be employed by different organizations irrespective of sectoral differences. These propositions can be further tested using other methodological approaches such as a large survey. (p. 174)

Rialp et al (2005)

Rialp and his three colleagues, all based in Spain, focus on the 'born global' phenomenon in industry, whereby newly established businesses rapidly internationalise from their foundation. They examine four recently established small or medium-sized enterprises in Catalonia, two of which fit the 'born global' pattern while the other two are developing in a more incremental fashion. They argue that:

multiple case-based research may serve as a basis for either empirically testing previous theories or building new theoretical explanation of the phenomenon being researched. In addition, analytical – not statistic – generalisation of the results of the several cases being used to other contexts with similar theoretical conditions can be obtained by means of applying replication logic – both literal and theoretical – and the so-called pattern-matching analytical procedure. Literal replication enables researchers to capture subtle similarities and differences within groups of cases related to a specific expected pattern, whereas theoretical replication allows researchers to identify key differences between groups of ... cases associated with different expected patterns. Therefore, they are expected to differ among themselves but for *a priori* predictable reasons. (pp. 139, 141)

They adopted what they term a conceptual (i.e. purposive) sampling approach, which:

allowed us to introduce some degree of variance in our case selection criteria by including both low- and high-technology-based companies of relatively different size, within different sectors (manufacturing and service industries), and belonging to diverse local geographic areas (urban or rural). However, to be consistent with previous research on entrepreneurial firms which are regarded as typically young and small in size, all firms in the purposeful sample had to be small, independently managed, and recently created (less than 7 years old). (p. 141)

Data collection centred on interviews with company leaders, backed up by company documentation and other secondary data. The four cases were examined on their own first, and then collectively, looking in particular for instances of literal and theoretical replication. While not small-scale, this was not a large project, and would be well within the scope of a single researcher – or a small team as here – to explore, given the time and access.

Vellema et al (2013)

Vellema and his three colleagues are based in the Netherlands, and focus on partnerships between companies and non-governmental organisations, designed to incorporate smallholder farmers into value chains (hence their term 'value chain partnerships'), and thus contribute to development. Their two case studies of value chain partnerships are based in Uganda and Rwanda. They employ a case study design because:

Case studies, understood as an intensive, in-depth study of a relatively bounded phenomenon lend themselves to making cautious causal inferences about the mechanisms of change triggered by the intervention, in this instance, value chain collaboration. Our two case studies allowed us to investigate partnering as 'situated action'. This individual case research provides a basis for a cross-case analysis that aims to distil more generic causal inferences about partnering activities. (p. 306)

They employed a three-stage approach to the use of case studies: (1) descriptive inference within cases; (2) developing hypotheses regarding the individual cases; (3) theorising regarding institutional change from both cases. Tellingly, given their focus on improving practice, they also describe their work as action research (see also the discussion of the use of action research with case study in a combined design in

Chapter 6). They conclude that 'The use of case studies enabled us to identify how underlying dynamics and processes can be either conducive or obstructive to achieving desired developmental outcomes' (p. 317).

Some Conclusions

These examples re-emphasise a series of important points, points which have already been made on a number of occasions in this book, but which are worth continually stressing:

- Case study as a research design is commonly applied in a wide range of disciplines. The examples discussed here include studies related to business and management, counselling, development, education, nursing, psychotherapy, social work and sociology (see also Chapter 5).
- Case study is also employed as a research design internationally. The small number of examples discussed included, as well as the 'obvious candidates' (given the restriction to English language publications) of the UK and the USA, contributions from researchers based or working in Canada, India, Israel, Norway, Rwanda, Spain, Uganda and Thailand.
- While some of the case studies relied on a single method for data collection, typically interviews but in one example documents, others used multiple methods, including focus groups, observation (participant or otherwise), questionnaires and surveys, as well as assessments, measurements and tests. While most of the examples leant towards a predominantly qualitative analysis, there were a number which mixed qualitative and quantitative analysis, and one (Jones et al 1993) which relied primarily on quantitative data.
- While most of the examples identified themselves purely as case studies of different types, some combined case study with other research designs, including action research (Vellema et al 2013), ethnography (Baines and Cunningham 2013) and time series analysis (Jones et al 1993). See also the discussion of such combined research designs in Chapter 6.
- The number of cases examined varied from just one (three of the examples) up to nine (two examples), with other studies focusing on two, three, four, six or seven cases. This does not, however, give an adequate idea of the scale or ambition of some of the studies. Thus, one of the single case studies was an examination of the Israel/Palestine conflict (Mjoset 2006), while the third case study was focused on improving literacy in India (Garaway 1996).

Most of the examples used involved a small number of researchers, but in two of them (Garaway 1996 and Mjoset 2006) there was just one. A number of them engaged extensively with relevant theory. All produced interesting and worthwhile results, with suggestions for further work. All demonstrate the argument that case study is – or, at least, should be – small-scale research with meaning.

CONTRARY EXAMPLES

In this section, in contrast to the previous one, we will examine two contrary examples of research projects, ones which claim they are case study designs, even though many case study advocates might question this. In the first example, the doubts concern the scale of the project, which is clearly not small-scale research, while in the second example, the issue is whether it is a case study at all, or is simply being termed this for convenience.

Greenhalgh et al (2010)

Greenhalgh and her five co-authors, all based in health or medical departments in the UK, present what they term a mixed method, multi-level case study that aimed to evaluate a national programme designed to implement a system of centrally stored electronic medical records in the National Health Service in England. The research had been commissioned by the Department of Health. This was a major research project involving both quantitative and qualitative elements, extending the notion of case study design well beyond what most of its practitioners envisage.

The quantitative data comprised 416,325 records of encounters in primary care out-of-hours and walk-in centres. The qualitative data consisted of 140 interviews with policy-makers, managers, clinicians and software suppliers, as well as 2,000 pages of ethnographic field notes, including observations of 214 clinical consultations, plus 3,000 pages of documents. While the quantitative data were analysed statistically, the qualitative data was analysed thematically and interpretively. For the latter:

> Rigour was defined in terms of authenticity (immersion in the case through extended fieldwork), plausibility (developing explanations of local phenomena which made sense to participants and drawing these together into a coherent overall narrative), and criticality (systematically questioning assumptions that are taken for granted). (p. 3)

Greenhalgh et al adopted what they term a 'utilisation-focused evaluation' approach. They carried out an interpretive field study in a large-scale information system, emphasising 'continuous, iterative comparison of findings in one part of the project with an emerging overarching story of the whole' (p. 2). They came to the following general conclusions:

> Benefits of centrally stored electronic summary records seem more subtle and contingent than many stakeholders anticipated, and clinicians may not access them. Complex interdependencies, inherent tensions, and high implementation workload should be expected when they are introduced on a national scale. (p. 1)

Such a large project would be impossible to consider without specific government funding and support, with the access and ethical issues posed being particularly acute.

Perhaps most interesting in the present context is why the research was categorised as a case study. Or, in other words, what constitutes the case or cases? The focus of the analysis presented in the article was on three sites (primary care out-of-hours and walk-in centres); within those sites it was on the individual doctors and nurses involved. Each of the centres and each of the doctors and nurses working within them were considered as cases. Hence it was a multi-level case study.

While accepting that this research may be termed a multi-level case study, there remains a suspicion that this designation in some way 'under-sells' it, and that a different terminology – perhaps large-scale evaluation – might have been more appropriate. It is the sheer scale of the study that raises most doubt in this respect, as the project (even if it was scaled down from three to just one site) would clearly have been well beyond the single researcher, or pair of researchers, most commonly associated with case study research.

This study, then, usefully raises the question of whether case study research has to be small-scale (cf. the study by Payne et al, 2007, considered in Chapter 4, which, while not so large overall, was also mixed method and multi-level).

Jenkins et al (2001)

Jenkins and his six colleagues were based in health or medical research centres in the USA or Sweden. They describe a method for combining data from two or more longitudinal studies without the use of meta-analysis, which could not be employed because the data collection methods varied. Their study involved combining data from the 'Otsego-Schoharie healthy heart study conducted in upstate New York, USA and the Norsjo study conducted in Northern Sweden' (p. 41):

> The overall aim of this study was to combine data from two different public health interventions in a manner that would permit maximum analytic power and flexibility… the creation of a synthetic longitudinal follow-up group via pair matching resulted in a relatively conservative, but statistically powerful, ANOVA [analysis of variance] model. (p. 41)

Clearly, then, this was a useful piece of research, building on two comparable existing studies and producing a 'powerful' model to explain and predict what was going on.

Where it gets confusing is when the authors refer to their research, in their sub-title (as is so often done) as 'a case study'. Yet the term 'case study' is not used in the text of the article, and no case study literature is referred to. Calling the research a case study doesn't seem to add anything to it, and it can only be understood as such in a very general sense: i.e. this is a study of a particular piece of research (i.e. a case).

This study raises the question of whether it is always legitimate or useful to call any piece of research a case study. As was noted in the discussion of Is Everything a Case? in Chapter 3, 'Here and there, researchers will call anything they please a case study' (Stake 2005, p. 445). But we don't always have to agree with them.

Some Conclusions

These two 'contrary' examples have been discussed – not to be unduly critical of them, because each of them is a useful piece of research – to raise questions about the limits of case study research. Thus, on the one hand, is there a point where a research project becomes so large in scale that it is difficult to conceive of it any more as a case study, and some other designation is called for? And, on the other hand, if we adopt the label of case study for a research project, should we be expected to justify this usage and engage, if only to a limited degree, with the case study literature?

Of course, in addition to examining examples of research projects which claimed to be case studies, but where there was some reasonable doubt about their status, we might also have looked at research projects which didn't claim to be case studies, but might have been designated as such. There would, though, have been a far greater number of those to choose from.

SUMMARY

In this chapter, we have:

- discussed the vast amount of published material available on case studies, both discussions of case study as a research design and the larger volume of material reporting on specific case studies
- examined a number of existing meta-analyses or systematic reviews of case studies on particular topics, noting their usefulness in building towards generalisations
- explored how you might go about identifying published case studies relevant to your own interests
- considered how you might make best use of such published case studies in your research, and discussed some detailed examples.

KEY READINGS

Byrne, D, and Ragin, C (eds) (2009) *The Sage Handbook of Case-based Methods*. London, Sage.
David, M (ed.) (2006) *Case Study Research* (4 volumes). London, Sage.
Mills, A, Durepos, G, and Wiebe, E (eds) (2010) *Encyclopedia of Case Study Research* (2 volumes). Los Angeles, CA, Sage.
Tight, M (ed.) (2015) *Case Studies* (4 volumes). London, Sage.

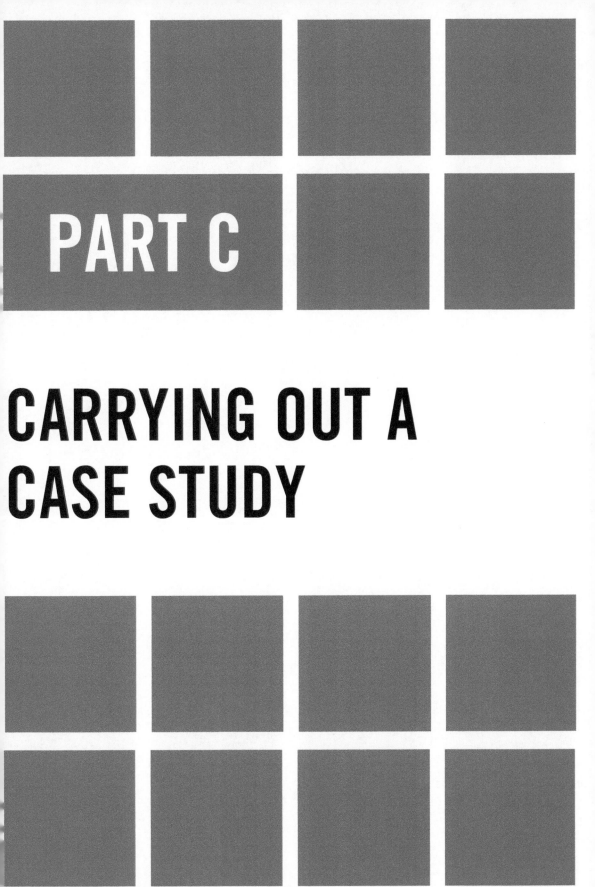

PART C

CARRYING OUT A CASE STUDY

8

Selection, Context and Theory in Case Study

INTRODUCTION

This chapter and the next one offer guidance on the issues you will need to consider in carrying out a case study. While this chapter focuses mainly on the issues you need to think about at the start, the next chapter focuses mainly on the issues you will face when actually carrying out the case study (there is, inevitably, some overlap).

This chapter starts by offering an overview of these issues, reviewing and adding to a number of the guides given by other authors. Your research question or questions are then discussed. Why are you doing this research, and what do you want to try to find out?

Sampling and selection issues are considered: which case or cases do you choose to study and how do you justify this choice? What questions of access does, or might, your study raise? Potential ethical concerns are then reviewed.

The importance of bounding the case study, and of understanding its relationship to the surrounding environment, is then addressed. This is significant both in principle – otherwise you will not be carrying out a case study – and in practical terms, to limit the scope of the research you plan to undertake.

The desirability, and implications, of locating the case study within a particular theoretical framework is discussed. Are you concerned with testing existing theory or building new theory? This is particularly important if you are researching your case study in an academic context and/or for academic credit.

The important distinctions between single case studies and multiple case studies are considered. While the former are more focused, the latter allow you to take a comparative perspective.

OVERVIEW

It should be stressed right at the beginning of this chapter that most, if perhaps not all, of the issues and processes involved in carrying out a case study – e.g. choosing what to study, how to study it and how to analyse your findings – are common to those faced when applying other research designs. The key difference is that in case study research we choose to focus in detail on a particular example or a small number of examples (though case study research is not, of course, the only form of small-scale but in-depth research).

This means that much guidance on the issues and processes involved in carrying out a case study can usefully be garnered from research methods texts that do not focus on case study, but consider qualitative and/or quantitative methods, or particular aspects of them, in general. It also means that much of the guidance offered in other texts that focus on case study (e.g. Stake 1995; Yin 2009), as in this one, is generic in nature.

Those who offer guidance specifically on doing case studies tend to organise – as I am doing in this chapter – their advice into a series of stages, steps, tasks or principles. Box 8.1 summarises the guidance given by seven recent sets of authors.

▪ ▪ ▪ Box 8.1 Guidance on Doing Case Studies ▪ ▪ ▪

Macpherson, Brooker and Ainsworth (2000, pp. 57–58) identify six principles for guiding the practice of case study research:

Regarding considerations of *purpose*:

1 *Contextuality*: Developing ways of collaborating and negotiating with research participants while acknowledging the reality of micropolitics that exist in all contexts and noting their implications in terms of the research purpose.

Regarding considerations of *place*:

2 *Sensitivity*: Developing methods of investigation with a sensitivity to, and empathy with the place, the participants and ethical matters.

Regarding considerations of *process*:

3 *Authenticity*: Developing ways of demonstrating a clear understanding of purpose, substantively and methodologically.*

4 *Applicability*: Developing ways of prioritising the focus (thinking big, but starting small) on specifically determined aspects of professional work.*

5 *Growth*: Developing ways of supporting and sustaining growth, in terms of the research partnership, and facilitating social transformation as an expression of the research purpose.

Regarding considerations of *product*:

6 *Communicability*: Implications of interacting and networking (including communication).**

* also applicable to purpose and place.

** also applicable to place and process.

Stuart et al (2002: 420) offer a five-step guide:

1 Define the research question
2 Instrument development
3 Data gathering
4 Analyse data
5 Disseminate

Stake (2005, pp. 459–460) identifies six 'major conceptual responsibilities of the qualitative case researcher':

1 Bounding the case, conceptualising the object of study
2 Selecting phenomena, themes or issues (i.e. the research questions to emphasise)
3 Seeking patterns of data to develop the issues
4 Triangulating key observations and bases for interpretation
5 Selecting alternative interpretations to pursue
6 Developing assertions or generalisations about the case

George and Bennett (2005, pp. 73–88) identify five tasks in the design of case study research:

1 Specification of the problem and the research objective
2 Developing a research strategy and specifying variables
3 Case selection
4 Describing the variance in variables
5 Formulation of data requirements and general questions

Rosenberg and Yates (2007, p. 449) provide nine 'clear and appropriate procedural steps to maintain the rigour and methodological integrity of the case study' (p. 448):

1 Pose the research question.
2 Identify the underpinning theories.
3 Determine the case – its context and the phenomena of interest.
4 Determine the specific case study approach.
5 Identify the data collection methods most suitable to answer the research questions.
6 Select analysis strategies appropriate to each of these data collection strategies.

(Continued)

(Continued)

7   Refine the analysed data through the analytical filter.
8   Use matrices to reduce data into manageable chunks and conceptual groupings.
9   Determine conclusions and develop a case *description*.

Pan and Tan's (2011: 164) eight step guide to what they call a 'structured-pragmatic-situational' approach to conducting case studies:

1   Access negotiation
2   Conceptualising the phenomenon
3   Collecting and organising the additional data
4   Constructing and extending the theoretical lens
5   Confirming and validating data
6   Selective coding
7   Ensuring theory–data–model alignment
8   Writing the case report

Thomas and Myers (2015, pp. 121–129) provide a three-phase design:

1   Locating a subject and an object
2   The kind of study
3   Intuition, theorisation and analysis

Six of these summaries – Stuart et al's five 'steps' (2002), Stake's six 'major conceptual responsibilities' (2005), George and Bennett's five 'tasks' (2005), Rosenberg and Yates' nine 'procedural steps' (2007), Pan and Tan's eight 'steps' (2011), and Thomas and Myers' three 'phases' (2015) – can be seen as broadly similar and analogous to the approach taken in this chapter. The number of points identified and the labels given to them differ, however, and George and Bennett focus on the design of the study only, not its implementation. But all of these authors present a sequential listing of tasks to be undertaken, from defining the research question, through developing a data collection strategy, data gathering, seeking patterns in the data, coding, aligning theory and data, to writing up and disseminating the results.

Nevertheless, each of these authors places particular emphasis on some of these tasks or processes. Thus, Stuart et al stress instrument development, Stake emphasises the bounding of the case and data triangulation, George and Bennett identify developing a strategy and describing the variance in the variables as particular tasks, Rosenberg and Yates – in the longest of the lists – advocate the use of matrices in analysis, Pan and Tan draw attention to negotiating access, constructing a theoretical lens and coding, and Thomas and Myers note the important role played by intuition.

Macpherson, Brooker and Ainsworth (2000) present a rather different summary from any of the others included in Box 8.1. They use the notions of purpose, place, process and product to develop some principles of practice for case study research: contextuality, sensitivity, authenticity, applicability, growth and communicability. What they are offering is guidance not so much on how to do a case study, but how to behave while you are doing it.

Each of these summaries of guidance on doing a case study, or some combination of them, would be a useful *aide-mémoire* to have at hand as a reminder while you were doing the case study. They would certainly be helpful in drawing up a schedule for your case study research, the subject of the next sub-section. You should, though, bear one thing clearly in mind. These are guidelines, ideals; they are not what usually happens in practice.

Scheduling Your Research Project

It is normal, and will almost certainly be required if you are doing case study research for academic credit, to draw up a draft schedule, plan or timetable for your research at an early stage. This will probably make use of many of the terms or labels used in Box 8.1 and throughout this chapter and the following one, arranged on one side of a table or chart, with the weeks or months you have to complete the research strung out along the other side. Such scheduling can be very helpful, both in working out what might be feasible at the start, and in checking on your progress, and perhaps doing a little re-scheduling, at regular intervals along the way.

Remember, however, that your actual experience of the research project – as it is set out in your schedule or written up at the end – is seldom as clear-cut and sequential as that. You may find yourself doing a number of tasks at the same time, jumping from one to the other, or going back and forth, as needs or feasibility dictate. You may even feel lost and confused, unclear about what to do next. Don't worry: this is normal. Almost any worthwhile research project involves compromises or changes in plan.

Doing research can be a messy and slippery business, and neither the guidance given in books such as this, nor the articles and reports which result from the writing up of the research, are an accurate or completely honest account of the process and experience. How could they be? The former are attempts to give guidance to thousands of researchers tackling varied topics in widely differing situations, while the later are brief accounts written to a fairly strict template. So view both the textbooks and the articles with a degree of critique and scepticism.

RESEARCH QUESTIONS

Interestingly, only three of the seven sets of authors included in Box 8.1 – Stuart et al, Stake, and George and Bennett (although they call it the research objective; others, particularly scientists and quantitative researchers, use the term hypothesis) – draw specific attention to the importance of your research question or questions to the process of undertaking research. Yet many researchers, whether focusing on case study, some other research design or more generally, would argue that your research question or questions are the key starting point, and should drive all your other research decisions:

> A question is the starting point for your research. Begin with a question, not a presupposition that you are going to do a case study. A case study should follow logically from your question or else you should not do one. (Thomas 2011a, p. 30)

It would be unusual to conduct research without any idea of what you were researching and why, though it is not unknown for both novice and experienced researchers to do so (and there might be good reasons for this: you might initially be searching around for something to research, or unsure of what questions you might ask). Most researchers, however, will have at least a general idea of what they are interested in and what they would like to find out. Even so, having only a general idea gives you quite a lot of scope for wasted time and effort, prevarication and going up blind alleys. Hence the importance of being as specific as possible about what you want to research as early as you can in your research project.

Research questions should ideally be short and specific, and should be clearly answerable. It is sensible, particularly in small-scale research, to keep your research questions down to a minimal number. Examples taken from reported research projects are listed in Box 8.2. Note that, in each of the examples illustrated, only two or three questions are identified, although in some of these, there are clearly sub-questions as well. Some of the questions are rather long-winded, while others might have been phrased more clearly, but each example gives a reasonably clear idea of what the researchers are seeking to find out.

▪ ▪ ▪ Box 8.2   Examples of Research Questions
from Case Studies ▪ ▪ ▪

1   To identify the range of methods used in barrier analyses and the range of methods used to adjust improvement interventions to the information provided by barrier analyses.
2   To compare purely educational improvement interventions to interventions involving a combination of educational and organizational improvement interventions with respect to these methods. (Bosch et al 2007, p. 162)

1   How may an extended role of informants contribute to enhance interpretivist case study research in IS [information systems]?
2   What are the conditions where this type of approach is appropriate? (Bygstad and Munkvold 2011, p. 33)

1   What is the usability, use, functionality, and impact of the SCR [summary case record], and what explains variation in its adoption and use?
2   How have the fortunes of the SCR programme been shaped and constrained by influences at the macro, meso, and micro level?
3   What are the transferable lessons for practice and policy? (Greenhalgh et al 2010, p. 2)

1   What are the formally defined domains of the internationalization process in the HEO [higher education organization]?
2   Why and how the formally defined domains are changed over time?
3   Why and how novel domains are added to the internationalization process over time? (Kondakci and Van den Broeck 2009, p. 444)

1   What are the different types of risks or potential risks in a retail supply chain?
2   What are the mitigation strategies required to manage these risks? And which of these are generic and which are specific to a particular type of risk? (Oke and Gopalakrishnan 2009, p. 168)

Your research questions, like your research schedule, are something you should aim to draft early on in your project, and then return to regularly. Looking at them, and reviewing both them and your progress towards answering them, should be a useful exercise. Always bear in mind, however, that research questions are not immutable or unchanging.

You may find that, as your research progresses, you have successfully addressed some of your research questions but not others, or you may feel that you have answered slightly different questions from those you set out initially. Do not worry: this is normal. It is quite acceptable to revise your research questions so that they better reflect what you have actually done and achieved. Indeed, not to do so would be foolish and potentially misleading. Depending on the intended audience for your research, and the kind of research report you are writing, you might want to acknowledge that you have revised your original research questions, and briefly explain why.

It would also be unrealistic to expect to have produced the definitive or final answer to any meaningful research question, so do not be overly concerned if you have not achieved all you set out to do. One of the key outputs of any research project is usually an identification of directions for future research, perhaps to be taken up later by you, or perhaps by another researcher following in your footsteps.

SAMPLING AND SELECTION ISSUES

Sampling and selection are fundamental processes in almost any research project, whether qualitative or quantitative; that is, unless you plan to study every example of the particular population (e.g. primary schools, car manufacturing plants, nations) of interest to you. In practice, many employing case study designs ignore or underplay these issues, sometimes going so far as to argue that they only apply when one is using a statistical or multivariate research design, but serious researchers should not do so.

Sampling and selection are important even if you are doing a single case study and have already identified the case you intend to study. Thus, many small-scale researchers select their own case – e.g. the primary school or car manufacturing plant they work in, the nation of which they are a member – or have it selected for them by their funder or employer. Even in such cases, however, you should carefully consider other options, if possible, and be aware of both the consequences of engaging in 'insider' research and the comparative characteristics of your case (i.e. its typicality or unusualness). You should then be able to justify and explain your choice.

Uprichard (2013) argues that there are three basic assumptions underlying sampling of cases:

> [T]he necessary presuppositions underpinning any sampling design might be said to rest on the following three-pronged configuration: (a) the ontology of the case(s); (b) the epistemological assumptions underpinning what properties are necessary to know the case(s) and (c) the logistics involved in… the processes of 'casing' the case(s). These three components interact recursively with one another throughout the research and are only determined in the context of the field. (p. 2)

She points out that the weight given to these three assumptions differs between probability (typically applied in quantitative research) and non-probability (typical for qualitative, and much case study, research) sampling. This also means, particularly for the latter, that the adequacy of the sample can only be assessed as the research is underway:

> [W]hile it is understandable that one might want a neat list of criteria that can be used to assess the validity of a sample, the reality is the criteria used to assess the validity of a sample are themselves dependent on the interplay between which cases are selected, what it means to know them and why it is deemed important to know about those particular ones. (p. 7)

Taking a more pragmatic view, Thomas (2011a) identified three main reasons for choosing a particular case to study:

> You may choose it because you know a great deal about the case in question and you want to understand some feature of that subject. This is your object. Alternatively, you may choose it because it provides a particularly good example of something. The other option is that the case may reveal something interesting because it is different from the norm. (pp. 95–96)

The first of these reasons applies when you choose, or are directed, to study your own institution. Often, of course, the motivation of familiarity is accompanied by a desire to improve some aspect of the institution's operation: its performance, efficiency or output. By studying the case in detail, you expect or hope to better understand its operation and be able to make practical recommendations for the improvement of this.

Thomas's other two options might be described as more 'researcherly'. Here, your choice is determined more by whether your findings might be of wider interest, either because the case studied is more typical or because it is unusual.

Meyer (2001) argues that sampling strategies in case study research, which she wrongly considers as being wholly qualitative in approach, are necessarily different from those in quantitative research:

> The logic of sampling cases is fundamentally different from statistical sampling. The logic in case studies involves theoretical sampling, in which the goal is to choose cases that are likely to replicate or extend the emergent theory or to fill theoretical categories and provide examples for polar types. Hence, whereas quantitative sampling concerns itself with representativeness, qualitative sampling seeks information richness and selects the cases purposefully rather than randomly. (p. 333)

This is akin to taking the second or third of the options outlined by Thomas (2011a).

Mahoney and Goertz (2004), in the context of political science, offer guidance on the selection of what they call negative cases, that is, examples of cases where the outcome of interest (e.g. improved student performance, company merger, national revolution) did not occur. This may be particularly helpful in shedding light on those cases where this outcome did occur. They structure case selection in terms of what they call the possibility principle and its associated rules of inclusion and exclusion:

> Possibility Principle: Choose as negative cases those where the outcome of interest is possible...

> Rule of Inclusion: Cases are relevant if their value on at least one independent variable is positively related to the outcome of interest...

> Rule of Exclusion: Cases are irrelevant if their value on any eliminatory independent variable predicts the non-occurrence of the outcome of interest. This rule takes precedent over the Rule of Inclusion. (pp. 657–658)

Another way of looking at this is in terms of the sort of case study or case study design you are planning (see also the discussion of different Types of Case Study in Chapter 2). Seawright and Gerring (2008), for example, discuss how to select cases for the following sorts of case study design: typical case, diverse cases, extreme case, deviant case, influential case, most similar/most different cases. Deviant case analysis, 'the study of particular cases which are anomalous with respect to a given hypothesis' (Molnar 1967, p. 1), has a long history.

The Role of Access

A key issue in sampling and selection is having or gaining access to the people, institutions, documents or whatever it is that you want or need to study to understand the case. Clearly, gaining only limited access, or being refused access at the beginning of (or, probably rather worse, part way through) your study, will not be conducive to successfully answering your research question(s) (for a cautionary warning, see Canen 1999; this article is discussed in Chapter 5 in the section on Education).

This also helps to explain why so many small-scale researchers opt to research within their own institution or setting, because access (often erroneously) seems to be assured. Yet, once again, it should be stressed that this is not the only factor of importance:

> You need sufficient access to the potential data, whether to interview people, review documents or records, or make observations in the 'field'. Given such access to more than a single candidate case, you should choose the case(s) that will most likely illuminate your research questions. (Yin 2009, p. 26)

Selecting cases for study solely on the basis of convenience and ease of access may severely limit the usefulness of the case study or studies you carry out. The greater effort, and possible delays, involved in going beyond the familiar may, in contrast, yield significant insights and benefits in the longer run:

> In reading numerous comparative accounts that use case studies or ethnographies of schools and classrooms, it is evident that insufficient concern is often given to the choice of research sites. Far too often it seems that researchers settle for research sites to which they can easily gain convenient and ready access rather than thinking through the implications of particular choices. The result is that there are too many comparative case studies where the choice of both the countries involved and the more micro-sites and case studies do not appear to be closely related to any theoretical objectives of the study. It is recognised that when selecting sites, researchers have to consider the time, financial and personal costs involved in conducting fieldwork in what might be distant and inconvenient locations. Additionally, and obviously, ethnographic and case study research can only proceed where access has been achieved, and this is not always straightforward. But, however difficult access may be, it is crucial that obtaining access is not seen as the primary consideration in selecting an appropriate site. (Walford 2001, p. 151)

Selecting the right case or cases for study may involve you in quite a bit of preliminary work, negotiation and extra effort, but it should be worth it when you finish.

One other issue in gaining access, which researchers sometimes overlook until it is too late and access is being denied, is their own characteristics. Your age, gender, class, ethnicity, physical condition and appearance may all impact on your gaining access, affecting whether those you are planning to research feel comfortable with your presence. Language and culture may also present barriers, even if you are researching within your own country. So be aware of the effect you may have on others, and be ready to be flexible.

Other Issues in Sampling and Selection

As in the case of overall guidance, on research or on the case study design in particular, there are also authors who have set out the issues that should be addressed by the researcher in deciding upon sampling and selection.

In a classic and much referenced text on qualitative data analysis, Miles and Huberman (1994) set out six general criteria for sampling practice in qualitative research:

1. The sampling strategy should be relevant to the conceptual framework and the research questions addressed by the research.
2. The sample should be likely to generate rich information on the type of phenomena which need to be studied.
3. The sample should enhance the 'generalizability' of the findings.
4. The sample should produce believable descriptions/explanations.
5. Is the sample strategy ethical?
6. Is the sampling plan feasible? (p. 34)

These criteria appear so generic that they could be applied well beyond qualitative research as well, so have relevance for all kinds of case study designs.

Curtis et al (2000; this study is discussed further in Chapter 5 in the section on Geography and Environmental Studies) apply these criteria to three case studies of their own concerning the geography of health. They come to the conclusion that 'The six criteria proposed by Miles and Huberman (1994) do appear relevant for the development of a sampling strategy in the examples of research in geography of health considered here' (p. 1013).

Poulis, Poulis and Plakoyiannaki (2012) take a slightly different stance, in stressing the role of context in case study selection:

First, researchers need to consider what the population is and which cases within this population are more suitable for exploring a study's research questions. This concern becomes especially important in cross-cultural settings, where researchers typically face limitations in selecting cases from a largely unknown population or may lack the skills or knowledge for carefully reading and understanding country data and local idiosyncrasies... Second, researchers need to consider why some cases are chosen while others, despite their potential criticality for the issue under investigation, may not be considered... neglecting conceptually significant cases can result in the emergence of problems in theorising and interpretation across contexts... Third, it is worthwhile stating that a universally accepted sampling frame that can safeguard the case selection process is neither feasible nor desirable. (p. 312)

In other words, while the ideal selection strategy may be unrealisable (and perhaps unknowable), the researcher should always be aware of, and be prepared to justify, the factors they took into account in making their selection, and what the limitations on that were.

From the perspective of a political scientist undertaking cross-national research, Anckar (2007; see also Most and Starr 1982) considers problems typically encountered in sampling and how they might be overcome. He notes that:

Very few focused comparative studies in political science employ several parallel sets of nations. Rather, the testing of different questions through the use of the one and same set of nations appears a rule. (pp. 58–59)

An oversimplified selection method of this sort undermines the comparable cases strategy.

If you are carrying out a multiple case study, examining two or more cases in a comparative fashion, there are a range of factors to bear in mind in sampling and selection (see also the section later in this chapter on Single and Multiple Case Studies). Thus, Small (2009) recommends two strategies for ethnographic researchers concerned to address wider audiences: Mitchell's extended case method (which involves studying the chosen case longitudinally over an extended period of time; see also the discussion of Time Series Designs in Chapter 6) and sequential interviewing (i.e. studying further selected cases until no new interpretation emerges, or until 'saturation' has been achieved).

Arnold (1970) outlines what he terms dimensional sampling, 'an approach for studying a small number of cases':

Briefly, the approach is a three-step one: (1) explicitly delineate the universe to which you eventually wish to generalize; (2) spell out what appear to be the most important dimensions along which the members of this universe vary and develop a typology that includes the various combinations of values on these dimensions; (3) use this typology as a sampling frame for selecting a small number of cases from the universe, typically drawing one case from each cell of the typology. (p. 147)

This approach does, of course, require some knowledge of the population or universe of cases from which you are selecting a small number for study.

Where this knowledge is lacking, McClintock (1985) recommends the use of what he calls the case cluster method:

The case cluster method is used when it is impractical to develop a complete list of processes from which to sample. The sample is drawn by firstly selecting naturally occurring 'clusters' in which the processes are expected to reside, enumerating them, and then defining and selecting the final units of analysis (i.e. the processes of interest). There may be several levels of stratification of process clusters before the final definition and selection stage. (p. 207)

In his view, 'The case cluster method offers a way to structure case study research so that data collection, analysis and reporting can be accommodated in a more focused manner' (p. 220).

Selection Bias

Another way of looking at sampling and selection issues is in terms of selection bias:

[C]hoosing cases for study on the basis of their scores on the dependent variable may bias the conclusion one reaches. Apparent causes that all the selected cases have in common may turn out to be just as common among cases in which the effect they were supposed to have caused has not occurred. Relationships that seem to exist between causes and effects in a small sample selected on the dependent variable may disappear or be reversed in a sample uncorrelated with position on the dependent variable. Arguments that seem plausible if a historical study or time-series ends at a particular date may seem ludicrous if the years included in the study are changed. (Geddes 1990, pp. 148–149)

Selection bias is also involved in what has been called the 'too few cases/too many variables' problem in studying the implementation of political decisions (Goggin 1986). Three proposed solutions to this problem are to reduce the number of variables, increase the number of cases, or select cases on the basis of similarity and comparability. These solutions still have their problems, however, leading Goggin to argue:

[Y]et as long as the number of cases remains relatively small, this type of comparative study will possess neither the randomization and multivariate analysis used in statistical correlation studies nor random selection and assignment and the use of control groups of experiments. Hence, there is still no assurance that an investigator can assess the unique effects of different independent variables, control for extraneous variables in a multivariate analysis, and generalize from the particular finding. (p. 334)

He therefore suggests two further strategies: combining small and large n studies, and conducting experiments and quasi-experiments. All of these comments, of course, serve to illustrate the potential weaknesses of the case study approach.

ETHICAL CONCERNS

Closely bound up with issues of access are those of ethics. Researchers – even small-scale researchers – particularly those doing research for academic credit or in an academic context, are expected to address these carefully before starting data collection, and then bear them in mind throughout their research. They may need to do so even after the research project has 'finished', for example, in ensuring that the data they have collected continues to be protected or is destroyed.

In recent decades, the medical model of oversight has been extended to cover all forms of research, even those in the humanities and social sciences where ethical risks are comparatively small. In the fields of medicine and health care, ethics are obviously a key concern for researchers, as the well-being of the patient or client is of paramount importance (see, for example, McLeod 2010, especially Chapter 4). While they are clearly not so pressing in other disciplines, they remain important and need to be explicitly addressed.

In an academic or institutional context, ethical approval may now have to be sought from two or more bodies, with a good deal of paperwork completed to an approved standard before consent is given. This may add significantly to the preparatory time needed before a project can get underway, so should be budgeted into your proposed research schedule (see the earlier section on Scheduling Your Research Project).

May (2001) offers a useful definition of what is meant by ethics in a research context:

> Ethics is concerned with the attempt to formulate codes and principles of moral behaviour... Ethical decisions are not being defined in terms of what is advantageous to the researcher or the project on which they are working. They are concerned with what is right or just, in the interests of not only the project, its sponsors or workers, but also others who are the participants in the research. (p. 59)

There are, of course, many issues that might be addressed in an ethical code or set of guidelines. Box 8.3 summarises the issues identified in four texts. It can readily be seen that these vary a good deal in terms of detail and the number and extent of the issues covered. Many national research associations or learned societies – e.g. in the UK, the British Educational Research Association, the British Sociological Association and the British Psychological Society, to name just three – also provide lists of guidelines, and these can be accessed online through their websites. If you are a student in one of these disciplines, or others that produce similar guidelines, you will most probably be expected to follow their guidelines scrupulously.

■ ■ ■ **Box 8.3   Alternative Formulations of Ethical Principles and Frameworks** ■ ■ ■

1   Bryman (2004, p. 509)

harm to participants; lack of informed consent; invasion of privacy; deception

2   Burns (2000, pp. 18–22)

voluntary and involuntary participation; informed consent; deception; role-playing; debriefing; privacy and confidentiality; the right to discontinue; experimenter obligations; publication of findings; stress; intervention studies

3   Kent (2000, pp. 63–65)

autonomy; beneficence; non-maleficence; justice; veracity; privacy; confidentiality; fidelity

4   Cohen, Manion and Morrison (2007, p. 51)

informed consent; gaining access to and acceptance in the research setting; the nature of ethics in social research generally; sources of tension in the ethical debate, including non-malefi-cence, beneficence and human dignity, absolutist and relativist ethics; problems and dilemmas confronting the researcher, including matters of privacy, anonymity, confidentiality, betrayal and deception; ethical problems endemic in particular research methods; ethics and evaluative research; regulatory ethical frameworks, guidelines and codes of practice for research; personal codes of practice; sponsored research; responsibilities to the research community

In essence, all of these codes, guidelines and checklists boil down to four main ethical principles:

1.   That any persons involved in a research project give their consent to be involved and know what they are consenting to (the principle of informed consent).
2.   That persons involved in a research project will suffer no harm or disadvantage from being involved (the principle of safety; note that this applies to the researcher as well).
3.   That persons involved in a research project have the right to discontinue or with-draw from the project at any time (the principle of withdrawal).
4.   That persons involved in a research project have the right of confidentiality, such that their contribution and identity will not be identifiable (the principle of confidentiality) – unless, of course, they want to be identified.

If your case study involves collecting data from other people, therefore, you will need to carry it out in a way that ensures that they give their informed consent, are kept safe and have the right to withdraw at any time, and that their contribution remains confidential.

However, while these are reasonable principles, their practice can be much more problematic. It can be difficult to predict how, for example, an interview may impact upon the interviewee. You may ask what seems to you to be an innocuous question which triggers a disturbing memory or response.

If you are carrying out your case study in your own organisation, where you are well known to your participants (and perhaps have some managerial or collegial relationship to them), it may be difficult for them to deny consent or withdraw. If you later write up and publish the results of your case study, it may be tricky to hide the identity of the organisation(s) studied, particularly as, since so much small-scale research is done within one's own organisation, readers may assume it is your own even if you attempt to anonymise it.

These practical problems do not, however, diminish the importance of paying close attention to ethical issues in planning and undertaking your research. At a minimum, you need to be aware of the issues and demonstrate that awareness through the care that you take:

> [T]he main ethical issues and debates... are not readily capable of resolution. This is why the ethical debate has scarcely moved on since the 1960s. What *is* crucial is to be aware of the ethical principles involved and of the nature of the concerns about ethics in social research. It is only if researchers are aware of the issues involved that they can make informed decisions about the implications of certain choices. (Bryman 2004, p. 507)

THE CASE STUDY IN CONTEXT: BOUNDARY, ENVIRONMENT AND UNIT OF ANALYSIS

> [M]aking something into a case or 'casing' it can bring operational closure to some problematic relationship between ideas and evidence, between theory and data. Casing, viewed as a methodological step, can occur at any phase of the research process, but occurs especially at the beginning of a project and at the end. (Ragin 1992b, p. 218)

Given the importance that case study researchers accord to bounding the case, and understanding its place and role within the surrounding environment, it is surprising how little explicit attention is given to these issues in discussions of case study design and process (but see Carter and Sealey 2009; Ragin 1992b, 1997). However, reports of case study research occasionally note the problems this can pose. For example, Wells et al (1995), in a study of detracking reforms in American schools (tracking is where pupils are grouped by ability), state that:

> in our search for a balance between researching a specific and well-defined 'case' and researching its context, we came to understand that they are one and the same. We also learned that these contextualized cases cannot be predetermined

as a set of categories of people who need to be interviewed; rather, we must co-construct each case, guided by our theoretical framework and our own personal subjectivities, with the help of our initial respondents in the schools. In this way, we built outward from each school site, identifying those people in the community who had the most influence on or the most distinct insight into the detracking phenomenon that is our unit of analysis. This meant that in the end, each of our 10 cases was a different shape and size and contained different categories of people; these cross-case differences were in some ways our most interpretive and significant findings about the normative, technical, and political struggles inherent in detracking reform. (p. 24)

Similarly, in the context of medicine, Griffiths (2009) notes that:

There is no clear, consistent boundary to the case in medicine both in space and time. Case-ness can fluctuate very rapidly or be very stable in time. It is difficult to know where to draw the boundary of a case in medicine, even though medicine tends to focus on individual people, as the nature of each person and their health is at least in part formed through their relationships with their social and physical environment. (p. 451)

The limited attention paid to bounding the case in the research methods literature may be at least partly because, as with so much about case study, the notion of bounding the case is simply specialist terminology for what is a much more generic process in research. All researchers, after all, have to place limits on their research projects, because they literally cannot research everything. This is particularly so in small-scale research, where limiting or focusing the research is of key importance if it is to be manageable and deliverable within time and resource constraints. The same considerations are involved in bounding the case.

This is readily apparent in the advice given by Baxter and Jack (2008, pp. 546–547): 'Suggestions on how to bind a case include: (a) by time and place; (b) time and activity; and (c) by definition and context. Binding the case will ensure that your study remains reasonable in scope.' To take the first two of Baxter and Jack's suggestions, you might bind, bound – or define – your case in terms of when and where it occurred (e.g. the Olympic Games 2012, Boston 1945–1953, Penns Lane in the summer of 2014), and what was of interest (e.g. tactics in the men's marathon race at the Olympic Games 2012, the growth of shipping in Boston 1945–1953, the impact of the tornados in Penns Lane in the summer of 2014).

Baxter and Jack's third suggestion, by definition and context, sounds very like case and environment; in other words, you need to carefully define what the case is and the environment it exists in. To further develop the three example cases used in the previous paragraph, this might involve:

- definition: the men's marathon race at the Olympic Games 2012; context: other Olympic marathon's races, the Olympic Games 2012
- definition: shipping entering and leaving the main port of Boston, USA, between the years 1945 and 1953; context: the history of Boston shipping, the history of Boston and its role as a port
- definition: Penns Lane, Sutton Coldfield, West Midlands, UK, June to August 2014, tornado events; context: changing weather patterns in the West Midlands, the history of tornados in the West Midlands

It is clear from this just how important it can be to bound or define the case(s) you are interested in as precisely as possible, while always bearing in mind that, if you had bound or defined them somewhat differently, your findings might be significantly different.

Bounding or binding the case is not necessarily a straightforward process. Arriving at an initial boundary may seem simple, but collecting data may show this to be inadequate, and the boundary may change over time as the research progresses, until a more acceptable and workable definition is settled upon. Wilson and Gudmunsdottir's research (1987; this is discussed further in the section on Education in Chapter 5) provides a good example of this process.

Closely associated with the notion of binding or defining the case is the issue of the unit of analysis. Again, this is a general concern in research, not just in case study. The unit of analysis 'refers to what is studied, which could be an individual, family, community, organisation, a state or even a nation' (Gangeness and Yurkovich 2006, p. 11). Or as Yin (2009) expresses it:

> As a general guide, your tentative definition of the unit of analysis (which is the same as the definition of the 'case') is related to the way you have defined your initial research questions... Selection of the appropriate unit of analysis will start to occur when you accurately specify your primary research questions. If your questions do not lead to the favouring of one unit of analysis over another, your questions are probably either too vague or too numerous – and you may have trouble doing a case study. (p. 30)

This rather simple equation of the unit of analysis with the case is challenged by Grunbaum (2007):

> The conceptual separation of the case from the unit of analysis has not been given much attention so far... It is in this paper argued that the case can be divided into layers that surround the unit of analysis or the 'heart' of the case. A unit of analysis must in any study always be identified as this process will intensify the purpose of the study. The unit of analysis will be on a lower abstraction level than the case layers, and will constitute specific information about the unknown that the research wants to enlighten. It thus becomes imperative to understand how a unit of analysis can be understood and how it can be identified in a given study. (p. 88)

In other words, the unit of analysis is the reason why you choose to study a particular case or cases; it is what you are focusing on trying to understand within the case. To pursue the three examples given above a little further, the units of analysis in these cases are marathon running tactics, shipping growth and tornado impacts.

It would be fair to say, of course, that many small-scale researchers work the other way around from that suggested by Yin. That is, they start with the case or unit of analysis that they wish to study – often, as we have argued, their own organisation or a part/aspect of it – and then specify their research questions. There is a third alternative approach, in which research questions and the case(s) to be studied emerge virtually simultaneously. All of these approaches are feasible; the key is to be as clear as possible about the case(s) and unit(s) of analysis to be studied, the research questions to be addressed, and thus the purpose of the research project.

CASE STUDIES AND THEORY

Thomas and Myers (2015) offer a clear perspective on the position of theory in case study research:

> [A] case study must comprise two elements:
>
> 1. a 'practical, historical unity', which we shall call the *subject* of the case study; and
> 2. an analytical or theoretical frame, which we shall call the *object* of the study. (p. 55)

Other researchers would, of course, be a little less dogmatic, and perhaps rather more flexible. However, as with any research design, the relationship between case study and theory is important. Research – especially academic research – is usually expected to take place within a theoretical framework, and is seen as being, at least in part, about developing and/or testing theory.

Critics of case study would, though, argue that, because it is small-scale, case study is not suitable for either theory development or testing. The proponents of case study, on the other hand, contend that, precisely because it is so in–depth, case study is well suited to theory development, and that, when suitably expanded through multiple case studies (discussed further in the next section), case studies may also test theories.

More pragmatically orientated or driven researchers, and especially those under-taking research outside an academic context, might not see such a pressing need to develop and use a theoretical framework. They may be content with just doing the case study research, and seeking to find out whatever it is that is of interest to them.

What is Theory?

Of course, a lot depends on what we mean by 'theory', and the position is further complicated or confused when we take into account the range of terms – such as concept, framework, hypothesis, idea or model – often used as synonyms for theory. One explanation of the varied ideas on theory was put forward a few decades ago by Eckstein, a political scientist, though it has resonance throughout the social sciences and beyond:

> Two polar positions on what constitutes theory in our field can be identified…
> On one extreme (the 'hard' line on theory) is the view that theory consists solely
> of statements like those characteristic of contemporary theoretical physics… On
> the other pole (the 'soft' line), theory is simply regarded as any mental construct
> that orders phenomena or inquiry into them. (1975, p. 86)

In other words, are we dealing with a theory which is, or seeks to be, universally applicable (such as, for example, theories about relativity or gravity), or are we instead talking about a hypothesis or summary which seeks to explain a pattern of behaviour we have just observed, or are we perhaps somewhere in between these positions?

A more recent, and more finely nuanced, interpretation has been put forward by three educational researchers, Adams, Cochrane and Dunne (2012):

> Theory has a multitude of meanings, not all of which can be easily reconciled,
> making it a concept open to wide appropriation. For example, theory can simply
> mean an idea about a social configuration, or it can mean an intellectual formula
> that enables one to structure experience (or data, in terms of research); sometimes
> it is used broadly and is synonymous with philosophy, or it is used specifically as
> an interpretative description of experience. Theorizing can be an expansive busi-
> ness, in that it can be thought of as an act that generates new ways of thinking
> about the way the world is configured, and may be generalized and transferred
> to a multitude of new concepts in the expectation that it will throw light on
> them. (p. 1)

Others have expressed the same idea somewhat differently, referring, for example, to high-level, medium-level and low-level theories, or to grand and everyday (or common-sense) theory.

However, it would probably be accurate to say that the majority of the theories put forward in the social sciences are towards the soft end of the spectrum Eckstein alludes to. Or, in Adams, Cochrane and Dunne's terms, most 'theoretical' discussion is at the level of 'an idea about a social configuration' or 'an interpretative description of experi-ence'. There are examples, though, of case study research being discussed in relation to higher level theories, for example, actor network theory (Hansen 2011).

Hammersley (2012) argues, reasonably enough, that the relationship between case study and theory depends crucially on what type of theory you are talking about and/or what you mean by theory. Like Adams, Cochrane and Dunne, he produces a more comprehensive classification than Eckstein, identifying a number of interpretations of theory: theory in relation to practice; theory versus fact; theory as abstraction as against concrete particulars; theory as concerned with the macro, as against accounts of the local; theory by contrast with description; theory as explanatory language; theory as an approach or 'paradigm'. He also distinguishes between case studies which focus on explaining and those concerned with theorising. He concludes:

> Whether theory is important… and for what purpose, depends upon which sense of the term is being employed. Furthermore, all these varieties of theory involve serious methodological and philosophical issues… theory should not be treated as a sacred cow, but there are many important questions associated with the concept of theory that demand attention. (p. 402)

Thomas (2010) offers a further, and refreshing, perspective in suggesting that we should be seeking to link case study to phronesis – an ancient Greek term referring to practical wisdom – rather than theory:

> If case study is concerned with phronesis rather than theory – if it is de-coupled from the inductive frame of theoretical analysis – what are the consequences? We are left with a view of case study's validation coming no longer through reference to a body of theory or generalized knowledge. Its validation comes through the connections and insights it offers between another's experience and one's own. The essence comes in understandability emerging from phronesis – in other words, from the connection to one's own situation. (p. 579)

While perhaps a less demanding interpretation than high-level theory, this still sets standards for the practice of case study research.

Theory Building with Case Study

Eisenhardt (1989), in a much cited article (see Ravenswood 2011), offers a roadmap for building theories from case study research. The roadmap involves a series of steps: getting started, selecting cases, crafting instruments and protocols, entering the field, analysing within-case data, searching for cross-case patterns, shaping hypotheses, enfolding literature, reaching closure. This roadmap is very similar to the general guidance on doing case studies provided by other authors (see Box 8.1 and the Overview section in this chapter).

Placing the emphasis firmly on the role of case studies in building theory, however, Eisenhardt argues that:

> The process of building theory from case study research is a strikingly iterative one. While an investigator may focus on one part of the process at a time, the process itself involves constant iteration backward and forward between steps. (p. 546)

It is also clear from her presentation that, while theory building may begin from the analysis of a single case, to progress further additional case studies need to be undertaken or examined. Theory building and theory testing, the subject of the next sub-section, are clearly linked.

Dooley (2002) takes a more measured view, accepting some of the limitations for theory building that many view as innate to case study research, yet arguing that it is still possible, just difficult:

> From the perspective of case study research, theory building is an arduous process. Case study research generally does not lend itself well to generalization or prediction. The researcher who embarks on case study research is usually interested in a specific phenomenon and wishes to understand it completely, not by controlling variables but rather by observing all of the variables and their interacting relationships. From this single observation, the start of a theory may be formed, and this may provoke the researcher to study the same phenomenon within the boundaries of another case, and then another, and another (single cases studied independently), or between individual cases (cross-case analysis) as the theory begins to take shape. (p. 336)

Dooley then produces a classification of the possible relations between case study research and theory, allowing for the application of an existing theory to a case or cases, the testing of an existing theory using a case or cases, the development of a new theory or the further development of an existing theory:

> Case study research can logically fulfill four specific roles in meeting the... requirements of the general method of theory building in applied disciplines...
>
> Role 1. Case application of an already conceptualized and operationalized theory (single or multiple cases)...
>
> Role 2. Confirmation or disconfirmation of an already conceptualized and operationalized theory (single or multiple cases)...
>
> Role 3. Case application for the purpose of creating or advancing the conceptualization and operationalization of a theory (single or multiple cases)...
>
> Role 4. Continuous refinement and development of a fully developed theory (single or multiple cases). (pp. 349–351)

Note that, for each role, Dooley at least holds open the possibility that this might be achieved through a single case study, even if multiple case studies might be preferable.

Based on a qualitative content analysis of published articles using case study design in international business, Welch et al (2011) identified four methods of theorising from case studies:

- case study as inductive theory building (inducing new theory from empirical data)
- case study as natural experiment (using deductive logic to test propositions)
- case study as interpretive sense-making (seeking to understand the particular rather than the general)
- case study as contextualised explanation (understanding how an outcome was brought about in a particular case).

These methods vary in terms of their emphasis on contextualisation and causal explanation. Welch et al argue for more use of the fourth of these methods:

[W]e have proposed that the method of contextualised explanation, while rarely found in our dataset of published case studies, holds promise in that it offers a high degree of contextualisation without sacrificing the goal of causal explanation. We would argue that, above all, the value of this approach lies in its different view of how to generate theories about the social world: the rejection of the regularity model of causation, scepticism towards the possibility of meaningful law-like generalisations, and a defence of context as being an essential component of, rather than a hindrance to, explanation. As a result of redefining the theorising process in this way, proponents of contextualised explanation seek to explain 'without laws'. They offer a way of reconciling context and explanation by acknowledging the complexity of the social world, the bounded scope and contingency of causal relationships, and the simultaneous operation of multiple interaction effects. (pp. 757–758)

Hoon (2013), by contrast, argues for the use of meta-synthesis or meta-analysis – in essence carrying out or analysing multiple case studies (meta-analysis is discussed further in Chapter 7) – for building theory from qualitative case studies. She comes to three main conclusions:

First, a meta-synthesis of qualitative case studies is proposed to have major potential in synthesizing qualitative evidence on a particular topic to build theory… Second, building theory out of published case studies holds great potential especially if a reliable synthesis process is augmented through the application of the rigorous procedures described here… Third, the greatest challenge that a qualitative synthesis faces is viewed in the heterogeneity inherent in the primary studies' underlying paradigmatic perspectives, methods, and quality. (p. 543)

Christensen and Carlile (2009) take a different tack altogether, describing a process for theory building using case studies which they have applied in teaching, as opposed to researching, management. This involves just two stages – descriptive and prescriptive – in each of which theory building proceeds through three steps: observation, classification and defining relationships. By applying their method, management courses become 'theory-building enterprises'.

Box 8.4 summarises some published examples of theory development from case studies. It is clear that these tend towards the 'soft' rather than the 'hard' end of the spectrum of theoretical articulation, as it was outlined at the beginning of this section.

■ ■ ■   Box 8.4   Published Examples of Theory Building from Case Study Research   ■ ■ ■

1   Fletcher et al (2009) researched how schools might influence young people's drug use through semi-structured interviews with purposively sampled students. They came up with three related explanations (theories) for this relationship:

> Various pathways may plausibly underlie school effects on drug use. In some school environments, young people may initiate and/or increase their drug use: as an alternative source of bonding and identity once they are marginalized from mainstream markers of achievement, to ensure acceptance and safety, and/or as a form of stress relief and 'escape.' Identification of these pathways should enable 'whole-school' interventions aiming to reduce drug use to target the most critical factors. (p. 131)

2   Haunschild and Eikhof (2009) researched the German theatrical employment system, using semi-structured interviews and participant observation. They arrive at the following theorisation of what their data and analysis showed:

> [W]e again took up the perspective of the theory of employment systems and asked what role the identified lifestyle plays in regulating and shaping inter-organizationally shared work and employment practices. The above mentioned elements of the bohemian lifestyle allow (theatre) artists to perceive themselves as fully dedicated to *artistic* production processes, to accept the disadvantages of a work-dominated life and, most importantly, to disguise economic rationales and market forces and integrate artistic and management activities. The bohemian lifestyle therefore helps to maintain artistic work motivation, which is the key input of theatre as a creative industry. While it can be interpreted as an individual coping strategy in a specific situation of work and employment, it thus also fulfils an important function for organizations and the industry on the whole: It allows them to keep work arrangements temporary and flexible, to offer less extrinsic incentives and to benefit from devotion and creativity and thus makes creative production viable. (p. 118)

3   Hashim (2010) studied information system project implementation in local government in Malaysia, carrying out interviews in twelve organisations:

> [T]he analysis resulted in 175 issues or patterns that were systematically inventoried in the issue database. Based on the issue descriptions, these patterns were matched and clustered under common themes or categories...The cross-case analysis actually searches for issues involved in ICT [information and communication technology] implementation. Subsequently these brought about four emergent themes. Inherently, the theme that occurred most (through counting) provided the leverage for theory

building… The findings obtained from the rigorous analyses of the interview transcripts, resulted in the tabulation of the categories and sub-issues which were then transformed or morphed into a micro framework or model on ICT implementation. (pp. 303–304)

4 Tibben (2015) describes a qualitative project in which 'theory triangulation was used to systematically compare multiple cases to develop theory' (p. 628). The cases were derived from the work of a community technology centre programme in Australia, with development as the theoretical framework. Tibben concludes that:

> The rival theoretical perspectives of populist, enterprise and statist identify different actors as central to the development process – namely, the community, the private sector and the government. The method of theory triangulation uses each of these perspectives to make sense of each case study. In applying each perspective to common cases, the relative strengths and weaknesses of each theoretical perspective become clearer. As a consequence, there is a rational basis by which to propose new initiatives, policies and theories in order to capitalize on the observed strengths of these perspectives while seeking to reduce the impact of contradictions between the reality of observed cases and theory. (p. 649)

5 Zonzi et al (2014) report on a theory-building case study which examined the theory of the zone of proximal development (ZPD). The case of a woman in her 40s undergoing psychodynamic-interpersonal therapy is examined, with a focus on the psychotherapist seeking to engage the client in play. They conclude that:

> [S]eeing the therapeutic ZPD as a playing zone within which the client can move around in creative ways emphasizes the close relationship between the content accessible to the clients and the quality of the therapist interventions. When the zone is too narrow, there is no place to play, and therapeutic progress is slow and difficult. (p. 459)

Theory Testing with Case Study

As well as using case studies to build or develop theory, they may also be employed to test theory. Theory testing and theory building are, unsurprisingly, closely linked, and the methods discussed in the previous sub-section in connection with theory building also have relevance for theory testing. Theory testing also brings in the notion of causation, and whether we can infer from our study of a particular case or cases that one thing is causing another (Rohlfing 2012).

Yin (2009) links theory testing with the issue of generalisation, arguing that case studies may be used to perform what he terms 'analytic generalization':

> [T]he mode of generalization is *analytic* generalization, in which a previously developed theory is used as a template with which to compare the empirical results of the case study. If two or more cases are shown to support the same

theory, replication may be claimed. The empirical results may be considered yet more potent if two or more cases support the same theory but do not support an equally plausible, *rival* theory. (pp. 38–39, emphasis in original)

By building up more and more case studies – or instances – theory may, in this way, be tested and verified, or rejected and then modified.

Given the close linkage between theorising and multiple case study designs made by many authors, it seems highly appropriate to close this chapter by considering multiple case studies in more detail.

SINGLE AND MULTIPLE CASE STUDIES

For those committed to the case study approach to research – which, as we saw in Chapter 5, includes significant numbers of researchers in a wide range of disciplines – one of the key decisions concerns moving from single case studies to carrying out and/or analysing multiple case studies. The decision to undertake, or at least analyse, multiple case studies is bound up with a whole range of issues, including generalisation (discussed in Chapter 3) and theory development and testing (discussed in the previous section of this chapter), as well as with building up the credibility of case studies when compared to other, larger-scale, research designs. These issues are of long standing, and researchers have grappled with the demands of multiple case study designs for many years.

For example, over 40 years ago, Lijphart (1975) defined what he referred to as the comparative method, which he presented as an alternative to the statistical method:

[T]he method of testing hypothesized empirical relationships among variables on the basis of the same logic that guides the statistical method, but in which the cases are selected in such a way as to maximize the variance of the independent variables and to minimize the variance of the control variables. (p. 164)

In other words, by selecting similar sorts of cases for study, the researcher would be able to assess whether the same sorts of relationships between variables could be observed within them, and thus provide support, or otherwise, for their hypotheses or theories about how these relationships worked. This is sometimes referred to as cross-case or across-case analysis (e.g. Ayres, Kavanaugh and Knafl 2003), to distinguish it from within-case analysis, which is confined to a single case study.

More recently, Odell (2001) has argued that single case studies, multiple case studies (employing the comparative method) and statistical methods lie on a spectrum, with multiple case studies somewhere between the other two designs:

Between single case methods on one end of the spectrum and large-n statistical methods on the other stand comparative case methods. They add the analytical leverage that comes from comparison to the strengths of the case study. (p. 167)

George and Bennett (2005) develop the strategy for carrying out multiple case studies further, emphasising the importance of structured and focused comparison:

> The method and logic of structured, focused comparison is simple and straightforward. The method is 'structured' in that the researcher writes general questions that reflect the research objective and that these questions are asked of each case under study to guide and standardize data collection, thereby making systematic comparison and cumulation of the findings of the cases possible. The method is 'focused' in that it deals only with certain aspects of the... cases examined. The requirements for structure and focus apply equally to individual cases since they may later be joined by additional cases. (p. 67)

They also make the point that such studies are made easier when, assuming this is feasible, the work is all undertaken by a single researcher:

> In comparative case studies, structure and focus are easier to achieve if a single investigator not only plans the study, but also conducts all of the case studies. Structured, focused comparison is more difficult to carry out in collaborative research when each case study is undertaken by a different scholar. (p. 71)

If this is not feasible, however, and the scale or the nature of the research planned necessitates the involvement of a number of researchers, then the importance of training, piloting and calibrating the work done by the research group becomes critical. This will be even more so if the research group is international in scope, and/or has varied linguistic and cultural origins.

Gerring and McDermott (2007) seek to provide what they term an experimental template for comparative case study research, proposing four alternative designs: dynamic comparison (involving the use of both temporal and spatial variation), longitudinal (i.e. temporal) comparison, spatial comparison and counterfactual (imagined) comparison. They conclude that:

> this framework may offer a significant clarification of methodological difficulties commonly encountered in case study research. Thus, when constructing a research design we suggest that the following questions be highlighted. First, what sort of evidence may be enlisted to shed light upon the presumed covariation of X and Y? Is there (a) temporal and (b) spatial variation, just (a), just (b), or neither? Second, what ceteris paribus conditions are, or might be, violated in the analysis of this identified covariational pattern? (p. 698)

Larsson (1993) takes the discussion in a different direction, towards what are commonly termed meta-analysis or synthesis strategies (discussed further in Chapter 7). This also takes us away from what one researcher or a small team might be able to carry out themselves in terms of empirical data collection, focusing instead on the reanalysis of what a whole host of case study researchers may have achieved. Larsson refers to this approach as the case survey method:

The case survey is an inexpensive and potentially powerful method of identifying and statistically testing patterns across studies. It is particularly suitable when case studies dominate an area of research, when the unit of analysis is the organization, when a broad range of conditions is of interest, and when an experimental design is impossible or otherwise fails to capture situations relevant to managerial practice. The basic procedure of the case survey is (1) select a group of existing case studies relevant to the chosen research questions, (2) design a coding scheme for systematic conversion of the qualitative case descriptions into quantified variables, (3) use multiple raters to code the cases and measure their interrater reliability, and (4) statistically analyze the coded data. (pp. 1516–1517)

It is difficult to avoid the conclusion that, if the usefulness of case study research is to be fully realised, researchers need to be thinking beyond their own case study to comparable and cumulative case studies.

SUMMARY

In this chapter, we have:

- considered case study research in relation to sampling and selection issues
- discussed the issues involved with access and ethics
- examined the questions of bounding, or binding, the case study, and the unit of analysis
- reviewed the relationship between case study research and theory building and testing
- considered the advantages of moving on from single case study to multiple case studies.

KEY READINGS

Bryman, A (2004) *Social Research Methods* (2nd edition). Oxford, Oxford University Press.

Denzin, N, and Lincoln, Y (eds) (2005) *The Sage Handbook of Qualitative Research* (3rd edition). Thousand Oaks, CA, Sage.

George, A, and Bennett, A (2005) *Case Studies and Theory Development in the Social Sciences.* Cambridge, MA, MIT Press.

Hancock, D, and Algozzine, B (2011) *Doing Case Study Research: A practical guide for beginning researchers* (2nd edition). New York, Teachers College Press.

9

Method, Analysis and Report
in Case Study

INTRODUCTION

This chapter follows on from the previous one in offering practical advice on carrying out a case study. It starts by offering an overview of the issues involved.

The choice of methodology and method – and the relationship between these two constructs – is considered. This relates both to your overall perspective on knowledge creation and the practicalities of data collection. Will you be taking a quantitative or qualitative approach, or perhaps using mixed methods?

The processes involved in collecting and analysing your data are then examined. Will you be using software to help analyse your data, or doing it manually?

A final section focuses on reporting your findings, that is, writing up the case study. This may be for personal use, or for use within your organisation, or you may want to share your findings and interpretation with a wider academic audience.

OVERVIEW

So, you have decided on doing a case study, you have drafted your initial research questions (bear in mind that these may change as you proceed with your project), you have chosen the case or cases you intend to study and you have an idea of the theoretical framework you will adopt. If some or none of these are true please look at or go back to the previous chapter where they are all discussed in detail.

Having sketched out your overall research strategy in this way, you are now about to embark on the more practical side of the work involved in doing a case study. This is the most time-consuming aspect of research – actually doing it – so it helps if you have carefully thought through and planned what you intend to do in advance. This does not mean, of course, that research is simply a matter of rolling out your plans without further thought or adjustment. In any research project, particularly perhaps in the social sciences, realities intrude and things change. Even the best laid plans will need some adaptation, and it is possible that the focus of your project will change quite radically in the light of circumstances. In the end, you can only research what is practically possible.

The practical side of research, whether doing a case study or something else, typically involves a lot of routine and fairly repetitive work. Yes, there are, or should be, moments of insight and elation – when something has gone particularly well, when you discover something surprising, when you think you are beginning to understand what is going on – but a lot of your time will be spent on tasks that aren't that demanding (and which tend to become easier the more you do them).

Because research involves repetitive and 'administrative' work, you need to be persistent and thorough, and learn to keep good records. You also need to be wary that the work doesn't become too routine, and that you maintain high-quality work. For this reason, it is a good idea both to vary what you do (e.g. mix periods of data collection with periods of analysis or literature searching; in any event, this is often driven by the demands of the research) and to regularly reflect upon how it is going, and whether you need to change your practice.

The other point to stress about the practical side of doing a case study, a point which has already been made a number of times in this book, is that the practice is much like that of research generally. The research design may be different, but the methods used for collecting data – interviews, surveys, observation, documents – and analysing data – the whole suite of qualitative and quantitative techniques – and what you then do with your results, are common issues to all forms of research.

What this means is that, if you do not find the detailed advice that you want here, you do not need to confine yourself to looking at other books or articles that focus on case study. There is a vast literature on social research, and the particular specialist techniques, some of which will be referred to in this chapter, that may be applied within it. The key readings listed at the end of this chapter, therefore, deliberately include a number of generic social science research texts which do not focus solely on case study research.

METHODOLOGY AND METHODS

A key early decision in carrying out a case study, or any other piece of research (whether small-scale or large-scale), is the choice of a suitable methodology and an appropriate method or range of methods for collecting and then analysing the data. The purpose of this section is to guide you through these choices.

There are some who argue that the methodology and methods you employ are determined by your view of the world – and, in particular, your view of knowledge and how it is constructed – and your research questions. Cohen, Manion and Morrison (2011) usefully summarise this perspective:

> [O]ntological assumptions (assumptions about the nature of reality and the nature of things) give rise to epistemological assumptions (ways of researching and enquiring into the nature of reality and the nature of things); these, in turn, give rise to methodological considerations; and these, in turn, give rise to issues of instrumentation and data collection. (p. 3)

For example, if you are a positivist (we will discuss the meaning of this and other related terms later in this section), you will tend to take a scientific view of the world and utilise quantitative methods to allow you to measure items and/or test hypotheses. And if you are an interpretivist, you will take a constructivist view of the world and use qualitative methods, most notably semi-structured interviews, to build up a deep and rich picture of particular issues or experiences.

Box 9.1, from Crotty (1998, p. 4), offers a more developed view of these relations, linking epistemologies, theoretical perspectives, methodologies and methods. It shouldn't be read, however, as implying a direct linear link between the four columns, and it is only meant to be indicative: thus Crotty himself notes that 'It is not an exhaustive listing'! Note also that in this formulation – which is, of course, subject to debate – case study is listed as a method rather than a methodology or a research design (as argued in this book).

Others, including the present author, take a different view on the relations between methodology, methods, theory and epistemology. This view might be characterised as less deterministic, more flexible or pragmatic, arguing that it is possible, indeed desirable, to employ a range of methodologies and methods. From this perspective, it is difficult to conceive a research question that could not be addressed in a variety of ways, which might either reveal different things or confirm the findings arrived at using an alternative approach.

What are probably a much stronger influence on your choice of methodology and method, however, are your personal preferences. These will be bound up with your past experience of research and learning more generally, the expertise you may have developed in particular areas, as well as your perceived deficiencies in other areas. Some people, for example, are averse to, or anxious about, using statistics, and many prefer talking to their respondents, while others would do anything to avoid engaging directly with other people and prefer to carry out their research 'at a distance'. These mindsets obviously lend themselves to particular research approaches.

If you are undertaking your research in an academic and/or work context, the preferences of your colleagues, manager and supervisor will also have an impact upon

Box 9.1 Epistemologies, Theoretical Perspectives, Methodologies and Methods

Epistemology	Theoretical Perspective	Methodology	Methods
Objectivism	Positivism (and post-positivism)	Experimental research	Sampling
Constructionism		Survey research	Measurement and scaling
Subjectivism (and their variants)	Interpretivism	Ethnography	
	- Symbolic interactionism	Phenomenological research	Questionnaire
	- Phenomenology	Grounded theory	Observation
	- Hermeneutics	Heuristic inquiry	- participant
	Critical Inquiry	Action research	- non-participant
	Feminism	Discourse analysis	Interview
	Postmodernism	Feminist standpoint research	Focus group
	etc.		Case study
		etc.	Life history
			Narrative
			Visual ethnographic methods
			Statistical analysis
			Data reduction
			Theme identification
			Comparative analysis
			Cognitive mapping
			Interpretative methods
			Document analysis
			Content analysis
			Conversation analysis
			etc.

Source: Crotty 1998, p. 5.

your choices. Alternatively, however, it may be that you want to use your case study research to learn about and practise methodologies and methods (including, perhaps, the use of data analysis software) that you are less familiar with.

Whatever the position, it is sensible to consider and review your options regarding methodology and method before you get too far in and committed to your research project and approach.

Distinguishing between Methodology and Method

In practice, it has to be admitted that the terms 'methodology' and 'method' are frequently used in overlapping ways, which has led some, including the present author, to use the compound term method/ology to cover both interchangeably. But there are meaningful distinctions which may be drawn between the two terms. For example, Punch (1998, p. 3) defines methods as 'the techniques or procedures used to gather and analyse data related to some research question or hypothesis', and methodology as 'the strategy, plan of action, process or design lying behind the choice and use of particular methods and linking the choice and use of methods to the desired outcomes'. Cohen, Manion and Morrison (2007), to take a second example, put it slightly differently:

> By methods, we mean that range of approaches used... to gather data which are to be used as a basis for inference and interpretation, for explanation and prediction... If methods refer to techniques and procedures used in the process of data-gathering, the aim of methodology then is to describe approaches to, kinds and paradigms of research. (p. 47)

While these distinctions are helpful, they are perhaps not as clear-cut as they might be, as is suggested, for example, by Cohen, Manion and Morrison's use of the term 'approaches' in their definitions of both methodologies and methods.

Nevertheless, the distinction between the overall strategy employed (i.e. the methodology) and the specific techniques (i.e. the methods) used to pursue it is fairly clear, and that is the distinction that will be applied here. It makes sense, then, to consider each of these in turn, starting with methodology.

Alternative Methodological Approaches: Positivist and Interpretivist Strategies

If you read the research methodology literature to any extent, you will soon realise that there is a plethora of methodological approaches that have been developed and applied (see Box 9.1 for some examples). In practice, many of these overlap, sometimes with different terms being used to mean much the same thing, or they relate to very specific approaches to research employed by a relative handful of researchers.

Overall, therefore, I would suggest that there are two main underlying methodological approaches, for which I will use the terms positivist and interpretivist. Note that Crotty (1998 – see Box 9.1) calls these theoretical perspectives and identifies a number of others, such as post-positivism, phenomenology and critical inquiry. Farquhar (2012), to give another example, recognises critical realism as a third approach, alongside positivism and interpretivism. Since these other approaches are either less popular, closely related to or share the essential characteristics of positivism or intepretivism, I shall focus on these two main approaches.

While these two underlying approaches could be – indeed, often are – seen as competing, I wouldn't go so far as to call them oppositional or incompatible. They do relate to alternative ways of thinking about and understanding (i.e. researching) the world, but both may be applied by the same individual researcher, though perhaps for understanding different sorts of things.

This might be illustrated by two common-sense examples. Thus, when flying in an aeroplane, I am reassured to think that the pilots are operating in a positivist, or at least post-positivist, fashion: we presume that there are standard or 'best practice' ways of flying, using a wide range of instruments and communication devices, and that trained pilots will know and practise them. On the other hand, when listening to a political debate, I am quite prepared to accept that the alternative explanations and policies advocated by spokespersons from different parties may each make a certain amount of sense without imagining for one moment that any of them represent the 'whole truth' about the matter in question.

In research terms, therefore, one might adopt a positivist approach to uncover what would commonly be regarded as 'the facts' about a particular situation: for example, how much do individuals earn each year? How many and what kinds of cars do they own? And what is the relationship between these variables? Approaching the same subject from an interpretivist perspective, one might wish to inquire how people feel about their cars and what ownership of a particular car, or cars, means to them. Using both of these approaches should lead to a more rounded understanding of what was going on in terms of car ownership.

Positivism is closely associated with what is called the scientific method, and is based on the belief that we live within a reality which can be definitively known. Post-positivism tweaks this belief a little, in arguing that, while there is a reality, we may not be able to comprehensively and definitively understand it, perhaps because we cannot observe it all, and perhaps because our intellectual powers are insufficient.

The purpose of research – to a positivist or post-positivist – is, then, to add to our knowledge and understanding of reality, with discoveries building on each other in a more or less cumulative fashion for most of the time, but with the occasional huge leap forward in understanding (e.g. with Darwin's theories about evolution, or Einstein's about relativity). Classically, in the 'hard' or 'pure' sciences, research proceeds through observation, experiment and measurement, putting forward hypotheses and testing them, building up theoretical frameworks to explain things. Clearly, this is easier to do with non-human, and preferably inanimate, materials.

Positivist approaches are, however, widely used in studying humans and their societies. Large-scale surveys, typically but not wholly quantitative in nature, are extensively used to measure human attributes, opinions, experiences and perceptions, with the resulting data sets interrogated for patterns and relationships using a wide variety of multivariate statistical techniques.

The patterns identified through such studies may be correlational rather than causal: that is, we cannot infer directly from the numbers themselves why they are, or appear to be, related; we may need to adopt more interpretivistic approaches to understand this. Nevertheless, such studies – largely because of their size and the apparent exactitude conveyed by numbers – are highly influential, particularly with policy-makers and funders.

But such studies and their findings are scarcely 'objective' (I have placed the term 'objective' in quotation marks because it is often used loosely and inappropriately). Thus, for example, the decisions made on what to measure and how to measure it may be questioned; it may not be possible to directly measure what we wish to, so an alternative characteristic might be measured as a substitute; or the statistical techniques we use to analyse the data collected may not be entirely appropriate.

Positivist analyses are also far from providing complete explanations of the issues they study. The amount of variation explained by the models arrived at may not be great – indeed, it will typically be less than half of the total variance – suggesting that there is a lot more going on that we do not yet understand.

Interpretivism offers an alternative perspective on research to positivism, and has become increasingly popular among social scientists, particularly outside North America, in recent decades. While the underlying purpose of such research – increasing our knowledge and understanding – is much the same as it is with positivism, views on whether there is a single reality to be known, and whether we can know it, are more varied and qualified.

In understanding the human and social world, interpretivism recognises that things may look different to different individuals, and that a range of explanations and positions may be taken on understanding a given phenomenon. And, bearing in mind that most phenomena worth researching are complex and multifaceted, interpretivists have to accept that there may be no overriding explanation of a particular phenomenon that is convincing and acceptable to all parties concerned.

In interpretivist research, data collection and analysis are likely to be on a smaller scale, but will aim to go deeper and be more holistic. It will be mostly qualitative, and obtained through interviews and/or observations. Researcher and researched may be seen as co-creating data through their interaction, with the former checking and rechecking their understanding of what the latter is doing or saying.

It would be wrong, however, at least in my view, to dismiss this as a fundamentally subjective approach, although it is undeniably subjective, like all research. The researchers involved may have a fairly clear idea of what they are looking for, and will likely – as with positivist research – be building on a substantive existing body of knowledge on (and assumptions about) the topic in question.

Interpretivist researchers are likely, therefore, to engage much more closely with the objects of their research – participants or respondents – than positivist researchers. There will likely be far fewer of them, but more time will be spent with them in gathering, or creating, the research data. For some interpretivists, the research endeavour will be seen as shared between the researcher and the researched, with both interested in the outcomes of the research and their possible use in improving some aspect of their lives.

While these brief summaries of the nature of positivist and interpretivist perspectives, coupled with your previous experiences of research, may lead you to favour one or the other in undertaking a case study, I would stress that either or both (sequentially or in combination) are possible. This is not a clear, hard-and-fast dichotomy and many variations are available.

Choice of Methods: Qualitative, Quantitative or Mixed?

Having decided on your methodological approach, at least provisionally, you also need to consider the specific methods you propose to use in order to collect or create data for your case study.

Like positivist and interpretivist methodologies, quantitative and qualitative methods are often thought of as being fundamentally distinct, even opposed. The link is typically made between positivism and quantitative methods, on the one hand, and between interpretivism and qualitative methods, on the other. And, as we have seen in other chapters, but misguidedly in my view, particular authors sometimes confine case study designs to qualitative methods.

But these are, I would argue, overly simplistic ways of looking at the issues, and, in practice, the qualitative and the quantitative have a habit of eliding into each other. The key difference between the two can be simply stated:

> Quantitative research is empirical research where the data are in the form of numbers. Qualitative research is empirical research where the data are not in the form of numbers. (Punch 2005, p. 3)

Qualitative methods may focus, therefore, on everything or anything else but numbers (e.g. words, pictures, diagrams, etc.). It is, however, extremely difficult just to focus on numbers or not-numbers. So quantitative researchers will, of necessity, use many words in analysing and reporting on their work, while qualitative researchers will often discuss their findings in terms of the proportion of the sample to which they apply (e.g. 'most', 'the majority', 'about one-third', etc.), i.e. pseudo-quantitatively.

While it might be difficult to conceive of carrying out and reporting on a piece of research in a wholly qualitative or wholly quantitative fashion, therefore, we can also think of the relationship between the quantitative and the qualitative in a more positive light. Numbers, words and other forms of representation have alternative or complementary messages to convey to us, and we might well reach a fuller understanding by using them in combination: in other words, making use of mixed methods.

We will consider qualitative, quantitative and mixed methods in a little more detail in turn.

Qualitative Methods

We have already noted Punch's definition of qualitative research as being 'empirical research where the data are not in the form of numbers' (2005, p. 3). It is not, however, entirely satisfactory to define something in terms of what it isn't, rather than what it is. Advocates of qualitative research have therefore come up with much more positive statements or definitions, for example:

> Qualitative research is a situated activity that locates the observer in the world. It consists of a set of interpretive, material practices that make the world visible. These practices transform the world. They turn the world into a series of representations, including field notes, interviews, conversations, photographs, recordings, and memos to the self... qualitative researchers study things in their natural settings, attempting to make sense of, or inter-pret, phenomena in terms of the meanings people bring to them. (Denzin and Lincoln 2005b, p. 3)

Here, Denzin and Lincoln place the emphasis upon the researcher operating within the world, in the 'natural setting' that is of interest. In this definition, there is still a sense, though, of qualitative research being defined in terms of its distinction from quantitative research. It takes place in the world, in a natural setting, rather than in the laboratory using experimental (i.e. un-natural) methods.

Emphasis is also placed on interpretation and making meaning, and on the study of people (rather than objects or non-human life). The qualitative researcher observes, participates, questions, listens, records and interprets in order to make meaning of what is going on. A diverse range of objects and forms of data may be created and/or used in this process, with the focus on arriving at a more or less convincing overall interpreta-tion (rather than a formula).

Wellington (2015) offers a related definition of qualitative research, which both use-fully breaks it down and adds some more elements:

There are several important features of qualitative research:

1. It is usually an exploratory activity.
2. Data are usually collected in a real-life, natural setting and are therefore often rich, descriptive and extensive.
3. The human being or beings involved are the main research 'instrument'.
4. The design of a study emerges or evolves 'as you go along' – sometimes leading to a broadening or blurring of focus, at other times leading to a narrowing or sharp-ening focus.
5. The typical methods used are observation, focus groups, interviews, collection of documents and sometimes photography or video recording.

> These features of qualitative research lead to one major consequence: qualitative research produces large amounts of data! (p.259)

Here Wellington places the emphasis on the typically exploratory nature of qualitative research. You have an idea, an interest or a question, and you start exploring it. Though you will probably have some kind of plan, your exploration may lead you in unexpected directions, and the nature of your research (and of your research questions) may change significantly as you proceed.

Of course, qualitative research is not alone in producing large amounts of data, as Wellington also notes. This, to my mind, is more a function of how much data collection is undertaken and how much detail is sought. Quantitative research can also yield vast amounts of extremely detailed and rich data.

One aspect of qualitative research which these definitions do not really bring out is that, like quantitative research, it is what we might call a 'broad church', i.e. there are a huge variety of methods and techniques included under this banner. Denzin and Lincoln (2005b, p. 23), in the introduction to their magisterial *Handbook of Qualitative Research*, which comes in at over 1200 pages, identify a wide range of both research strategies and methods of collection and analysis (see Box 9.2).

■ ■ ■   **Box 9.2   Research Strategies and Methods of Data Collection and Analysis within Qualitative Research** ■ ■ ■

Research Strategies

- Design
- Case Study
- Ethnography, participant observation, performance ethnography
- Phenomenology, ethnomethodology
- Grounded theory
- Life history, *testimonio*
- Historical method
- Action and applied research
- Clinical research

Methods of Collection and Analysis

- Interviewing
- Observing
- Artifacts, documents and records
- Visual methods
- Autoethnography
- Data management methods
- Computer-assisted analysis
- Textual analysis
- Focus groups
- Applied ethnography

Denzin and Lincoln (2005b, p. 23)

But this is only an overview and summary, and these strategies and methods could be added to and broken down further. For example, from the perspective of case study, which Denzin and Lincoln identify as a research strategy (analogous to my designation of it as a research design), all of the other strategies identified, as well as all of the methods (and others besides), could be employed within a case study research design.

Another aspect of qualitative research that is worth stressing at this point, which again relates to its comparison with quantitative research and perceived lack of rigour in that context, is the way in which particular authors or schools of practice have attempted to draw up rules of guidance for practice. An example is given in Box 9.3. Here Mason (1996) offers a series of guidelines for what qualitative research should and should not be. While such guidance may undeniably be helpful, particularly for the novice researcher, it can also become rather dogmatic and unnecessarily constraining. All of Mason's guidelines could, after all, be critiqued and varied.

■ ■ ■   Box 9.3   What Should Qualitative Research Be?   ■ ■ ■

Qualitative research should be systematically and rigorously conducted...

Qualitative research should be strategically conducted, yet flexible and contextual...

Qualitative research should involve critical self-scrutiny by the researcher, or active reflexivity...

Qualitative research should produce social explanations to intellectual puzzles...

Qualitative research should produce social explanations which are generalizable in some way, or which have a wider resonance...

Qualitative research should not be seen as a unified body of philosophy and practice, whose methods can simply be combined unproblematically. Similarly, qualitative research should not be seen as necessarily in opposition to, and uncomplementary to, quantitative research. The distinction between quantitative and qualitative methods is not entirely clear cut...

Qualitative research should be conducted as an ethical practice, and with regard to its political context.

Mason (1996, pp. 5–6)

That this is so is evident when we consider how different research designs or strategies have developed over time, with alternative and competing schools of thought coming into existence. Chapter 3 of this book, in particular, has demonstrated how this has affected case study as a research design, but the same could be said for many others. For example, we may take another of the strategies identified by Denzin and Lincoln

(2005b), grounded theory, a strategy quite frequently applied within case study research (see also the discussion in Chapter 6).

Grounded theory was originally developed by Glaser and Strauss (1967), and in its initial formulation involved the researcher in exploring a given topic without any preconceptions, reviewing the data they had collected, coming to preliminary findings, and then collecting further data in order to check or modify them. However, Glaser and Strauss came to have differences of opinion over the best way to develop and practise grounded theory, with Glaser staying true to the original formulation and Strauss developing a less restrictive alternative with a new co-author (Strauss and Corbin 1990). This, in turn, has also now been superseded, as the original authors' careers have come to their natural close, and Charmaz (2006) now offers what is probably the most popular contemporary formulation.

Quantitative Methods

By comparison to qualitative research, quantitative research may seem more straightforward to define, but it would be just as limiting to think of it as being solely about numbers as it is to conceptualise qualitative research as being not about numbers. There is a broader, more encompassing set of ideas about the nature of research here as well.

Thus, Bryman (2004) identifies four key elements to quantitative research: measurement, causality, generalisation and replication:

> There are three main reasons for the preoccupation with measurement in quantitative research. Measurement allows us to delineate *fine differences* between people in terms of the characteristic in question… Measurement gives us a *consistent device* or yardstick for making such distinctions… Measurement provides the basis for *more precise estimates of the degree of relationship between concepts*… Quantitative researchers are rarely concerned merely to describe how things are, but are keen to say why things are the way they are… In quantitative research the researcher is usually concerned to be able to say that his or her findings can be generalized beyond the confines of the particular context in which the research was conducted… This concern reveals itself in social survey research in the attention that is often given to the question of how one can create a representative sample… the possibility of a lack of objectivity and of the intrusion of the researcher's values would appear to be much greater when examining the social world than when the natural scientist investigates the natural order. Consequently, it is often regarded as important that the researcher spells out clearly his or her procedures so that they can be replicated by others, even if the research does not end up being replicated. (pp. 66, 75–77, emphasis in original)

These key elements of measurement, causality, generalisation and replication may be seen to parallel those set out by some qualitative researchers. Thus, Mason

(1996; see Box 9.3) writes about the importance of being systematic and rigorous, and of seeking explanations which are 'generalizable in some way'. But, with the focus on quantities rather than qualities, issues of precision and representation also come more to the foreground.

When researchers are dealing with humans and their social worlds, however, these elements and issues take on a rather different hue, and it becomes much more difficult for the quantitative researcher to argue – though some still do – that they are proceeding 'objectively' in search of 'the facts'. Measurement of people's attitudes and perceptions, for example, is not so straightforward as measuring their height or weight. Quantitative researchers may develop instruments and scales for these purposes, but whether they are measuring the right thing is often debatable, and their interpretation by respondents will usually be varied.

Causality can also pose problems for the quantitative researcher, even if they are conducting carefully constructed experiments (which are much less common, partly for ethical reasons, in social research). Analyses of quantitative data may indicate correlations between particular variables, but ascertaining whether these are causal, occur because both variables under consideration are correlated with some other variable, or are misleading may take further (and perhaps qualitative) research.

Quantitative research, like qualitative research, is also a vast and contested terrain, and the researchers involved have a huge array of multivariate and statistical methods or techniques available, at least potentially, to them. Box 9.4 provides a list of some of these. The key point about this list is that quantitative methods are of varying complexity.

Simpler techniques, such as frequencies and proportions, averages and ranges, and cross-tabulating variables against each other to assess what kinds of relationships they might have with each other (e.g. do attitudes on, or perceptions of, a particular topic vary between men and women, or between people of different ages?), can be very revealing. These techniques may be adequate for addressing your research questions, and should be accessible and intelligible to anyone.

■ ■ ■ Box 9.4   Forms of Quantitative Analysis ■ ■ ■

Simpler Forms of Quantitative Analysis

- Frequencies
- Proportions and percentages
- Charts, diagrams and graphs
- Measures of central tendency (averages)
- Measures of dispersion (ranges)
- Cross-tabulations

(Continued)

(Continued)

More Complicated Forms of Quantitative Analysis

- Regression and correlation
- Analysis of variance
- Discriminant analysis
- Structural equation modelling
- Factor analysis
- Cluster analysis
- Inferential statistics

Many more complex multivariate and statistical techniques are available, however, for those quantitative researchers who wish to interrogate large data sets in greater detail. These include, for example, the use of inferential statistics, regression analysis, structural equation modelling and factor analysis. While these may seem less accessible to some, their basic principles are not difficult to grasp and they are all supported by widely available software. Rather, the key issue for case study researchers will be whether their research has generated sufficient quantitative data of the right kinds to make their use worthwhile.

Mixed Methods

Given the ways in which they are often falsely contrasted or dichotomised, it is worth stressing the similarities and potential overlaps between qualitative and quantitative methods. As Punch (2005) points out:

> [Q]uantitative research is thought to be more concerned with the deductive testing of hypotheses and theories, whereas qualitative research is more concerned with exploring a topic, and with inductively generating hypotheses and theories. While this is often true, these stereotypes can be overdone. (p. 235)

The potential overlaps between qualitative and quantitative techniques, and the mutual support that they can give to each other, become even clearer when we consider mixed methods. While some would still wish to argue that qualitative and quantitative techniques remain in some sense incompatible, other, more pragmatic, researchers are increasingly advocating their joint use (Tashakkori and Teddlie 1998, 2010; Teddlie and Tashakkori 2009; see also the discussion of combined research designs in Chapter 6).

There are, of course, a variety of ways in which qualitative and quantitative methods may be used or mixed together in practice, and it will frequently be the case that one or the other will dominate. The order in which the different methods are employed will also vary. For example, a limited number of targeted interviews might be carried out as the first part of a research project in order to identify the questions to be asked in a large-scale survey and test their wording. Or survey respondents could be asked to provide their contact details if they are willing to be approached for a follow-up interview, the purpose of which would be to clarify and provide more detail for some of their responses.

Qualitative and quantitative methods can also be employed contemporaneously. For example, it is common for interviewees to be asked to fill in a short questionnaire, giving their demographic and/or other details, immediately before, during or immediately after their interview. Surveys, for their part, may contain a mix of question types, some of which ask the respondent to mark the option that applies to them from a given list, others that allow them to write in an individual and open-ended response. Many other variants are possible.

Dunning et al (2008) report on the use of mixed methods in case study research concerning the geography of health. This involved the use of qualitative interviews and quantitative telephone surveys. Interestingly, in examining four common questions from the interviews and surveys, they came up with divergent rather than confirming results, which might lead some to question the use of qualitative and quantitative techniques for confirming or triangulating evidence. For Dunning et al, however, this divergence was not unexpected, demonstrating both the different strengths of interview and survey methods, and the complexity of the issues which the research was examining, something which the use of a single method may tend to simplify. They concluded that:

> seven distinct benefits were derived from using a mixed methods approach in this study: (1) It identified possible questions to be added in future iterations of the survey; (2) It revealed variation in how participants in surveys and interviews respond to questions; (3) It revealed variation in definition of a neighbourhood condition; (4) It necessitated awareness of other data sources; (5) It operationalized confirmation and comprehension [issues of concern to the research]; (6) It revealed variation in how people define neighbourhood; and (7) It revealed variation in how people define friendly. Ultimately, using mixed methods was an iterative process and therefore the list of benefits is not an exhaustive one. (p. 155)

This then led them to suggest four guidelines for others using mixed methods approaches:

1. Define a research purpose and question.
2. Make a conscious choice to use a mixed method design.
3. Prepare in advance for dissonant results.
4. Be clear ('transparent') about the methodology used for: (a) mixed method project design; (b) achieving confirmation and/or comprehension; and (c) interpreting confirming or 'unconfirming' (dissonant) results. (p. 156)

Leaving aside the focus on 'mixed method design', this seems like pretty good general guidance for research.

COLLECTING AND ANALYSING DATA

Having decided on your methodological approach, and on the method or methods you will be using to collect data for your case study, it is time, of course, to proceed with data collection and its analysis. I link data collection and analysis together deliberately here, because, while it may seem logical to wait until you have collected all (or at least most) of your data before you start to analyse it, in practice it may well be sensible to start your analysis as soon as you have a reasonable amount of data to examine.

Indeed, unless you are an extremely self-disciplined person, you may find it impossible to stop thinking about what your data imply or mean as soon as you have collected some. Don't worry, such initial analysis can help to confirm that you are working on the right lines and suggest possible avenues for additional data collection while you still have time and resource to do so.

There are at least two golden rules so far as data collection is concerned. The first of these is that data collection almost always takes longer than you think it will: there may be delays in gaining access or ethical approval, appointments may need to be postponed or rearranged, response rates may initially be inadequate, documents may prove hard to source, and so forth. So it makes sense to allow for some slippage and to be flexible in the scheduling of the different aspects of your research project.

The second golden rule is that it is normal to collect more data than you can possibly analyse and use in the time you have available for your project. Indeed, you should probably deliberately aim for this state of affairs. This is, after all, a far more comfortable position to be in than to not have enough data. You can then be more selective in what you choose to analyse now, and can hold back data for subsequent analysis when the current project is finished.

Guidance on Analysis from Exponents of Case Study

Two useful assessments of the different strategies for analysing case studies are provided by Yin (2009) and Swanborn (2010). These are particularly interesting because Swanborn builds upon and extends Yin's categorisation. Even so, neither – in my view – covers all of the possibilities (see also the next sub-section).

Yin (2009) emphasises the need to have an analytic strategy, noting that:

> The analysis of case study evidence is one of the least developed and most difficult aspects of doing case studies. Too many times, investigators start case studies without having the foggiest notion about how the evidence is to be analyzed. (p. 127)

He recommends and discusses five analytic techniques: pattern matching, explanation building, time-series analysis, logic models and cross-case synthesis. These are outlined in more detail in Box 9.5. Two things are immediately notable about this classification. First, they are all essentially variants of his first, pattern-matching technique, something that Yin himself acknowledges. In other words, the basic analytical strategy offered is to compare what is observed in the case or cases studied with what was expected (for theoretical or logical reasons) or observed elsewhere (e.g. in another case).

The second point to be highlighted about Yin's formulation is that, while he does take the position that either or both qualitative or quantitative data may be analysed, the language and logic employed is essentially post-positivist in nature, owing a great deal to the classic scientific method (see also Boblin et al 2013). Yin's strategy involves the careful analysis of cases to provide evidence to support given expectations or explanations.

Swanborn (2010) also offers a fivefold categorisation of what he terms the 'traditions' of case study analysis:

Research literature in the field of case study data analysis is rather diversely oriented, depending on the definition of 'case study'. Roughly, we distinguish five traditions:

1. Analysis of data collected in the field of changing organisations, according to Yin.
2. Analysis of data collected in one of the qualitative traditions, especially the grounded theory approach of Strauss and Corbin.
3. Data analysis and presentation according to the work of Miles and Huberman.
4. Time-series analysis.
5. Data analysis according to Ragin's method, using Boolean logic and fuzzy-set theory. (pp. 114–115)

Again, these are explained in more detail in Box 9.5.

■ ■ ■ Box 9.5 Analysing Case Studies according to Yin and Swanborn ■ ■ ■

A: According to Yin (2009)

Pattern Matching

For case study analysis, one of the most desirable techniques is to use a pattern-matching logic. Such a logic compares an empirically based pattern with a predicted one (or with several alternative predictions). (p. 136)

Explanation Building

The explanation-building process… is likely to be a result of a series of iterations:

- Making an initial theoretical statement or an initial proposition about policy or social behavior
- Comparing the findings of *an initial case* against such a statement or proposition
- Revising the statement or proposition

(Continued)

(Continued)

- Comparing other details of the case against the revision
- Comparing the revision to the facts of *a second, third, or more cases*
- Repeating this process as many times as is needed. (p. 143, emphasis in original)

Time-Series Analysis

[T]he important… objective is to examine some relevant 'how' and 'why' questions about the relationship of events over time, not merely to observe the time trends alone. (p. 148)

Logic Models

The logic model deliberately stipulates a complex chain of events over an extended period of time. The events are staged in repeated cause-effect-cause-effect patterns, whereby a dependent variable (event) at an earlier stage becomes the independent variable (causal event) for the next stage. (p. 149)

Cross-case Synthesis

Cross-case syntheses can be performed whether the individual case studies have previously been conducted as independent research studies (authored by different persons) or as a predesigned part of the same study. (p. 156)

B: According to Swanborn (2010)

Research in the Field of Changing Organisations according to Yin (i.e. the five approaches identified above)

Yin's approach fits the empirical-analytical tradition completely. (p. 115)

Analysis of Data Collected in One of the Qualitative Traditions

Within this category we corral together symbolic-interactionist, phenomenological, ethno-methodological and many other approaches. (p. 117)

Data Analysis and Presentation according to the Work of Miles and Huberman

They suggest that all data collected within the frame of a case study (by way of several sources, such as documents, informants, observation) is laid down – in principle – in a temporary 'monster-matrix'. The cells in this matrix are not filled with numbers, however, but with written notions of various kinds: quotations, abbreviations, acronyms, etc. (p. 122)

Time-series Analysis

The analysis of data based on repeated measurements of a small number of precise variables originates in the health sciences and psychology. Studying the effects of a medication or intervention by monitoring a patient or a client on some important health variables in an experimental setting is the core of this type of research. (pp. 123–124)

> ### Data Analysis according to Ragin's Method
>
> Ragin uses Boolean logic to discover under which combination of conditions a phenom-enon occurs. In this way, he tries to frame causal conclusions on the basis of data from only a small number of units… Ragin's 'fuzzy-set method' is also used for the analysis of causal relations in a restricted number of cases. (pp. 91, 93)

Swanborn's categories are primarily linked to particular researchers and disciplines. Indeed, his first category, dedicated to Yin, encompasses the five variants of case study analysis that Yin identifies, and which we have just discussed. Intriguingly, one of Swanborn's categories, times-series analysis, shares the same title as one of Yin's, but the two authors are referring to different things, with Swanborn's time-series analysis relating to quantitative studies of treatment in health care and psychology.

Swanborn's analysis is particularly useful for demonstrating that there are particular forms of analysis that have developed to examine case study data in different disciplines. While each of these has not been much used outside their originating disciplines, there is no reason, as Swanborn points out, why they should not be, providing the data coll-ected are appropriate.

Other Approaches

What Yin and Swanborn have done here is to identify and categorise the approaches to case study data analysis that have become popular in particular disciplinary areas. Their lists of alternative approaches are, therefore, by no means exhaustive, as any form of qualitative or quantitative analysis could – at least potentially – be applied to case study data. What limits their application is solely the amount and nature of the data that has been collected on a particular case or cases, and whether this matches the assumptions of the form of analysis selected.

Boxes 9.1, 9.2 and 9.4 identify many of the more popular forms of qualitative and quantitative analysis that could be applied to case study data, although, like Yin's and Swanborn's formulations, they are not exhaustive lists by any means. General texts on qualitative and quantitative data analysis (some examples are given in the Key Readings section at the end of this chapter), and specialist texts focusing on particular analytical techniques, will provide much more detail.

Using Software for Analysis

One key issue to bear in mind before you get deep into the analysis of your collected case study data is whether to use computer software. In the case of quantitative data, of course, and certainly where the amount of quantitative data collected is beyond a bare minimum, the use of software is almost compulsory. With large data sets, any but the most basic analyses would be far too time consuming, and subject to human error, to be worth considering without software. And there are many established software program suites, such as SPSS and Matlab, which are easy to learn and use, and which will undertake extremely complex analyses speedily, providing masses of output for consideration.

Software usage has not yet advanced so far for qualitative data analysis, but it is growing fast. Qualitative software packages like Atlas.ti and NVivo are now well established and widely used by experienced qualitative researchers. Many qualitative researchers, particularly those less experienced, still, however, opt or prefer to do their analyses manually. For a relatively small case study, this may be a time-efficient approach, but for those undertaking larger or multiple case studies, or who envision themselves repeatedly engaging in qualitative research, it would surely be worthwhile to at least explore the possibilities of qualitative software.

If you do not have access to, and/or cannot afford a licence for, an appropriate specialist software analysis package, bear in mind that standard computer software packages, such as Word and Excel, do offer considerable facilities for application in this way.

One other point to bear in mind, whether you are doing quantitative or qualitative analysis, is that – if you are using computer software for this purpose – it is still important to do some analysis manually. This should both give you a better feel for the analysis to be undertaken and act as a check that your software analysis is producing appropriate results.

REPORTING YOUR FINDINGS

Having (hopefully with a reasonable amount of success) completed your case study, there are still two key actions to be undertaken: assessing the worth of what you have achieved and then writing it up for publication and/or dissemination. Both are important, and the latter particularly so, if your research is to have a wider and longer-term impact.

Assessing Your Work

A number of authors of case study texts provide checklists for judging the worth of a completed case study. These may, of course, be used to assess published case studies (see also the discussion in Chapters 4 and 7) as well as your own. Two of these (Thomas 2011a; Yin 2009) were discussed in Chapter 4 in the section on What Makes a Meaningful Case Study? To these were added four key questions:

- Can you understand what the researchers have done and why?
- Does their interpretation of their findings seem reasonable and defensible?
- Can you relate the case study to other research on the topic?
- Does the study suggest plausible change actions and/or further research directions?

These questions were then applied in an assessment of some examples of published case study research.

These checklists provide a useful set of questions that you might use in attempting to assess the worth of your own case study. If you find it difficult to get an honest angle on these questions, you might ask yourself, if you were starting again from scratch, how might you do your case study differently?

In assessing your work, you need not rely solely on your own evaluation of the significance, quality and so forth of what you have done. It makes sense to seek the opinions of others as well, such as colleagues, friends and fellow researchers, who know of you and your work, and who are prepared to spend some time reading your drafts, discussing them with you, and making suggestions on where and how they might be improved. This, of course, links closely to the subject of the next sub-section, writing up for publication. Particularly if you are inexperienced in the business of publication, it is important to get as much guidance as you can before you commit to seeking publication.

Writing Up for Publication

Writing up and seeking to publish your case study is also, of course, another way of assessing the quality of a case study, as it usually involves the judgement of your work by one or more people, or reviewers, who have specialist expertise and knowledge of your research area. Academic publishing is a competitive practice, and almost always requires the author(s) to undertake some significant revision of what they originally drafted, in the light of comments made by reviewers, if they are to proceed to publication. Successful publication in a reputable academic journal is, however, a significant achievement and a strong (if by no means foolproof) indication of the quality of a piece of work.

Due to its focused nature and the need to present an argument that is of more general interest:

> ...case study research can be difficult to write up so that it is suitable for publication in academic journals. When reporting case studies for this purpose, it is useful to follow a recognized case study reporting structure that has been used in published case study research literature within the field. This assists potential reviewers in readily understanding the research and its results. An exemplary case study paper may also be used as a template for presentation of case data and research results. (Darke, Shanks and Broadbent 1998, p. 286)

As Darke, Shanks and Broadbent point out, one obvious way to get a grip on what is involved in writing up your case study for publication is to examine previous examples (see also Chapters 4 and 7). Whatever genre of publication you are attempting – e.g. an academic journal article, a book chapter, a report, a conference paper or perhaps a dissertation – there will be existing, more or less successful, examples you can access and study. Get advice, if you can, on particularly good examples (and, perhaps, also particularly bad ones) or, if you can't get any advice, focus on those which are highly cited (typically for positive but also sometimes for negative reasons) by other researchers. Look at the way in which the writing up of the research has been organised, how it has been divided into sections, and the balance of space devoted to the different sections. Note the kind of language used, the way references to other publications are brought in, and how the author(s) puts forward their argument.

Alternatively, there are also guides available to writing up. For example, Pan and Tan (2011) recommend that a case study paper should contain six sections: introduction, literature review, research method, results, discussion and conclusion. That is a perfectly reasonable structure to adopt for writing up a case study, but it is wholly generic, and would do just as well for many other kinds of research (there is a more general literature focused on the practice of academic writing: see, for example, Murray 2013).

Lyons (2009) offers what he calls a prescriptive approach for publishing case studies on learning facilitated by information and communication technology in higher education. While this may seem a very specific area of study, the guidance given is also fairly generic in nature and could be applied in many other contexts. He argues that:

> Content of case studies should be framed to facilitate analysis. An individual case study may provide a small body of data that provides insights but also accretes to provide the basis of a theoretical contribution. (p. 30)

He then outlines a seven-stage approach for reporting the case study: discussion of the organisational context; a description of what has happened; technical specification of the project; discussion of pedagogy; implementation; evaluation; and limitations of data. This could easily be adapted to reporting other sorts of case studies in other disciplines as well. Don't be afraid, though, to move away from such formulaic approaches if you think a different structure would suit your material better.

If you are seeking academic publication and have identified a journal – or, perhaps, a small number of journals – that you would like to target with an article, there are two further things that you must do before you submit your article for consideration.

First, visit the journal's website, as this will contain useful guidance on all kinds of relevant matters, from the journal's focus and coverage, and its editors and editorial board, through to details of permissible word lengths, expected section headings and approved referencing style. There will probably be a pdf document entitled *Guidance for Authors*, or something similar, which you can download and study. Read all of this carefully and take their guidance on board. The editor or editors may also be open to direct queries from potential authors.

Second, access and read recent copies of the journal in question, ideally going back at least a decade. This is essential to check what they have published that is of relevance to your research, and to ensure that you refer to relevant articles from the journal in your article and reference them. If you don't do this, it will both seem impolite and cast doubt on your thoroughness as a researcher. After all, why would you be targeting a journal unless it published material directly relevant to your topic and interests?

One final point if you are seeking academic publication: be prepared for some knock-backs, but don't let them put you off. Academic reviewers can be pretty tough and many journals have high rejection rates. However, if you persevere and take the comments made on your article on board, there is a good chance you will get it published somewhere in time.

SUMMARY

In this chapter, we have:

- discussed the nature of alternative positivist and interpretivist methodologies
- reviewed the range of qualitative, quantitative and mixed methods that may be employed in undertaking case study research
- argued that qualitative and quantitative methods pose many of the same issues, and overlap, in practice, such that mixed methods approaches may be fruitfully employed
- explored the practicalities involved in collecting and analysing data
- stressed the importance of writing up, reporting on and seeking to publish your findings on completion of your case study research.

KEY READINGS

Black, T (1999) *Doing Quantitative Research in the Social Sciences: An integrated approach to research design, measurement and statistics.* London, Sage.

Bryman, A (2012) *Social Research Methods* (4th edition). Oxford, Oxford University Press.

Cohen, L, Manion, L, and Morrison, K (2011) *Research Methods in Education* (7th edition). London, Routledge.

Denzin, N, and Lincoln, Y (eds) (2005) *The Sage Handbook of Qualitative Research* (3rd edition). Thousand Oaks, CA, Sage.

Hamilton, L, and Corbett-Whittier, C (2013) *Using Case Study in Education Research.* London, Sage.

Hancock, D, and Algozzine, B (2011) *Doing Case Study Research: A practical guide for beginning researchers* (2nd edition). New York, Teachers College Press.

Thomas, G, and Myers, K (2015) *The Anatomy of the Case Study.* London, Sage.

Vaus, D de (2002) *Analyzing Social Science Data: 50 key problems in data analysis.* London, Sage.

10

Conclusion

INTRODUCTION

The purpose of this final chapter is to briefly gather together the discussion in the book, and to offer some speculations regarding how case study might develop as a research design in the future. The chapter, therefore, contains two main sections.

In the first of these sections, a synthesis is provided of the arguments that have been presented in the book. In the second main section, we then look forward and consider the directions in which case study might be headed.

THE CONTEMPORARY STATE OF CASE STUDY

This book has discussed:

- the nature of case study
- the debates that continue about it
- its value as a research design
- its varied use in a wide range of different disciplines
- its application in combination with other research designs
- what and how we can learn from published case studies
- the practical issues involved in carrying out a case study.

There is a need for care in defining what is a case study and what isn't. While all research can be said to study cases, this does not mean that all research projects are case studies. Case study involves the study of a particular case, or a number of cases (multiple case study), where the case is complex and bounded, is studied in its context, and the analysis seeks to be holistic. Case study is *small-scale research with meaning*.

There are three major factors to bear in mind when considering examples of case studies: whether they focus on a single case or involve a comparative study of two or more cases; whether they confine themselves to description or engage with theory; whether they are intended primarily to support teaching or research. The focus of this book has been on case study as used in research.

Case study has a long history, having been employed as a research design for well over a century. Although it has often, because of its small-scale nature, been seen, primarily or wholly, as a qualitative research design, it lends itself equally well to the application of quantitative methods of data collection and analysis.

Throughout its history, case study has, like many research designs, been the subject of extensive debate. For its proponents – of which there are many – case studies have considerable advantages: they are detailed, in-depth and particular; they adopt a holistic approach to the case, rather than focus on a limited number of variables; the case studied may be typical or exemplary, or critical or extreme; and they are bounded and small-scale, and thus more feasible for the small-scale researcher to undertake.

On the other hand, critics of case study research – of which there are also many – draw particular attention to its perceived lack of generalisability, reliability and validity. In these ways, it is compared unfavourably with positivist and quantitative research designs which underpin the classical scientific method. Case study researchers have to take on board these criticisms, ensuring and stressing the trustworthiness, credibility, transferability and confirmability of their research.

Viewing case study as small-scale research with meaning, we may assess how meaningful individual case studies are by assessing whether:

- we can understand what the researchers have done and why they have done it
- their interpretation of their findings seems reasonable and defensible
- the case study can be related to other research on the topic
- the study suggests plausible change actions and/or further research directions.

Case study has been extensively applied as a research design in a wide range of disciplines and sub-disciplines. These include, most notably, different areas of business and management, education and health. They also include other professional disciplines, such as development, information systems, law, library and information studies, and social work, and other 'pure' disciplines, such as geography and environmental studies, philosophy, political science, psychology and sociology.

Case study has also been extensively applied in combination with a variety of other research designs, demonstrating its flexibility and facility. These have included action and other participatory forms of research, complexity science and network theory, constructionism and critical realism, content analysis, ethnography, evaluation, experiment, grounded theory, surveys, system designs and time series designs.

Whether you are carrying out a case study yourself or not, there is a great deal that can be learned from published case studies. They can be used to inform your research design, methodology and methods; to inform your theoretical framework; to compare your practice, findings and conclusions with; and to enable you to generalise further. Because there are thousands and thousands of published case studies available, you will need, however, to search carefully for those most appropriate to your interests. This may be done using search engines; by consulting existing meta-analyses, systematic reviews and literature reviews; by using published articles, books and reports; and by consulting theses and dissertations.

Carrying out a case study involves many of the same issues and processes that are encountered in other forms of research. At the beginning, the researcher has to consider the questions they wish to address, and plan out a feasible schedule for the project. There are issues over sampling and selection of the case or cases, and concerns about access and ethics to consider.

The context of the case, its boundary and the unit of analysis also need definition, and – particularly if the research has an academic context – the theoretical framework for, and aims of, the research will require thought. Alternative methodological approaches (positivist or interpretivist?) and methods (qualitative, quantitative or mixed?) need to be considered, decided upon and justified.

Then there is the process of data collection itself: are primary and/or secondary data being collected? How are the data to be analysed, and will software packages be used? And then, finally, there are the decisions about what to do when the case study has been completed: writing up, presenting and seeking publication.

All in all, then, case study has been, and remains, a robust, flexible and successful research design. For those interested in, or limited by resource constraints to, in-depth small-scale research, it can be an ideal fit. Carefully and thoughtfully pursued, it can result in meaningful findings. These can then be built upon over time through further case study research and/or through comparison with existing published case studies or other forms of research.

POSSIBLE FUTURE DIRECTIONS

Clearly, the future for case study research looks promising. With so many committed practitioners worldwide, distributed within so many disciplines, it can only be expected to thrive and develop further. But are there any particular directions in which we might anticipate this further development to occur? I would hazard some speculations in three areas, though it has to be said that these represent how I would like case study to develop at least as much as how I think it will.

First, while recognising that there have been considerable advances in this area already (see Chapter 7), I would like to see more meta-analyses and systematic reviews of the case study research that has been completed and published on particular topics. Indeed, this could be extended further by linking the findings from case study research on particular topics to those from other research designs.

Second, and linked to that last point, it would be healthy to see more use of case study in combination with other research designs (see Chapter 6). This would serve to strengthen the research, adding significantly to both its acceptability and explanatory power.

Third, and finally, we might see greater uses of case study research designs in comparative studies. In part, this simply means more use of multiple case study designs, but there is also a call here for using case study in international studies more often.

Whether case study does develop in these or other directions, however, its position as a valuable and meaningful research design is secure for the foreseeable future.

References

Abbato, S (2015) The Case for Evaluating Process and Worth: Evaluation of a programme for carers and people with dementia. pp. 107–131 in J Russell, T Greenhalgh, and S Kushner (eds) *Case Study Evaluation: Past, present and future challenges*. Bingley, Emerald.

Achen, C, and Snidal, D (1989) Rational Deterrence Theory and Comparative Case Studies. *World Politics*, 41, 2, pp. 143–169.

Adams, J, Cochrane, M, and Dunne, L (2012) Introduction. pp. 1–10 in J Adams, M Cochrane, and L Dunne (eds) *Applying Theory to Educational Research: An introductory approach with case studies*. Chichester, Wiley-Blackwell.

Adams, J, and Tyson, S (2000) The Effectiveness of Physiotherapy to Enable an Elderly Person to Get Up from the Floor: A single case study. *Physiotherapy*, 86, 4, pp. 185–189.

Adelman, C (2015) Case Study, Methodology and Educational Evaluation: A personal view. pp. 1–18 in J Russell, T Greenhalgh, and S Kushner (eds) *Case Study Evaluation: Past, present and future challenges*. Bingley, Emerald.

Adelman, C, Jenkins, D, and Kemmis, S (1976) Re-thinking Case Study: notes from the second Cambridge conference. *Cambridge Journal of Education*, 6, 3, pp. 139–150.

Alvesson, M (2003) Methodology for Close Up Studies: Struggling with closeness and closure. *Higher Education*, 46, 2, pp. 167–193.

Anaf, S, Drummond, C, and Sheppard, L (2007) Combining Case Study Research and Systems Theory as a Heuristic Model. *Qualitative Health Research*, 17, 10, pp. 1309–1315.

Anckar, D (2007) Selecting Cases in Cross-national Political Research. *International Journal of Social Research Methodology*, 10, 1, pp. 49–61.

Anderson, R, Crabtree, B, Steele, D, and McDaniel, R (2005) Case Study Research: The view from complexity science. *Qualitative Health Research*, 15, 5, pp. 669–685.

Andrade, A (2009) Interpretive Research Aimed at Theory Building: Adopting and adapting the case study design. *The Qualitative Report*, 14, 1, pp. 42–60.

Anthony, S, and Jack, S (2009) Qualitative Case Study Methodology in Nursing: An integrative review. *Journal of Advanced Nursing*, 65, 6, pp. 1171–1181.

Arnold, D (1970) Dimensional Sampling: An approach for studying a small number of cases. *The American Sociologist*, 5, 2, pp. 147–150.

Atkinson, P, and Delamont, S (1985) Bread and Dreams or Bread and Circuses? A critique of 'case study' research in education. pp. 26–45 in M Shipman (ed.) *Educational Research: Principles, policies and practices*. London, Falmer.

Ayres, L, Kavanaugh, K, and Knafl, K (2003) Within-case and Across-Case Approaches to Qualitative Data Analysis. *Qualitative Health Research*, 13, 6, pp. 871–883.

Baines, D, and Cunningham, I (2013) Using Comparative Perspective Rapid Ethnography in International Case Studies: Strengths and challenges. *Qualitative Social Work*, 12, 1, pp. 73–88.

Bair, C (1980) Teaching Community Diagnosis to Medical Students: Evaluation of a case study approach. *Journal of Community Health*, 6, 1, pp. 54–64.

Barzelay, M (1993) The Single Case Study as Intellectually Ambitious Inquiry. *Journal of Public Administration Research and Theory*, 3, 3, pp. 305–318.

Bassey, M (1981) Pedagogic Research: On the relative merits of search for generalization and study of single events. *Oxford Review of Education*, 7, 1, pp. 73–94.

Bassey, M (1983) Pedagogic Research into Singularities: Case studies, probes and curriculum innovations. *Oxford Review of Education*, 9, 2, pp. 109–121.

Bassey, M (1999) *Case Study Research in Educational Settings*. Buckingham, Open University Press.

Bassey, M (2001) A Solution to the Problem of Generalisation in Educational Research: Fuzzy prediction. *Oxford Review of Education*, 27, 1, pp. 5–22.

Bates, M (2008) The Responsive Case Study: Action research and action learning in short courses. *Educational Action Research*, 16, 1, pp. 97–108.

Battleson, B, Booth, A, and Weintrop, J (2001) Usability Testing of an Academic Library Website: A case study. *Journal of Academic Librarianship*, 27, 3, pp. 188–198.

Baxter, P, and Jack, S (2008) Qualitative Case Study Methodology: Study design and implementation for novice researchers. *The Qualitative Report*, 13, 4, pp. 544–559.

Benbasat, I, Goldstein, D, and Mead, M (1987) The Case Research Strategy in Studies of Information Systems. *MIS Quarterly*, September, pp. 369–386.

Bennett, A, and Elman, C (2006) Qualitative Research: Recent developments in case study methods. *Annual Review of Political Science*, 9, pp. 455–476.

Beverland, M, and Lindgren, A (2010) What Makes a Good Case Study? A positivist review of qualitative case research published in *Industrial Marketing Management*, 1971–2006. *Industrial Marketing Management*, 39, 1, pp. 56–63.

Black, T (1999) *Doing Quantitative Research in the Social Sciences: An integrated approach to research design, measurement and statistics*. London, Sage.

Blaxter, L, Hughes, C, and Tight, M (2006) *How to Research*. Maidenhead, Open University Press.

Blencowe, N, Blazeby, J, Donovan, J, and Mills, N (2015) Novel Ways to Explore Surgical Interventions in Randomised Control Trials: Applying case study methodology in the operating theatre. *Trials*, 16, 589, 9pp.

Boblin, S, Ireland, S, Kirkpatrick, H, and Robertson, K (2013) Using Stake's Qualitative Case Study Approach to Explore Implementation of Evidence-based Practice. *Qualitative Health Research*, 23, 9, pp. 1267–1275.

Bonoma, T (1985) Case Research in Marketing: Opportunities, problems and a process. *Journal of Marketing Research*, 22, 2, pp. 199–208.

Borgatti, S, and Halgin, D (2011) On Network Theory. *Organization Science*, 22, 5, pp. 1168–1181.

Bosch, M, van der Weijden, T, Wensing, M, and Grol, R (2007) Tailoring Quality Improvement Interventions to Identified Barriers: A multiple case analysis. *Journal of Evaluation in Clinical Practice*, 13, 2, pp. 161–168.

Braun, V, and Clarke, V (2006) Using Thematic Analysis in Psychology. *Qualitative Research in Psychology*, 3, 2, pp. 77–101.

Brennan, K (1988–89) The Influence of Cultural Relativism on International Human Rights Law: Female circumcision as a case study. *Law and Inequality*, 7, pp. 367–398.

Brewer, J (2000) *Ethnography*. Buckingham, Open University Press.

Bryar, R (1999) An Examination of Case Study Research. *Nurse Researcher*, 7, 2, pp. 61–78.

Bryman, A (ed.) (2001) *Ethnography* (4 volumes). London, Sage.

Bryman, A (2004) *Social Research Methods* (2nd edition). Oxford, Oxford University Press.

Bryman, A (2012) *Social Research Methods* (4th edition). Oxford, Oxford University Press.

Burgess, E (1927) Statistics and Case Studies as Methods of Sociological Research. *Sociology and Social Research*, 12, 103–120.

Burgess, E (1941) An Experiment in the Standardization of the Case-Study Method. *Sociometry*, 4, 4, pp. 329–348.

Burns, R (2000) *Introduction to Research Methods* (4th edition). London, Sage.

Burrawoy, M (1998) The Extended Case Method. *Sociological Theory*, 16, 1, pp. 4–33.

Bygstad, B, and Munkvold, B (2011) Exploring the Role of Informants in Interpretive Case Study Research in IS. *Journal of Information Technology*, 26, 1, pp. 32–45.

Byrne, D, and Ragin, C (eds) (2009) *The Sage Handbook of Case-based Methods*. London, Sage.

Canen, A (1999) The Challenges of Conducting an Ethnographic Case Study of a United Kingdom Teacher Education Institution. *Journal of Teacher Education*, 50, 1, pp. 50–56.

Carden, F (2009) Using Comparative Data: A systems approach to a multiple case study. pp. 331–344 in D Byrne and C Ragin (eds) *The Sage Handbook of Case-based Methods*. London, Sage.

Carter, B, and Sealey, A (2009) Reflexivity, Realism and the Process of Casing. pp. 69–83 in D Byrne and C Ragin (eds) *The Sage Handbook of Case-based Methods*. London, Sage.

Casanave, C (2003) Looking Ahead to More Socio-politically Oriented Case Study Research in L2 Writing Scholarship (but should it be called 'post-process'?). *Journal of Second Language Writing*, 13, 1, pp. 85–102.

Casey, D, and Houghton, C (2010) Clarifying Case Study Research: Examples from practice. *Nurse Educator*, 17, 3, pp. 41–51.

Caulley, D, and Dowdy, I (1987) Evaluation Case Histories as a Parallel to Legal Case Histories: Accumulating knowledge and experience in the evaluation profession. *Evaluation and Program Planning*, 10, pp. 359–372.

Cavaye, A (1996) Case Study Research: A multi-faceted research approach for IS. *Information Systems Journal*, 6, 3, pp. 227–242.

Charmaz, K (2006) *Constructing Grounded Theory: A practical guide through qualitative analysis*. London, Sage.

Chesney-Lind, M, and Chagnon, N (2016) Criminology, Gender and Race: A case study of privilege in the academy. *Feminist Criminology*, ahead of print: DOI: 10.1177/1557085116633749.

Chetty, S (1996) The Case Study Method for Research in Small and Medium-sized Firms. *International Small Business Journal*, 15, 1, pp. 73–85.

Christensen, C, and Carlile, P (2009) Course Research: Using the case method to build and teach management theory. *Academy of Management Learning and Education*, 8, 2, pp. 240–251.

Cohen, L, Manion, L, and Morrison, K (2007) *Research Methods in Education* (6th edition). London, Routledge.

Cohen, L, Manion, L, and Morrison, K (2011) *Research Methods in Education* (7th edition). London, Routledge.

Contardo, I, and Wensley, R (2004) The Harvard Business School Story: Avoiding knowledge by being relevant. *Organization*, 11, 2, pp. 211–231.

Cooper, D, and Morgan, W (2008) Case Study Research in Accounting. *Accounting Horizons*, 22, 2, pp. 159–178.

Corcoran, P, Walker, K, and Wals, A (2004) Case Studies, Make-your-case Studies and Case Stories: A critique of case-study methodology in sustainability in higher education. *Environmental Education Research*, 10, 1, pp. 7–21.

Cottrell, L (1941) The Case-Study Method in Prediction. *Sociometry*, 4, 4, pp. 358–372.

Cowell, I, and Phillips, D (2002) Effectiveness of Manipulative Physiotherapy for the Treatment of a Neurogenic Cervicobrachial Pain Syndrome: A single case study – experimental design. *Manual Therapy*, 7, 1, pp. 31–38.

Crasnow, S (2011) Evidence for Use: Casual pluralism and the role of case studies in political science research. *Philosophy of the Social Sciences*, 41, 1, pp. 26–49.

Crotty, M (1998) *The Foundations of Social Research: Meaning and perspective in the research process*. London, Sage.

Crowe, S, Cresswell, K, Robertson, A, Huby, G, Avery, A, and Sheikh, A (2011) The Case Study Approach. *BMC Medical Research Methodology*, 11, 100, 9pp.

Cunningham, J (1997) Case Study Principles for Different Types of Cases. *Quality and Quantity*, 31, 4, pp. 401–423.

Curtis, S, Gesler, W, Smith, G, and Washburn, S (2000) Approaches to Sampling and Case Selection in Qualitative Research: Examples in the geography of health. *Social Science and Medicine*, 50, 7–8, pp. 1001–1014.

Darke, P, Shanks, G, and Broadbent, M (1998) Successfully Completing Case Study Research: Combining rigour, relevance and pragmatism. *Information Systems Journal*, 8, 4, pp. 273–289.

David, M (ed.) (2006) *Case Study Research* (4 volumes). London, Sage.

Denscombe, M (2014) *The Good Research Guide for Small-scale Social Research Projects* (5th edition). Maidenhead, Open University Press.

Denzin, N, and Lincoln, Y (eds) (2005a) *The Sage Handbook of Qualitative Research* (3rd edition). Thousand Oaks, CA, Sage.

Denzin, N, and Lincoln, Y (2005b) Introduction: The discipline and practice of qualitative research. pp. 1–32 in N Denzin and Y Lincoln (eds) *The Sage Handbook of Qualitative Research* (3rd edition). Thousand Oaks, CA, Sage.

Diefenbach, T (2009) Are Case Studies More than Sophisticated Storytelling? Methodological problems of qualitative empirical research mainly based on semi-structured interviews. *Quality and Quantity*, 43, 6, pp. 875–894.

Dion, D (1998) Evidence and Inference in the Comparative Case Study. *Comparative Politics*, 30, 2, pp. 127–145.

Donmoyer, R, and Galloway, F (2010) Reconsidering the Utility of Case Study Designs for Researching School Reform in a Neo-scientific Era: Insights from a multiyear mixed-methods study. *Educational Administration Quarterly*, 46, 1, pp. 3–30.

Dooley, L (2002) Case Study Research and Theory Building. *Advances in Developing Human Resources*, 4, 3, pp. 335–354.

Doolin, B (1996) Alternative Views of Case Research in Information Systems. *Australasian Journal of Information Systems*, 3, 2, pp. 21–29.

Dube, L, and Pare, G (2003) Rigor in Information Systems Positive Case Research: Current practices, trends and recommendations. *MIS Quarterly*, 27, 4, pp. 597–635.

Dubois, A, and Gibbert, M (2010) From Complexity to Transparency: Managing the interplay between theory, method and empirical phenomena in IMM case studies. *Industrial Marketing Management*, 39, 1, pp. 129–136.

Dugard, P, File, P, and Todman, J (2012) *Single-case and Small-n Experimental Designs: A practical guide to randomization tests* (2nd edition). New York, Routledge.

Dul, J, and Hak, T (2008) *Case Study Methodology in Business Research*. Oxford, Elsevier.

Dunning, H, Williams, A, Abonyi, S, and Crooks, V (2008) A Mixed Method Approach to Quality of Life Research: A case study approach. *Social Indicators Research*, 85, 1, pp. 145–158.

Easton, G (2010) Critical Realism in Case Study Research. *Industrial Marketing Management*, 39, 1, pp. 118–128.

Eckstein, H (1975) Case Study and Thought in Political Science. pp. 79–137 in F Greenstein and N Polsby (eds) *Strategies of Inquiry*. Handbook of Political Science, Volume 7. Reading, MA, Addison-Wesley.

Edwards, D (1998) Types of Case Study Work: A conceptual framework for case-based research. *Journal of Humanistic Psychology*, 38, 3, pp. 36–70.

Edwards, D, Dattilio, F, and Bromley, D (2004) Developing Evidence-based Practice: The role of case-based research. *Professional Psychology: Research and Practice*, 35, 6, pp. 589–597.

Eisenhardt, K (1989) Building Theories from Case Study Research. *Academy of Management Review*, 14, 4, pp. 532–550.

Elliott, J, and Lukes, D (2008) Epistemology as Ethics in Research and Policy: The use of case studies. *Journal of Philosophy of Education*, 42, S1, pp. 87–119.

Elliott, R (2002) Hermeneutic Single Case Efficacy Design. *Psychotherapy Research*, 12, 1, pp. 1–21.

Ellis, L (2003) Illuminative Case Study Design: A new approach to the evaluation of continuing professional education. *Nurse Researcher*, 10, 3, pp. 48–59.

Ellram, L (1996) The Use of the Case Study Method in Logistics Research. *Journal of Business Logistics*, 17, 2, pp. 93–138.

Etherington, K, and Bridges, N (2011) Narrative Case Study Research: On endings and six session reviews. *Counselling and Psychotherapy Research*, 11, 1, pp. 11–22.

Evers, C, and Wu, E (2006) On Generalising from Single Case Studies: Epistemological reflections. *Journal of Philosophy of Education*, 40, 4, pp. 511–526.

Farquhar, J (2012) *Case Study Research for Business*. London, Sage.

Feagin, J, Orum, A, and Sjoberg, G (eds) (1991) *A Case for the Case Study*. Chapel Hill, NC, University of North Carolina Press.

Fidel, R (1984) The Case Study Method: A case study. *Library and Information Science Research*, 6, 3, pp. 273–288.

Fletcher, A, Bonell, C, Sorhaindo, A, and Strange, V (2009) How Might Schools Influence Young People's Drug Use? Development of theory from qualitative case-study research. *Journal of Adolescent Health*, 45, 2, pp. 126–132.

Flicker, S (2008) Who Benefits from Community-based Participatory Research? A case study of the Positive Youth Project. *Health Education and Behavior*, 35, 1, pp. 70–86.

Flyvbjerg, B (2004) Five Misunderstandings about Case Study Research. pp. 390–404 in C Seale, G Gobo, J Gubrium, and D Silverman (eds) *Qualitative Research Practice*. London, Sage.

Ford, J, Keskitalo, E, Smith, T, Pearce, T, Berrang-Ford, L, Duerden, F, and Smit, B (2010) Case Study and Analogue Methodologies in Climate Change Vulnerability Research. *WIREs Climate Change*, 1, pp. 374–392.

Foreman, P (1948) The Theory of Case Studies. *Social Forces*, 26, 4, pp. 408–419.

Forman, H (2006) Participative Case Studies: Integrating case writing and a traditional case study approach in a marketing context. *Journal of Marketing Education*, 28, 2, pp. 106–113.

Foster, P, Gomm, R, and Hammersley, M (2000) Case Studies as Spurious Evaluations: The example of research on educational inequalities. *British Journal of Educational Studies*, 48, 3, pp. 215–230.

Franz, Y, Tausz, K, and Thiel, S-K (2015) Contextuality and Co-creation Matter: A qualitative case study comparison of living lab concepts in urban research. *Technology Innovation Management Review*, 5, 12, pp. 48–55.

Funnell, P (2015) Drop-in Sessions as an Effective Format for Teaching Information Literacy: A case study in the medical and dental libraries at Queen Mary University of London. *Journal of Information Literacy*, 9, 2, pp. 62–83.

Gangeness, J, and Yurkovich, E (2006) Revisiting Case Study as a Nursing Research Design. *Nurse Researcher*, 13, 4, pp. 7–18.

Garaway, G (1996) The Case Study Model: An organizational strategy for cross-cultural evaluation. *Evaluation*, 2, 2, pp. 201–211.

Garvin, D (2003) Making the Case: Professional education for the world of practice. *Harvard Magazine*, 106, 1, pp. 56–65, 107.

Geddes, B (1990) How the Cases you Choose Affect the Answers you Get: Selection bias in comparative politics. *Political Analysis*, 2, 1, pp. 131–150.

George, A, and Bennett, A (2005) *Case Studies and Theory Development in the Social Sciences.* Cambridge, MA, MIT Press.

Gerring, J (2004) What is a Case Study and What is it Good For? *American Political Science Review,* 98, 2, pp. 341–354.

Gerring, J (2006) Single-outcome Studies: A methodological primer. *International Sociology,* 21, 5, pp. 707–734.

Gerring, J (2007) *Case Study Research: Principles and practices.* New York, Cambridge University Press.

Gerring, J, and McDermott, R (2007) An Experimental Template for Case Study Research. *American Journal of Political Science,* 51, 3, pp. 688–701.

Ghauri, P, and Firth, R (2009) The Formalization of Case Study Research in International Business. *Der Markt,* 48, 1, pp. 29–40.

Ghesquiere, P, Maes, B, and Vandenberghe, R (2004) The Usefulness of Qualitative Case Studies in Research on Special Needs Education. *International Journal of Disability, Development and Education,* 51, 2, pp. 171–184.

Gibbert, M, Ruigrok, W, and Wicki, B (2008) What Passes as a Rigorous Case Study? *Strategic Management Journal,* 29, 13, pp. 1465–1474.

Gilgun, J (1994) A Case for Case Studies in Social Work Research. *Social Work,* 39, 4, pp. 371–380.

Gillham, B (2000) *Case Study Research Methods.* London, Continuum.

Glaser, B, and Strauss, A (1967) *The Discovery of Grounded Theory: Strategies for qualitative research.* Chicago, IL: Aldine.

Goggin, M (1986) The 'Too Few Cases/Too Many Variables' Problem in Implementation Research. *Western Political Quarterly,* 39, 2, pp. 328–347.

Golden-Biddle, K, and Locke, K (1993) Appealing Work: An investigation of how ethnographic texts convince. *Organization Science,* 4, 4, pp. 595–616.

Gomm, R, Hammersley, M, and Foster, P (eds) (2000a) *Case Study Method: Key issues, key texts.* London, Sage.

Gomm, R, Hammersley, M, and Foster, P (2000b) Case Study and Generalization. pp. 98–115 in R Gomm, M Hammersley, and P Foster (eds) *Case Study Method: Key issues, key texts.* London, Sage.

Good, C (1942) The Sequence of Steps in Case Study and Case Work. *Educational Research Bulletin,* 21, 6, pp. 161–171.

Gottman, J (1973) N-of-one and N-of-two Research in Psychotherapy. *Psychological Bulletin,* 80, 2, pp. 93–105.

Greene, D, and David, J (1984) A Research Design for Generalizing from Multiple Case Studies. *Evaluation and Program Planning,* 7, 1, pp. 73–85.

Greenhalgh, T, Stramer, K, Bratan, T, Byrne, E, Russell, J, and Potts, H (2010) Adoption and Non-adoption of a Shared Electronic Summary Record in England: A mixed-method case study. *British Medical Journal,* 340:c3111.

Greenwald, R, Hedges, L, and Laine, R (1994) When Reinventing the Wheel is Not Necessary: A case study in the use of meta-analysis in education finance. *Journal of Education Finance,* 20, 1, pp. 1–20.

Griffiths, F (2009) The Case in Medicine. pp.441–453 in D Byrne and C Ragin (eds) *The Sage Handbook of Case-based Methods.* London, Sage.

Grima, N, Singh, S, Smetchska, B, and Ringhofer, L (2016) Payment for Ecosystem Services (PES) in Latin America: Analysing the performance of 40 case studies. *Ecosystem Services,* 17, pp. 24–32.

Grunbaum, N (2007) Identification of Ambiguity in the Case Study Research Typology: What is a unit of analysis? *Qualitative Market Research: An International Journal,* 10, 1, pp. 78–97.

Guba, E, and Lincoln, L (2005) Paradigmatic Controversies, Contradictions and Emerging Confluences. pp. 191–215 in N Denzin and Y Lincoln (eds) *The Sage Handbook of Qualitative Research* (3rd edition). Thousand Oaks, CA, Sage.

Gummesson, E (2007) Case Study Research and Network Theory: Birds of a feather. *Qualitative Research in Organizations and Management*, 2, 3, pp. 226–248.

Hagg, I (1979) 'Case Studies' in Accounting Research. *Accounting, Organizations and Society*, 4, 1–2, pp. 135–143.

Halinen, A, and Tornroos, J-A (2005) Using Case Study Methods in the Study of Contemporary Business Networks. *Journal of Business Research*, 58, 9, pp. 1285–1297.

Hamilton, L, and Corbett-Whittier, C (2013) *Using Case Study in Education Research*. London, Sage.

Hammersley, M (1992) *What's Wrong with Ethnography?* London, Routledge.

Hammersley, M (2001) On Michael Bassey's Concept of the Fuzzy Generalisation. *Oxford Review of Education*, 27, 2, pp. 219–225.

Hammersley, M (2012) Troubling Theory in Case Study Research. *Higher Education Research and Development*, 31, 3, pp. 393–405.

Hammersley, M, Gomm, R, and Foster, P (2000) Case Study and Theory. pp. 234–258 in R Gomm, M Hammersley, and P Foster (eds) *Case Study Method: Key issues, key texts*. London, Sage.

Hancock, D, and Algozzine, B (2011) *Doing Case Study Research: A practical guide for beginning researchers* (2nd edition). New York, Teachers College Press.

Hansen, A (2011) Relating Performative and Ostensive Management Accounting Research: Reflections on case study methodology. *Qualitative Research in Accounting and Management*, 8, 2, pp. 108–138.

Hanushek, E (1981) Throwing Money at Schools. *Journal of Policy Analysis and Management*, 1, 1, pp. 19–41.

Hanushek, E (1986) The Economics of Schooling: Production and efficiency in public schools. *Journal of Economic Literature*, 24, 3, pp. 1141–1171.

Hanushek, E (1989) The Impact of Differential Expenditures on School Performance. *Educational Researcher*, 18, 4, pp. 45–65.

Hanushek, E (1991) When School Finance 'Reform' May Not be a Good Policy. *Harvard Journal on Legislation*, 28, 2, pp. 423–456.

Harland, T (2014) Learning about Case Study Methodology to Research Higher Education. *Higher Education Research and Development*, 33, 6, pp. 1113–1122.

Hart, C (1998) *Doing a Literature Review: Releasing the social science research imagination*. London, Sage.

Hashim, R (2010) Theory-building from Multiple Case Study Research on Information System Project Implementation in Local Government. *International Journal of Interdisciplinary Social Sciences*, 5, 1, pp. 297–310.

Haunschild, A, and Eikhof, D (2009) From HRM to Employment Rules and Lifestyles. Theory development through qualitative case study research into the creative industries. *Zeitschrift für Personalforschung*, 23, 2, pp. 107–124.

Haydu, J (1998) Making Use of the Past: Time periods as cases to compare and a sequences of problem solving. *American Journal of Sociology*, 104, 2, pp. 339–371.

Hayes, S (1981) Single Case Experimental Design and Empirical Clinical Practice. *Journal of Consulting and Clinical Psychology*, 49, 2, pp. 193–211.

Healey, M, Jordan, F, Pell, B, and Short, C (2010) The Research-Teaching Nexus: A case study of students' awareness, experiences and perceptions of research. *Innovations in Education and Teaching International*, 47, 2, pp. 235–246.

Hilliard, R (1993) Single-Case Methodology in Psychotherapy Process and Outcome Research. *Journal of Consulting and Clinical Psychology*, 63, 3, pp. 373–380.

Hoon, C (2013) Meta-synthesis of Qualitative Case Studies: An approach to theory building. *Organizational Research Methods*, 16, 4, pp. 522–556.

Hopwood, N (2004) Research Design and Methods of Data Collection and Analysis: Researching students' conceptions in a multiple-method case study. *Journal of Geography in Higher Education*, 28, 2, pp. 347–353.

Järvensivu, T, and Tornroos, J-A (2010) Case Study Research with Moderate Constructionism: Conceptualization and practical illustration. *Industrial Marketing Management*, 39, 1, pp. 100–108.

Jauch, L, Osborn, R, and Martin, T (1980) Structured Content Analysis of Cases: A complementary method for organizational research. *Academy of Management Review*, 5, 4, pp. 517–525.

Jenkins, P, Weinehall, L, Erb, T, Lewis, C, Nafziger, A, Pearson, T, and Wall, S (2001) The Norsjo-Cooperstown Healthy Heart Project: A case study combining data from different studies without the use of meta-analysis. *Scandinavian Journal of Public Health*, 29 (suppl. 56), pp. 40–45.

Jensen, J, and Rodgers, R (2001) Cumulating the Intellectual Gold of Case Study Research. *Public Administration Review*, 61, 2, pp. 235–246.

Johnston, P (1985) Understanding Reading Disability: A case study approach. *Harvard Educational Review*, 55, 2, pp. 153–177.

Johnston, W, Leach, M, and Liu, A (1999) Theory Testing Using Case Studies in Business-to-Business Research. *Industrial Marketing Management*, 28, 3, pp. 201–213.

Jones, E, Ghannam, J, Nigg, J, and Dyer, J (1993) A Paradigm for Single-case Research: The time-series study of a long-term psychotherapy for depression. *Journal of Consulting and Clinical Psychology*, 61, 3, pp. 381–394.

Jones, E, and Windholz, M (1990) The Psychoanalytic Case Study: A method for systematic inquiry. *Journal of the American Psychoanalytical Association*, 38, 4, pp. 985–1015.

Jones, P, Trier, C, and Richards, J (2008) Embedding Education for Sustainable Development in Higher Education: A case study examining common challenges and opportunities for undergraduate programmes. *International Journal of Educational Research*, 47, 6, pp. 341–350.

Kazdin, A (1981) Drawing Valid Inferences from Case Studies. *Journal of Consulting and Clinical Psychiatry*, 49, 2, pp. 183–192.

Kennedy, M (1979) Generalizing from Single Case Studies. *Evaluation Quarterly*, 3, 4, pp. 661–678.

Kent, G (2000) Ethical Principles. pp. 61–67 in D Burton (ed.) *Research Training for Social Scientists*. London, Sage.

Khan, S (2008) The Case in Case-based Design of Educational Software: A methodological interrogation. *Educational Technology Research and Development*, 56, 4, pp. 423–447.

Kim, J, Price, M, and Lau, F (2014) The Case Study Research Method: Overview and proposed guidelines for reporting and evaluation illustrated with health informatics case studies. *International Journal of Health Information Management Research*, 2, 1, pp. 13–30.

Koenig, G (2009) Realistic Evaluation and Case Studies: Stretching the potential. *Evaluation*, 15, 1, pp. 9–30.

Kohlbacher, F (2006) The Use of Qualitative Content Analysis in Case Study Research. *Forum: Qualitative Social Research*, 7, 1, article 21, 30pp.

Kondakci, Y, and Van den Broeck, H (2009) Institutional Imperatives versus Emergent Dynamics: A case study on continuous change in higher education. *Higher Education*, 58, 4, pp. 439–464.

Koshy, E, Koshy, V, and Waterman, H (2011) *Action Research in Healthcare*. London, Sage.

Krippendorff, K (2012) *Content Analysis: An introduction to its methodology* (3rd edition). Thousand Oaks, CA, Sage.

Kyburz-Graber, R (2004) Does Case-study Methodology Lack Rigour? The need for quality criteria for sound case-study research, as illustrated by a recent case in secondary and higher education. *Environmental Education Research*, 10, 1, pp. 53–65.

Lakomski, G (1987) Case Study Methodology and the Rational Management of Interaction. *Educational Management, Administration and Leadership*, 15, 2, pp. 147–157.

Larsson, R (1993) Case Survey Methodology: Quantitative analysis of patterns across case studies. *Academy of Management Journal*, 36, 6, pp. 1515–1546.

Lee, A (1989a) Case Studies as Natural Experiments. *Human Relations*, 42, 2, pp. 117–137.

Lee, A (1989b) A Scientific Methodology for MIS Case Studies. *MIS Quarterly*, 13, 1, pp. 33–50.

Lee, E, Mishna, F, and Brennenstuhl, S (2010) How to Critically Evaluate Case Studies in Social Work. *Research on Social Work Practice*, 20, 6, pp. 682–689.

Leitenberg, H (1973) The Use of Single-case Methodology in Psychotherapy Research. *Journal of Abnormal Psychology*, 82, 1, pp. 87–101.

Levy, J (2008) Case Studies: Types, designs and logics of inference. *Conflict Management and Peace Science*, 25, 1, pp. 1–18.

Lijphart, A (1975) The Comparable-cases Strategy in Comparative Research. *Comparative Political Studies*, 8, 2, pp. 158–177.

Linos, K (2015) How to Select and Develop International Law Case Studies: Lessons from comparative law and comparative politics. *American Journal of International Law*, 109, 3, pp. 475–485.

Lipsey, M, and Wilson, D (2001) *Practical Meta-Analysis*. Thousand Oaks, CA, Sage.

Littell, J, Corcoran, J, and Pillai, V (2008) *Systematic Reviews and Meta-Analysis*. Oxford, Oxford University Press.

Llewellyn, S (1992) The Role of Case Study Methods in Management Accounting Research: A comment. *British Accounting Review*, 24, 1, pp. 17–31.

Lukoff, D, Edwards, D, and Miller, M (1998) The Case Study as a Scientific Method for Researching Alternative Therapies. *Alternative Therapies*, 4, 2, pp. 44–52.

Lundervold, D, and Belwood, M (2000) The Best Kept Secret in Counselling: Single case (N=1) experimental designs. *Journal of Counselling and Development*, 78, 1, pp. 92–102.

Lyons, H (2009) Case Study Research Methodology for Publishing Developments in ICT-facilitated Learning in Higher Education: A prescriptive approach. *Innovations in Education and Teaching International*, 46, 1, pp. 27–39.

Macpherson, I, Brooker, R, and Ainsworth, P (2000) Case Study in the Contemporary World of Research: Using notions of purpose, place, process and product to develop some principles for practice. *International Journal of Social Research Methodology*, 3, 1, pp. 49–61.

Mahoney, J (2000) Strategies of Causal Inference in Small-N Analysis. *Sociological Methods and Research*, 28, 4, pp. 387–424.

Mahoney, J, and Goertz, G (2004) The Possibility Principle: Choosing negative cases in comparative research. *American Political Science Review*, 98, 4, pp. 653–669.

Mason, J (1996) *Qualitative Researching*. London, Sage.

Massis, A de, and Kotlar, J (2014) The Case Study Method in Family Business Research: Guidelines for qualitative scholarship. *Journal of Family Business Strategy*, 5, 1, pp. 15–29.

Maxfield, F (1930) The Case Study. *Educational Research Bulletin*, 9, 5, pp. 117–122.

May, T (2001) *Social Research: Issues, methods and process* (3rd edition). Buckingham, Open University Press.

McAteer, M (2013) *Action Research in Education*. London, Sage.

McCarthy, J, Holland, J, and Gillies, V (2003) Multiple Perspectives on the 'Family' Lives of Young People: Methodological and theoretical issues in case study research. *International Journal of Social Research Methodology*, 6, 1, pp. 1–23.

McClintock, C (1985) Process Sampling: A method for case study research on administrative behaviour. *Educational Administration Quarterly*, 21, 3, pp. 205–222.

McClintock, C, Brannon, D, and Maynard-Moody, S (1979) Applying the Logic of Sample Surveys to Qualitative Case Studies: The case cluster method. *Administrative Science Quarterly*, 24, 4, pp. 612–629.

McCullough, J (1984) The Need for New Single-case Design Structure in Applied Cognitive Psychology. *Psychotherapy*, 21, 3, pp. 389–400.

McCutcheon, D, and Meredith, J (1993) Conducting Case Study Research in Operations Management. *Journal of Operations Management*, 11, 3, pp. 239–256.

McKenna, B (2015) The Collapse of 'Primary Care' in Medical Education: A case study of Michigan's Community/University Health Partnerships Project. pp. 133–156 in J Russell, T Greenhalgh, and S Kushner (eds) *Case Study Evaluation: Past, present and future challenges*. Bingley, Emerald.

McLeod, J (2010) *Case Study Research in Counselling and Psychotherapy*. London, Sage.

Merriam, S (1998) *Qualitative Research and Case Study Applications in Education*. San Francisco, CA, Jossey-Bass.

Meyer, C (2001) A Case in Case Study Methodology. *Field Methods*, 13, 4, pp. 329–354.

Miles, M, and Huberman, A (1994) *Qualitative Data Analysis*. Thousand Oaks, CA, Sage.

Mills, A, Durepos, G, and Wiebe, E (eds) (2010) *Encyclopedia of Case Study Research* (2 volumes). Los Angeles, CA, Sage.

Mitchell, C (1983) Case and Situation Analysis. *Sociological Review*, 31, 2, pp. 187–211.

Mitchell, C (1984) Case Studies. pp. 237–241 in R Ellen (ed.) *Ethnographic Research: A guide to general conduct*. London, Academic Press.

Mjoset, L (2006) A Case Study of a Case Study: Strategies of generalization and specification in the study of Israel as a single case. *International Sociology*, 21, 5, pp. 735–766.

Modell, S (2005) Triangulation between Case Study and Survey Methods in Management Accounting Research: An assessment of validity implications. *Management Accounting Research*, 16, 2, pp. 231–254.

Moliterno, T, and Mahony, D (2011) Network Theory of Organization: A multilevel approach. *Journal of Management*, 37, 2, pp. 443–467.

Molnar, G (1967) Deviant Case Analysis in Social Science. *Politics*, 2, 1, pp. 1–11.

Most, B, and Starr, H (1982) Case Selection, Conceptualizations and Basic Logic in the Study of War. *American Journal of Political Science*, 26, 4, pp. 834–856.

Murray, R (2013) *Writing for Academic Journals* (3rd edition). Maidenhead, Open University Press.

Nicholson-Crotty, S, and Meier, K (2002) Size Doesn't Matter: In defense of single-state studies. *State Politics and Policy Quarterly*, 2, 4, pp. 411–422.

Nonthaleerak, P, and Hendry, L (2008) Exploring the Six Sigma Phenomenon using Multiple Case Study Evidence. *International Journal of Operations and Production Management*, 28, 3, pp. 279–303.

Oberlack, C (2010) Determinants of the Capacity to Adapt to Climate Change in Multi-level Governance Systems: A meta-analysis of case study evidence. Paper given at the conference on the Human Dimensions of Global Environmental Change, Berlin, October.

Odell, J (2001) Case Study Methods in International Political Economy. *International Studies Perspectives*, 2, 2, pp. 161–176.

Ogulata, S, Koyuncu, M, and Karakas, E (2008) Personnel and Patient Scheduling in the High Demanded Hospital Services: A case study in the physiotherapy service. *Journal of Medical Systems*, 32, 3, pp. 221–228.

Oke, A, and Gopalakrishnan, M (2009) Managing Disruptions in Supply Chains: A case study of a retail supply chain. *International Journal of Production Economics*, 118, 1, pp. 168–174.

Otley, D, and Berry, A (1994) Case Study Research in Management Accounting and Control. *Management Accounting Research*, 5, 1, pp. 45–65.

Pan, S, and Tan, B (2011) Demystifying Case Research: A structured-pragmatic-situational (SPS) approach to conducting case studies. *Information and Organization*, 21, 3, pp. 161–176.

Parker, E, Myers, N, Higgins, H, Oddsson, T, Price, M, and Gould, T (2009) More than Experiential Learning or Volunteering: A case study of community service learning within the Australian context. *Higher Education Research and Development*, 28, 6, pp. 585–596.

Payne, S, Field, D, Rolls, L, Hawker, S, and Kerr, C (2007) Case Study Research Methods in End-of-Life Care: Reflections on three studies. *Journal of Advanced Nursing*, 58, 3, pp. 236–245.

Perren, L, and Ram, M (2004) Case-study Method in Small Business and Entrepreneurial Research: Mapping boundaries and perspectives. *International Small Business Journal*, 21, 1, pp. 83–101.

Piekkari, R, Welch, C, and Paavilainen, E (2009) The Case Study as Disciplinary Convention: Evidence from international business journals. *Organizational Research Methods*, 12, 3, pp. 567–589.

Platt, J (1992) 'Case Study' in American Methodological Thought. *Current Sociology*, 40, 1, pp. 17–48.

Poulis, K, Poulis, E, and Plakoyiannaki, E (2012) The Role of Context in Case Study Selection: An international business perspective. *International Business Review*, 22, 1, pp. 304–314.

Punch, K (1998) *Introduction to Social Research: Quantitative and qualitative approaches.* London, Sage.

Punch, K (2005) *Introduction to Social Research: Quantitative and qualitative approaches* (2nd edition). London, Sage.

Ragin, C (1992a) Introduction: Cases of 'what is a case'? pp. 1–17 in C Ragin and H Becker (eds) *What is a Case? Exploring the foundations of social inquiry.* Cambridge, Cambridge University Press.

Ragin, C (1992b) 'Casing' and the Processes of Social Inquiry. pp. 217–226 in C Ragin and H Becker (eds) *What is a Case? Exploring the foundations of social inquiry.* Cambridge, Cambridge University Press.

Ragin, C (1997) Turning the Tables: How case-oriented research challenges variable-oriented research. *Comparative Social Research*, 16, pp. 27–42.

Ragin, C (2000) *Fuzzy-Set Social Science.* Chicago, IL, University of Chicago Press.

Ragin, C, and Becker, H (eds) (1992) *What is a Case? Exploring the foundations of social inquiry.* Cambridge, Cambridge University Press.

Ravenswood, K (2011) Eisenhardt's Impact on Theory in Case Study Research. *Journal of Business Research*, 64, 7, pp. 680–686.

Reason, P, and Bradbury, H (eds) (2006) *Handbook of Action Research* (2nd edition). London, Sage.

Rialp, A, Rialp, J, Urbano, D, and Vaillant, Y (2005) The Born-Global Phenomenon: A comparative case study research. *Journal of International Entrepreneurship*, 3, 2, pp. 133–171.

Riege, A (2003) Validity and Reliability Tests in Case Study Research: A literature review with 'hands-on' applications for each research phase. *Qualitative Market Research*, 6, 2, pp. 75–86.

Ritchie, J (2001) Case Series Research: A case for qualitative method in assembling evidence. *Physiotherapy Theory and Practice*, 17, 3, pp. 127–135.

Rohlfing, I (2012) *Case Studies and Causal Inference: An integrative framework.* Basingstoke, Palgrave Macmillan.

Romm, T, and Mahler, S (1991) The Case Study Challenge: A new approach to an old method. *Management Learning*, 22, 4, pp. 292–301.

Rosenberg, J, and Yates, P (2007) Schematic Representation of Case Study Research Designs. *Journal of Advanced Nursing*, 60, 4, pp. 447–452.

Ruddin, L (2006) You Can Generalize Stupid! Social Scientists, Bent Flyvbjerg and Case Study Methodology. *Qualitative Inquiry*, 12, 4, pp. 797–812.

Runesson, P, and Host, M (2009) Guidelines for Conducting and Reporting Case Study Research in Software Engineering. *Empirical Software Engineering*, 14, 2, pp. 131–164.

Russell, J, Greenhalgh, T and Kushner, S (eds) (2015) *Case Study Evaluation: Past, present and future challenges*. Bingley, Emerald.

Ruzzene, A (2012) Drawing Lessons from Case Studies by Enhancing Comparability. *Philosophy of the Social Sciences*, 42, 1, pp. 99–120.

Scapens, R (1990) Researching Management Accounting Practice: The role of case study methods. *British Accounting Review*, 22, 3, pp. 259–281.

Schiele, H, and Krummaker, S (2011) Consortium Benchmarking: Collaborative academic-practitioner case study research. *Journal of Business Research*, 64, 10, pp. 1137–1145.

Schneider, K (1999) Multiple-case Depth Research: Bringing experience-near closer. *Journal of Clinical Psychology*, 51, 12, pp. 1531–1540.

Scholz, R, and Tietje, O (2002) *Embedded Case Study Methods: Integrating quantitative and qualitative knowledge*. Thousand Oaks, CA, Sage.

Schreier, M (2012) *Qualitative Content Analysis in Practice*. London, Sage.

Scott, D (2007) Resolving the Quantitative–Qualitative Dilemma: A critical realist approach. *International Journal of Research and Method in Education*, 30, 1, pp. 3–17.

Seawright, J, and Gerring, J (2008) Case Selection Techniques in Case Study Research: A menu of qualitative and quantitative options. *Political Research Quarterly*, 61, 2, pp. 294–308.

Seuring, S (2008) Assessing the Rigour of Case Study Research in Supply Chain Management. *Supply Chain Management*, 13, 2, pp. 128–137.

Shapiro, M (1966) The Single Case in Clinical-Psychological Research. *The Journal of General Psychology*, 74, 1, pp. 3–23.

Simons, H (ed.) (1980) *Towards a Science of the Singular*. Norwich, University of East Anglia, Centre for Applied Research in Education, Occasional Publication No. 10.

Simons, H (2009) *Case Study Research in Practice*. London, Sage.

Sleeter, C (2009) Developing Teacher Epistemological Sophistication about Multicultural Curriculum: A case study. *Action in Teacher Education*, 31, 1, pp. 3–13.

Sloane, R (2002) The Changing Face of Recognition in International Law: A case study of Tibet. *Emory International Law Review*, 16, pp. 107–186.

Small, M (2009) 'How Many Cases Do I Need?': On science and the logic of case selection in field-based research. *Ethnography*, 10, 1, pp. 5–38.

Snyder, C (2012) A Case Study of a Case Study: Analysis of a robust qualitative research methodology. *The Qualitative Report*, 17, Article 21, pp. 1–21.

Solomon, B, Klein, S, Hintze, J, Cressey, J, and Peller, S (2012) A Meta-analysis of School-wide Positive Behavior Support: An exploratory study using single-case synthesis. *Psychology in the Schools*, 49, 2, pp. 105–121.

Stake, R (1995) *The Art of Case Study Research*. Thousand Oaks, CA, Sage.

Stake, R (2005) Qualitative Case Studies. pp. 443–466 in N Denzin and Y Lincoln (eds) *The Sage Handbook of Qualitative Research* (3rd edition). Thousand Oaks, CA, Sage.

Stall-Meadows, C (1998) Grounded Meta-analysis of Qualitative Case Study Dissertations in Distance Education Pedagogy. EdD Dissertation, Oklahoma State University.

Stenhouse, L (1978) Case Study and Case Records: Towards a contemporary history of education. *British Educational Research Journal*, 4, 2, pp. 21–39.

Stenhouse, L (1979) Case Study in Comparative Education: Particularity and generalization. *Comparative Education*, 15, 1, pp. 5–10.

Stewart, R, and Chambless, D (2010) Interesting Practitioners in Training in Empirically Supported Treatments: Research reviews versus case studies. *Journal of Clinical Psychology*, 66, 1, pp. 73–95.

Stouffer, S (1941) Notes on the Case-Study and the Unique Case. *Sociometry*, 4, 4, pp. 349–357.

Strauss, A, and Corbin, J (1990) *Basics of Qualitative Research: Grounded theory procedures and techniques.* Thousand Oaks, CA, Sage.

Stuart, I, McCutcheon, D, Handfield, R, McLachlin, R, and Samson, D (2002) Effective Case Research in Operations Management: A process perspective. *Journal of Operations Management*, 20, 5, pp. 419–433.

Swanborn, P (2010) *Case Study Research: What, why and how?* London, Sage.

Sword, H (2012) *Stylish Academic Writing.* Cambridge, MA, Harvard University Press.

Symonds, P (1945) The Case Study as a Research Method. *Review of Educational Research*, 15, 5, pp. 352–359.

Taber, K (2000) Case Studies and Generalizability: Grounded theory and research in science education. *International Journal of Science Education*, 22, 5, pp. 469–487.

Tashakkori, A, and Teddlie, C (1998) *Mixed Methodology: Combining qualitative and quantitative approaches.* Thousand Oaks, CA, Sage.

Tashakkori, A, and Teddlie, C (eds) (2010) *Handbook of Mixed Methods in Social and Behavioral Research* (2nd edition). Thousand Oaks, CA, Sage.

Teddlie, C, and Tashakkori, A (2009) *Foundations of Mixed Methods Research: Integrating quantitative and qualitative approaches in the social and behavioral sciences.* Thousand Oaks, CA, Sage.

Thacher, D (2006) The Normative Case Study. *American Journal of Sociology*, 111, 6, pp. 1631–1676.

Thomas, G (2010) Doing Case Study: Abduction not induction, phronesis not theory. *Qualitative Inquiry*, 16, 7, pp. 575–582.

Thomas, G (2011a) *How to Do Your Case Study: A guide for students and researchers.* London, Sage.

Thomas, G (2011b) The Case: Generalization, theory and phronesis in case study. *Oxford Review of Education*, 37, 1, pp. 21–35.

Thomas, G (2011c) A Typology for the Case Study in Social Science Following a Review of Definition, Discourse and Structure. *Qualitative Inquiry*, 17, 6, pp. 511–521.

Thomas, G, and James, D (2006) Reinventing Grounded Theory: Some questions about theory, ground and discovery. *British Educational Research Journal*, 32, 6, pp. 767–795.

Thomas, G, and Myers, K (2015) *The Anatomy of the Case Study.* London, Sage.

Thomas, W, and Znaniecki, F (1918–1920) *The Polish Peasant in Europe and America: Monograph of an immigrant group* (5 volumes). Boston, MA, Gorham Press.

Tibben, W (2015) Theory Building for ICT4D: Systematizing case study research using theory triangulation. *Information Technology for Development*, 21, 4, pp. 628–652.

Tight, M (2012) *Researching Higher Education* (2nd edition). Maidenhead, Open University Press.

Tight, M (ed.) (2015) *Case Studies* (4 volumes). London, Sage.

Tripp, D (1985) Case Study Generalization: An agenda for action. *British Educational Research Journal*, 11, 1, pp. 33–43.

Uprichard, E (2009) Introducing Cluster Analysis: What can it teach us about the case? pp. 132–147 in D Byrne and C Ragin (eds) *The Sage Handbook of Case-based Methods.* London, Sage.

Uprichard, E (2013) Sampling: Bridging probability and non-probability designs. *International Journal of Social Research Methodology*, 16, 1, pp. 1–11.

Urinboyev, R (2011) Law, Social Norms and Welfare as Means of Public Administration: Case study of Mahalla institutions in Uzbekistan. *NISPAcee Journal of Public Administration and Policy*, 4, 1, pp. 33–57.

VanWynsberghe, R, and Khan, S (2007) Redefining Case Study. *International Journal of Qualitative Methods*, 6, 2, pp. 80–94.

Vaus, D de (2002) *Analyzing Social Science Data: 50 key problems in data analysis.* London, Sage.

Vellema, S, Ton, G, de Roo, N, and van Wijk, J (2013) Value Chains, Partnerships and Development: Using case studies to refine programme theories. *Evaluation*, 19, 3, pp. 304–320.

Verschuren, P (2003) Case Study as a Research Strategy: Some ambiguities and opportunities. *International Journal of Social Research Methodology*, 6, 2, pp. 121–139.

Visconti, L (2010) Ethnographic Case Study (ECS): Abductive modelling of ethnography and improving the relevance in business marketing research. *Industrial Marketing Management*, 39, 1, pp. 25–39.

Vissak, T (2010) Recommendations for Using the Case Study Method in International Business Research. *The Qualitative Report*, 15, 2, pp. 370–388.

Voss, C, Tsikriktsis, N, and Frohlich, M (2002) Case Research in Operations Management. *International Journal of Operations and Production Management*, 22, 2, pp. 195–219.

Walford, G (2001) Site Selection within Comparative Case Study and Ethnographic Research. *Compare*, 31, 2, pp. 151–164.

Walshe, C (2011) The Evaluation of Complex Interventions in Palliative Care: An exploration of the potential of case study research strategies. *Palliative Medicine*, 25, 8, pp. 774–781.

Watson, T (2009) Narrative, Life Story and Manager Identity: A case study in autobiographical identity work. *Human Relations*, 62, 3, pp. 425–452.

Weerd-Nederhof, P de (2001) Qualitative Case Study Research. The case of a PhD research project on organizing and managing new product development systems. *Management Decision*, 39, 7, pp. 513–538.

Welch, C, Piekkari, R, Plakoyiannaki, E, and Paavilainen-Mantymaki, E (2011) Theorising from Case Studies: Towards a pluralist future for international business research. *Journal of International Business Studies*, 42, 5, pp. 740–762.

Wellington, J (2015) *Educational Research: Contemporary issues and practical approaches* (2nd edition). London, Bloomsbury.

Wells, A, Hirshberg, D, Lipton, M, and Oakes, J (1995) Bounding the Case within its Context: A Constructivist Approach to Studying Detracking Reform. *Educational Researcher*, 24, 5, pp. 18–24.

Williams van Rooij, S, and Zirkle, K (2016) Balancing Pedagogy, Student Readiness and Accessibility: A case study in collaborative online course development. *Internet and Higher Education*, 28, 1, pp. 1–7.

Wilson, I, Huttly, S, and Fenn, B (2006) A Case Study of Sample Design for Longitudinal Research: Young lives. *International Journal of Social Research Methodology*, 9, 5, pp. 351–365.

Wilson, S (1979) Explorations of the Usefulness of Case Study Evaluations. *Evaluation Review*, 3, 3, pp. 446–459.

Wilson, S, and Gudmundsdottir, S (1987) What is this a Case of? Exploring some conceptual issues in case study research. *Education and Urban Society*, 20, 1, pp. 42–54.

Woods, L (1997) Designing and Conducting Case Study Research in Nursing. *Nursing Times Research*, 2, 1, pp. 48–56.

Woodside, A (2010) Bridging the Chasm between Survey and Case Study Research: Research methods for achieving generalization, accuracy and complexity. *Industrial Marketing Management*, 39, 1, pp. 64–75.

Woolcock, M (2013) Using Case Studies to Explore the External Validity of 'Complex' Development Interventions. *Evaluation*, 19, 3, pp. 229–248.

Yin, R (1992) The Case Study Method as a Tool for Doing Evaluation. *Current Sociology*, 40, 1, pp. 121–137.

Yin, R (1997) Case Study Evaluations: A decade of progress? *New Directions for Evaluation*, 76, pp. 69–78.

Yin, R (1999) Enhancing the Quality of Case Studies in Health Services Research. *Health Services Research*, 34, 5, Part II, pp. 1209–1224.

Yin, R (2003) *Case Study Research: Design and methods* (3rd edition). Thousand Oaks, CA, Sage.

Yin, R (2009) *Case Study Research: Design and methods* (4th edition). Thousand Oaks, CA, Sage.

Yin, R (2013) Validity and Generalization in Future Case Study Evaluations. *Evaluation*, 19, 3, pp. 321–332.

Young, C (2013) Initiating Self-assessment Strategies in Novice Physiotherapy Students: A method case study. *Assessment and Evaluation in Higher Education*, 38, 8, pp. 998–1011.

Zhao, J (1996) Using Case Studies for International Business Communication Training. *Business Communication Quarterly*, 59, 4, pp. 11–24.

Zonzi, A, Barkham, M, Hardy, G, Llewelyn, S, Stiles, W, and Leiman, M (2014) Zone of Proximal Development (ZPD) as an Ability to Play in Psychotherapy: A theory-building case study of very brief therapy. *Psychology and Psychotherapy: Theory, Research and Practice*, 87, 4, pp. 447–464.

Index